William Symington

On the Atonement and Intercession of Jesus Christ

William Symington

On the Atonement and Intercession of Jesus Christ

ISBN/EAN: 9783743382640

Manufactured in Europe, USA, Canada, Australia, Japa

Cover: Foto ©Lupo / pixelio.de

Manufactured and distributed by brebook publishing software (www.brebook.com)

William Symington

On the Atonement and Intercession of Jesus Christ

ON THE

ATONEMENT

AND

INTERCESSION OF JESUS CHRIST.

BY

WILLIAM SYMINGTON, D.D.,
GLASGOW.

Fifth Thousand.

NEW YORK:
ROBERT CARTER & BROTHERS
No. 530 BROADWAY.

1868

PREFACE.

The subjects discussed in the following pages are, without doubt, the most deeply interesting that can engage the thoughts or feelings of men. Of the manner in which they are treated others must judge. To prevent disappointment, it may be remarked, that it was not so much the Author's intention to treat them practically, as to explain, establish, and vindicate them, as grand leading TRUTHS of the Gospel of the Son of God, which are, unhappily, much misunderstood, neglected, and impugned in the present day.

The writers, to whose labors he has been indebted for assistance, will be found referred to, and the extent of his obligations acknowledged, in the course of the work itself. He has often, since he commenced this undertaking, had occasion to regret the remoteness of his situation, at a distance from those stores of learning to which he might otherwise have had access, and from which he might have been enabled to enrich his pages.

On the subject of Atonement, writers of the greatest eminence have, in every age, exerted their talents. The labors of Archbishop Magee, and of Dr. J. Pye Smith, stand pre-eminent in modern times. The former writer has accumulated a body of proof for the *reality* of the Atonement, which will serve to transmit to posterity his fame for biblical knowledge, acute thinking, and learned research. But, besides regretting that his varied materials had not been arranged in a more orderly and useful form, the friends of true religion have to lament that the opinions of this distinguished author, on some vital points, should have been not only defective but erroneous. These defects of the Archbishop have been supplied by the labors of Dr. Smith, who, in his Four Discourses, has given a masterly view of what may be called the *philosophy* of the Atonement.

There are other writers who treat, some of the *necessity*, and others of the *extent*, of the Atonement. But it appeared desirable that there should exist a work embracing a view of the whole subject; so comprehensive as not to fatigue the mind on any one topic, and yet so copious as not altogether to disappoint the serious and anxious inquirer, who should wish to obtain an adequate acquaintance with all the leading branches of this interesting and absorbing theme. To furnish such a work has been the aim of the present writer. He is not aware of the existence of any treatise on precisely the same plan. That of Dr. Dewar, he believes, comes nearest to it. This opinion, however, is formed, simply from the title of the doctor's volume. As it appeared, after the present undertaking was projected, the Author,—whether wisely or not he pretends not to say—abstained from reading so much as a sentence of it, as he did not reckon its publication any good reason why he should abandon his purpose, and he was anxious not to embarrass his mind with any coincidences that might exist betwixt that writer's plan and his own. The subject is of sufficient magnitude and importance to warrant the employment of many minds. It is but a narrow and contracted view that could lead any one to suppose, on such a subject, that because some had already written upon it, others should refrain from directing the attention of the public to it again. No. The theme is one on which all the moral creatures of God may profitably exert their powers without interruption. The subject is indeed exhaustless—it is a theme for eternity! Every writer, too, has his own mode of treating a subject, and his own proper circle of readers, who will peruse with interest what *he* has written, while the superior productions of others on the same topic may never be known to exist.

On the subject of the Intercession the number of writers has been much more limited. It is, of course, introduced in works of systematic theology, as one of the functions of the Saviour's priesthood; but it has seldom received a full and separate discussion. To be sure, it admits not of the same amplitude of remark as the other topic; but, in a practical and consolatory point of view, its interest is not exceeded even by the Atonement. The two are, however, inseparably connected; although we fear that, in this instance, men have not been sufficiently aware of the evil of putting asunder what God has joined together. The treatise of Charnock on this point is the most complete that has come under the Author's notice.

The present work was undertaken from the impulse of motives with which, perhaps, the reader is not greatly concerned. To supply what he conceived to be a desideratum in theological literature—to counteract the evils of prevalent erroneous sentiments—and to leave, in the district which has been the scene of his labors, some memorial of those official services which have been based on the principles of Atonement and Intercession, are among the inducements by which he was stimulated to enter upon, and to prosecute, this work. When it had been little more than begun, all progress was suspended for nearly a year, in consequence of bodily indisposition. And, even after it pleased God to give health to resume it, it has been carried forward only at such snatches of leisure as could be obtained, amid a considerable variety both of official avocation and domestic affliction.

The writer cannot close without giving expression to the gratitude he feels to Him who has permitted him to complete a work on which he had set his heart. And he now commends it, with all due humility, to the blessing of that divine Intercessor, who can render the feeblest services of his people useful to men, and acceptable to God.

W. S.

Stranraer, *May*, 1834.

CONTENTS.

Part I.—ATONEMENT.

SECTION I.

NATURE OF ATONEMENT.

	PAGE.
Introductory Remarks	9
The Three Systems	10
Socinian	ib.
Middle	11
Catholic	12
Definition of Atonement	ib.
Terms explained	13
Atonement	ib.
Reconciliation	14
Redemption	15
Propitiation	ib.
Satisfaction	16
Substitution	17
Vicarious	ib.
Expiation	ib

SECTION II.

OBJECTIONS TO ATONEMENT CONSIDERED.

I. Objec. It represents the Deity in an unfavorable light 20
Reply 1. The objection proceeds on a mistaken assumption of what the atonement is designed to effect 21
   2. It assumes, what is not proved, that God is ready to pardon sin without satisfaction 22
II. Objec. It is inconsistent with the Divine Immutability 24
Reply 1. The inspired writers use language which *seems* to imply a change in God .... ib.
   2. The change is not in God but in man 27
III. Objec. It is incompatible with the gracious nature of pardon 28
Reply 1. Justice and mercy are not opposed to one another 29
   2. The objection overlooks the origin of Christ's satisfaction 30
   3. The bestowment of pardon is an act of grace .... ib.
   4. Pardon could not be shown to be gracious without atonement 32
IV. Objec. It supposes the innocent to suffer for the guilty 33
Reply 1. The innocent *do* suffer for the guilty .... ib.
   2. The sentiment of our opponent supposes the same thing 35
   3. Christ was *legally*, though not personally guilty 36
   4. Christ suffered by divine authority and his own voluntary agreement. 37
   5. The ends of punishment are more completely subserved by this arrangement 38
   6. The case admits of a compensation 39
   7. The case altogether peculiar 41
V. Objec. An Atonement is unnecessary 42
Reply 1. The objection is presumptuous .... ib.
   2. There may be reasons for its necessity of which we are ignorant 43
   3. The objection supposes an inadequate view of the evil of sin 44
   4. It proceeds on an imperfect notion of the nature of salvation .... ib

SECTION III.

NECESSITY OF ATONEMENT.

	PAGE
Term *necessity* explained	47
Necessity proved from	
I. The perfections of God	48
Majesty	ib.
Truth	49
Holiness	50
Justice	ib.
Goodness	52
II. The nature of God's moral government	53
The letter of the law	ib.
The nature of the law	ib.
The law cannot be relaxed	54
The purposes of moral government	56
III. The inefficacy of every other thing to procure pardon of sin	57
Inefficacy of repentance	58
Inefficacy of future amendment	61
IV. The assertions of Holy Writ	64
Luke xxiv. 26	ib.
Heb. ii. 10	ib.
Heb. viii. 3	65
Heb. ix. 22, 23	ib.

SECTION IV.

PROOF OF ATONEMENT—ANCIENT SACRIFICES.

Antiquity of sacrifices	67
Universal prevalence of sacrifices	70
The ancient sacrifices expiatory	71
The origin of ancient sacrifices	75
Objections to their divine origin answered	85
The design of ancient sacrifices	88

SECTION V.

PROOF—LEVITICAL SACRIFICES.

Sacrifices a part of the Levitical services	94
The Jewish sacrifices propitiatory	95
Not in themselves sufficient to take away sin	98
Designed to prefigure Christ	101
Argument hence in favor of atonement	114

SECTION VI.

PROOF—PROPHECY.

Isaiah liii	118
Daniel ix. 24—27	125

SECTION VII.

PROOF—THE SUFFERINGS OF CHRIST.

The *facts* of the case	127
The *explanation* of the facts	130
Not explained on the principle of retributive justice	ib.
Not possibly disciplinary	ib.
Not merely confirmatory of his doctrine	131
Not only exemplary	133

SECTION VIII.

PROOF—NEW TESTAMENT WRITINGS.

Passages which speak of *atonement* or *reconciliation*	136
Passages which treat of *propitiation*	137

	PAGE.
Passages in which the term *ransom* or *redemption* occurs.	138
Passages in which Christ is said to be *made sin* or a *curse*.	140
Passages in which Christ is said to have been made a *sacrifice*.	141
Passages in which the language of *substitution* is employed.	142

SECTION IX.

MATTER OR SUBSTANCE OF ATONEMENT.

Christ's sufferings *alone*.	149
The *whole* of his sufferings.	153
The sufferings of his *soul*, and of the *concluding period* of his life in particular	155
The sufferings of Christ and those of the wicked in the place of woe not precisely the same.	158

SECTION X.

VALUE OF ATONEMENT.

Relation of cause and effect.	160
The circumstances which constitute the value of Christ's death are	
The dignity of his person	163
His relationship to man	169
His freedom from all personal obligation to the law.	170
His being at his own disposal.	175
His being voluntary.	176
His appointment of God.	179

SECTION XI.

EXTENT OF ATONEMENT.

I. Explanations.	184
The infinite intrinsic worth of Christ's atonement admitted on the one hand.	185
The limited application of it admitted on the other.	186
The divine intention with regard to the extent of its objects, is the point in dispute.	187
II. Arguments for a definite atonement.	188
The divine purpose	ib.
The rectitude of God	190
The covenant of grace.	191
The very nature of atonement.	192
The resurrection and intercession of Christ	193
The work of the Spirit.	195
The limited application and revelation of atonement.	196
The absurdity of all other suppositions.	198
The direct testimony of scripture.	201
III. Objections to a definite atonement considered	205
It is derogatory to the honor and merits of Christ	ib.
It supposes a redundancy of merit.	207
The universal Gospel offer.	209
The universal terms employed in scripture	214
The possibility of those perishing for whom Christ died.	227

SECTION XII.

RESULTS OF ATONEMENT.

It illustrates the character of God.	234
It vindicates the divine moral government	237
It demonstrates the evil of sin.	239
It secures a perfect and eternal salvation	240
It opens a way for the exercise of divine mercy, encourages sinners to rely on the mercy of God, and awakens in saints pious emotions.	244
It affects the divine dispensations towards our world.	248
It furnishes an eternal theme of contemplation to the whole universe of moral creatures.	254

Part II.—INTERCESSION.

Section I.
REALITY OF INTERCESSION.

	PAGE
Intercession the correlate of atonement	256
Necessary to the fulfilment of the covenant of grace	257
Supposed in the perfection of Christ's priesthood	ib.
The necessities of God's people require it	259
Not inconsistent with God's love to his people	260
Not derogatory to the honor of Christ	261

Section II.
NATURE OF INTERCESSION.

Terms explained	262
In what it consists	263
Appearing before God	ib.
Exhibiting his sacrifice	264
Intimating his will	266
Whether vocal or symbolical	267

Section III.
MATTER OF INTERCESSION.

The persons for whom Christ intercedes	
The elect only	269
All the elect	271
Each of the elect	272
The things for which he intercedes	
Being brought into a state of grace	ib.
Daily pardon of sin	275
Protection from Satan	276
Progressive sanctification	278
Peace and intercourse with God	280
Acceptance of services	281
Complete and eternal salvation	282

Section IV.
PROPERTIES OF INTERCESSION.

Skilful	284
Holy	285
Compassionate	286
Prompt	287
Earnest	289
Authoritative	290
Peculiar	291
Prevalent	293
Constant	295

Section V.
RESULTS OF INTERCESSION.

It displays the love of God and of Christ	296
It proves the divinity of Christ	297
It shows the efficacy of Christ's death	298
It affords security to the people of God	ib.
The sin of dishonoring Christ's intercession	299
The duty of daily seeking an interest in it	300

PART I

ATONEMENT.

SECTION 1.

NATURE OF ATONEMENT.

How can man be justified with God? This is the most important, by far, of all the questions that can ever awaken human inquiry. From the universal consciousness of guilt, it may be presumed, that every individual of our race has, at one time or another, been forced to utter a similar interrogation. The very language in which it is expressed conveys the idea of difficulty; and one can scarce conceive of its being used without being accompanied, in the countenance of the inquirer, with at least a look of deep anxiety, if not an air of utter despondency. It is a question, too, on which the mind of man, unassisted by revelation, finds itself utterly undone. The light of reason, the lamp of philosophy, the torch of science, have been unable to shed a single ray of hope on this momentous subject; and, left to these, we should have been doomed to the blackness of darkness forever. Not that there have been no attempts to answer, without the aid of inspiration, the all-momentous question; but the answers have ever been such as were calculated to bewilder and deceive, rather than to quiet the apprehensions of an awakened conscience, or to impart true peace of soul. The utmost that school-men, or philosophers, or natural religionists have been able to effect in this department, has tended only to apply palliatives to the wounded heart, or to administer stupefying opiates to the patient. "Forgers of lies, physicians of no value" were they all, leaving their patients, so soon as the temporary effect of their worthless expedients went off, as ready as ever to exclaim, in mental agony, *Is there no balm in Gilead? Is there no physician there?*

To the light of divine revelation alone does it belong to irradiate this moral gloom; to the wisdom of Jehovah was it reserved to point out a sovereign remedy for the deep-rooted malady of human guilt. This he has done in his word, which contains full, multifarious, and satisfactory information on the most important of all human inquiries. All who believe the Scriptures, profess to regard the work of Christ as the only remedy for moral evil. They all agree in considering that he has conferred the greatest possible benefit on the world, and that he is to be regarded as the only Saviour of men from sin and wrath. But by those who agree thus far very different views are taken respecting the *nature* of the remedy Christ has provided. These views may be conveniently reduced to three, which have been distinguished by the names of the Socinian, the Middle, and the Catholic.

The Socinian system is founded on the supposition, that pure goodness, or unmixed benevolence, constitutes the whole character of God. Discarding vindictive justice, the abettors of this opinion represent him as ready to forgive the sins of his creatures, simply on their repentance. Nothing requires to be done by Christ to *procure* pardon; he has only to *reveal* or make it known. His priestly office is obliterated, or merged into the prophetical. His work is to instruct mankind by doctrine and by example; and the sole value of his sufferings and death springs from their tendency to confirm his doctrinal testimony. To this system they ingeniously accommodate all the language of scripture regarding the Gospel remedy. When it is said, Christ "died for us," the meaning is, that he died for our benefit. He is called "Mediator," only because he came from God to make known the divine mercy to men. He "saves from sin" by the influence of his precepts and example, in leading men to the practice of holiness. His "blood cleanseth from all sin," because it was shed in confirmation of that doctrine which is the strongest incentive to virtue. "We have redemption through his blood, even the forgiveness of sins," inasmuch as we are led, by the consideration of his death, to that repentance which is sure to obtain forgiveness under the merciful constitution of the divine government. Respecting this system, it is only necessary, at present, to request our readers to consider how ill it accords with the views given in scripture of the exceeding malignity of sin ; how inconsistent it is with other features of the divine character; how much at variance with the letter and spirit of revelation; and how utterly irreconcilable with the exalted nature of the mediatory reward.

The Middle system rests on the supposition that a certain power to pardon sin was conferred on Christ in consequence of what he did. Like the former, it discards the idea of anything being done to procure pardon, but holds that Jesus, by his obedience and sufferings acquired a power to save. The friends of this system, while they allow that God could freely forgive the sins of his creatures without any satisfaction, conceive it right in itself that some distinction should be put between innocents and penitents—that, while the former are accepted for their own goodness, the acceptance of the letter should proceed on some principle which shall serve to mark their character as transgressors, and to prevent them from feeling on a perfect equality with those who have never deviated from the commandments of God. These purposes are supposed to be served by sinners being pardoned on profession of penitence, for the sake of something done by Christ, which entitles him to intercede for their deliverance as one friend intercedes on behalf of another. In some respects this scheme may be thought nearer the truth than the former, but it is open to substantially the same objections. It gives a most defective view of the divine character. It does not serve to explain the tenor of scripture language respecting the work of Christ: not to speak of its failing to account for the peculiarity and severity of the Redeemer's sufferings.

The Catholic system, so called because it seems to have been held by the great body of Christians since the days of the apostles, is founded on the principle that God is just as well as merciful. It maintains that the pardon of sin is procured by the work of Christ, by which he gave satisfaction to the justice of God on behalf of those to be redeemed. This is what is commonly known by the doctrine of ATONEMENT, deemed, in every age of the church, of such transcendent importance as to deserve the most complete and patient discussion. Such is the system which it is our object to explain, prove, and defend. In doing so, the others must, of course, necessarily fall to be refuted; and the objections against them, which have already been hinted at, will be more fully illustrated and confirmed.*

It is important, at the outset, to have a correct definite idea of the doctrine of which we are to treat. Many definitions have been given. Perhaps the substance may be comprehended in the following:—The Atonement means, THAT PERFECT SATISFACTION GIVEN TO THE LAW AND JUSTICE OF GOD, BY THE SUFFERINGS AND DEATH OF JESUS CHRIST, ON BEHALF OF ELECT SINNERS OF MANKIND, ON ACCOUNT OF WHICH THEY ARE DELIVERED FROM CONDEMNATION.

This statement supposes that mankind have offended against the law and Justice of God. The fact of man's sin cannot be denied. And that sin is an offence against the almighty moral Governor, which calls forth his high displeasure, cannot be questioned, without blasphemously supposing that he makes no distinction between moral good and moral evil; that obedience and disobedience, righteousness and sin, are to him objects of equal indifference or complacency.

That God, being offended, requires to be satisfied, is

---

* For a more complete delineation of the three systems, see Principal Hill's Lectures in Divinity, (vol. ii. pp. 398—434,) to which we have been indebted in drawing up the above abstract.

also supposed in the statement. This is a point, the evidence of which will fall to be presented afterwards. We now call the attention to it as a matter of fact, and content ourselves with remarking, that the contrary supposes either a want of truth in his professing to be offended, or a want of power to punish the offender.

It is farther supposed, in our definition of the doctrine, that the requisite satisfaction is given by a substitute, not by the offenders themselves. Satisfaction may be given by the offender himself, when what is required for this purpose is not previously due to the party offended ; but where this is the case, if satisfaction be given at all, it must be by a substitute. The case before us is of the latter kind. To whatever men can perform, the divine Lawgiver has a prior claim on other grounds, a claim as strong as he has to that the non-performance of which constitutes the original ground of offence. Into the scripture doctrine of atonement the idea of *substitution* enters as an essential element.

On account of the satisfaction given by the substitute, the party offended is pleased to pardon the offenders, and to be reconciled to them. This is another thing supposed in the doctrine. There could be no atonement without this. God is pleased to accept the satisfaction offered by his Son, and on this ground to dispense pardon and reconciliation to sinners.

The only other thing included in the definition is, that the persons on whose behalf the atonement is made, are a definite number of mankind ; not angels, but men ; not all men, but elect sinners of the human family.

To prevent ambiguity, it may be proper, before proceeding farther, to give a brief explanation of the principal terms in common use on this subject.

ATONEMENT. (כָּפַר—καταλλαγη.)—This is the characteristic appellation of the doctrine. It occurs frequently in our English translation of the Scriptures, but only once in the New Testament. The Hebrew, word which is so translated signifies a *covering*. The verb means to *cover*, to *draw over;* whence it comes by an easy and natural process, to signify to forgive, to expiate, to propitiate; that is, to cover an offence from the eye of offended justice by means of an adequate compensation. The term is applied to the mercy-seat, which was the lid or *covering* of the ark of the covenant, a divinely appointed symbol closely connected with the presentation of sacrifices on the day of expiation. The idea that seems to be expressed by this word, is that of averting some dreaded consequence by means of a substitutionary interposition. It thus fitly denotes the doctrine of salvation from sin and wrath, by a ransom of infinite worth.—The Greek word more closely harmonizes with the English term atonement. It signifies *reconciliation*, or the removal of some hinderance to concord, fellowship, or good agreement. This is the true import of the term AT-ONE-MENT, the act of reconciling or uniting parties at variance. 'The next day, he (Moses) showed himself unto them, as they strove; and would have set them AT ONE again, saying, Sirs, ye are brethren; why do ye wrong one to another?"* Sin has placed God and man *apart* from one another; all harmony between them has been broken up; and those who once dwelt together in perfect concord have been separated and disjoined. What Christ has done has had the effect of reconciling the parties—of restoring them to a state of *one-ness* with each other. The Deity is *at-oned;* God is brought to be *at-one* with his people; the work of the Redeemer is a proper *at-one-ment*. "We joy in God, through our Lord Jesus Christ, by whom we have received the AT-ONE-MENT."

RECONCILIATION.—This term occurs in both the Old and New Testaments several times. But it is generally, if not always, used as a translation of the original words above explained. Indeed, as has already been remarked, it is quite synonymous with the term atonement, involving the same ideas and serving the same purposes. It supposes bringing into a state of good

---

* Acts vii. 26.

agreement parties who have had cause to be at variance, as is the case with God and his sinful creature man. It may farther be understood to express the effecting of harmony between two seemingly incompatible principles in the character and government of the great Legislator—equity and sovereignty, justice and grace.

REDEMPTION. (פְּדוּת—ἀπολυτρωσις.)—This term is borrowed from certain pecuniary transactions among men, as the release of an imprisoned debtor by liquidating his debt, or the deliverance of a captive by paying a ransom. These are transactions with which mankind in general, and especially the Jews and primitive Christians, have been perfectly familiar. Accordingly, both in the Hebrew and Greek Scriptures, the deliverance of man from sin is frequently represented by language borrowed from such negotiations. The term before us is of this nature. It involves all the ideas included in atonement. It supposes sin, which is the cause of imprisonment or captivity. It supposes deliverance by a substitute, the captive or debtor being unable to effect his own escape. And, of course, it supposes also a clear emancipation or restoration as the result of the ransom being paid. "The Son of man came to give his life a ransom ($\lambda υτρον$) for many." "Ye were not redeemed ($ελυτρωθητε$) with corruptible things, as silver and gold, but with the precious blood of Christ."*

PROPITIATION. ($ιλαστηριον, ιλασμος$.)—In the three cases in which this term occurs in the New Testament, (which are the only cases in the Scriptures,) it is applied to him by whom atonement is effected.† It is the same word which the Seventy employ to translate כפר atonement. The cover of the ark, or mercy-seat, is called by them $ιλαστηριον$. The writer of the Epistle to the Hebrews makes the same use of it.‡ The verb ($ιλασκω$) from which it is derived, signifies to turn away wrath, to appease anger, to do whatever may

---

* Matt xx. 28. 1 Peter i. 18, 19. † Rom, iii. 25. 1 John 2.—iv. 10.
‡ Heb. ix. 5.

give the judicial authority a valid reason for pardoning an offender. It supposes, of course, an offence and the turning away of the offence—two ideas which, we have seen, are involved in the doctrine of atonement; while the use that is made of it in scripture connects it inseparably with sacrifice as the means by which the offence is taken away.

SATISFACTION.—Though not found in scripture, this term is of frequent use in connection with the subject under discussion. From certain misconceptions regarding its import, the grossest prejudices have been raised against its use. It properly denotes, that the sufferings borne by Christ were not the identical punishment required by the law, but a proper equivalent with which the great moral Governor was pleased to be *satisfied* in its place. What Christ endured was not the precise penalty of the law, but something equally *satisfactory*, serving the same purpose as far as the rectoral honor of God is concerned. " By satisfaction," says an accurate and learned theologian of the present day, " we mean, such act or acts as shall accomplish all the moral purposes which to the infinite wisdom of God, appear fit and necessary under a system of rectoral holiness, and which must otherwise have been accomplished by the exercise of retributive justice upon transgressors in their own persons. . . . If the work of Christ have that excellency and merit, which the unerring justice of heaven has seen to be an actual doing of that which was requisite to compensate for the injury perpetrated, and to restore the moral harmony which had been violated, it may with the utmost propriety be called a *satisfaction*." The theological use of the word was probably introduced from the Roman law. Tertullian, who was well acquainted with that science, says, *Christus peccata hominum omni satisfactionis habitu expiavit:* which may be, I conceive, justly translated, " Christ atoned for the sins of men by a satisfaction perfect in every respect." He clearly shows his understanding of the term, when he says that our Lord, by healing the wound of Malchus, repaired the injury.* It is scarcely necessary to add, that this term involves all the requisite ideas of our doctrine—sin, substitution, and pardon.

SUBSTITUTION.—Neither is this term to be found in the Bible, though in common use, and of great moment. The doctrine supposes, as has been said, that Christ takes the place of offending sinners, bearing their guilt, and suffering their punishment. As surety for men, he voluntarily places himself in their situation, as violators of God's holy, just, and good law; he holds himself responsible for all their guilt; and bears his bosom to the full reward of the threatened penalty due to *them* for sin. He substitutes himself in their stead, not merely in regard to punishment, but in respect of obligation to punishment. Christ submitted not only to be treated as a *sin-offering*, but to be made *sin* for us. He not only "bare our *griefs*, and carried our *sorrows*," but he "bare the *sin* of many." While his holy soul was free from all the moral contamination connected with a state of guilt; while personal guilt never could be charged upon him; he, nevertheless, behooved to have imputed to him the guilt for which he was to make atonement. This was necessary that his sufferings might partake of the nature of a *punishment*. Suffering, disconnected from guilt, is *calamity* or affliction, not *punishment;* to punishment, guilt is indispensably requisite. Christ had no guilt of his own; he was incapable, indeed, of contracting it; but " the Lord laid on him the *iniquity of us all.*"

VICARIOUS.—This word, as its Latin derivation imports, has the same meaning as that just explained. It signifies performing the functions, or standing in the place of another.

EXPIATION.—The annulling of guilt, or taking away of sin by some meritorious interposition, is the distinctive idea suggested by this term. Though not found in the Scriptures, no word is of more frequent use, or of greater significance, in connection with the subject of our present inquiry.

---

* Dr. Pye Smith's Discourses on Sacrifice, &c., pp. 287, 288.

Such, then, are the principal terms, scriptural and technical, which are in use on the subject now under review. It is of great importance that they be rightly understood, so that specific and distinctive ideas be attached to them respectively. In theology, as in other departments of science, we are in danger from that common law by which words and phrases in constant use come to be dissevered from the notions they are intended to represent. "This gravitation," as has been happily remarked by a powerful anonymous writer, " which brings the heavier substance (knowledge) down, as a *residuum*, and leaves the lighter (language) to float as a frothy crust on the surface, is to be counteracted only by *continual agitation of the mass*."* Let it be remarked, then, that the first three terms above explained, (atonement, reconciliation, and redemption,) direct our attention particularly to the *effects* of Christ's work; the next (propitiation), to the source of the sinner's *danger*, the wrath of God which needs to be appeased; the three next, (satisfaction, substitution, and vicarious,) to the *medium* of deliverance; and the (expiation), to its *nature* as a deliverance from guilt. Some of these terms involve the same ideas as others: but, generally speaking, there are nice shades of meaning which serve to distinguish them. A knowledge of these distinctions will at once serve to direct us in the choice of proper language in speaking on the subject ourselves, and tend to facilitate our right understanding of what is spoken by others. The terms are not to be regarded as mere synonymes or expletives. The death of Christ was at once expiatory, and vicarious, and propitiatory, and atoning. When we say it was *expiatory*, we mean that it was for sin that he died. When we say it was *vicarious*, we affirm that he died for the sins of others, not for his own. When we speak of it as *propitiatory*, we represent it as designed to appease the wrath of God, who is angry with sinners for their sins. And when we say it was *atoning*, we regard it as effecting a proper reconciliation.

* Saturday Evening; by the Author of the Natural History of Enthusiasm, p. 99.

Let the reader strive, before he proceeds, to fix in his mind correct notions of the language in use on this subject. Whatever be the matter of investigation, this is of vast moment; and more so, surely, when the theme, as in the present case, is one of such awful magnitude. Let the doctrine in question be clearly distinguished from others which have been substituted by heretics in its place. Let it be distinctly understood what is meant by Christ's atonement. Let the terms in customary use in treating of it be associated with definite conceptions. Thus may we expect the issue of our investigation to be satisfactory and profitable. But if we content ourselves with vain ambiguities, like persons in a mist, everything must appear to us dim and ill-defined; we are likely, at every step, to get more and more bewildered; and the result is sure to be darkness and confusion.

It may be proper to remind the reader of the necessity of bringing a candid, humble, and well-disciplined mind, to the investigation of this great question. A subject so high and difficult in itself, and withal so much controverted, is not to be approached under the influence of prejudice or passion. In such an inquiry much depends on the state of the moral feelings. In justice to the pure light of sacred truth, the dark mists of moral prejudice must be dissipated, and the soul freed from every unholy bias which the love or practice of sin is fitted to impart. Perfect submission ought to be given to the word of God as the sole standard and unerring guide. There should be humble reliance on the promised assistance of the divine Spirit, and the wrestlings of fervent prayer at the throne of mercy for light and direction. Care ought to be taken to view the subject as one, not of speculative research, but of practical and awful importance; affecting the very foundation of a sinner's hopes; the bond of Christian doctrine; the heart and life-blood of the religion of Jesus. Then will levity, self-confidence, and pride, be discarded; and the investigation be pursued in that lowly, pure, and reverential spirit, which cannot fail to be rewarded with ultimate success. *What man is he that feareth the Lord? him shall he teach in the way that he shall choose.*

SECTION II.

OBJECTIONS TO ATONEMENT CONSIDERED.

The view given, in the former section, of the nature of atonement, is strenuously opposed by many. The orthodox doctrine on the subject is disbelieved by not a few, who, nevertheless, lay claim to the Christian name. Their objections are at best but the specious cavils of a cold and speculative philosophy, and, in many cases, there is reason to fear, the natural result of criminal passions and irreligious prejudice, producing a secret dislike at those exalted views of the divine purity, and those humiliating sentiments of man's guilt and depravity, which the doctrine necessarily presupposes. But from whatever source they spring, the objections in question must be duly weighed. If found to be valid, it will be unnecessary to advance another step: if proved to be unfounded, the future discussion will be freed of no little incumbrance. To the candid consideration of these objections' let us, then, proceed.

I. It is objected that the doctrine of atonement represents the Supreme Being in an unamiable light, destroys the attribute of mercy, and resolves his whole character into stern and inexorable justice.

This it is supposed to do by representing the death of Christ as that which procures the mercy or love of God for sinners; that which renders him willing to pardon the sins of his creatures, and without which he would not be so willing: in short, as a motive, an inducement, a price, a bribe, a something which effects a change in the divine mind from stern and vindictive wrath to melting compassion. Now, say our opponents, so far from this being the case, God is uniformly spoken of in scripture as in his very nature merciful and gracious; as disposed to regard sinners with spontaneous benevolence; as perfectly reconciled, and instead of needing to be appeased, as " waiting to be gracious" and " ready to pardon." That such is the light in which the sacred writers exhibit the character of God, is not denied; and if the doctrine we maintain could be shown to be at variance with this view of the divine character, this must be regarded as an insuperable objection against it. But we beg attention to the following remarks.

1. The objection gives a mistaken view of what the atonement is understood to effect.

It is never supposed, by those who understand the subject, that the work of Christ is, in any sense, the *cause* of divine love, mercy, or grace; but the *medium* through which these perfections of God find expression to guilty creatures. It is never regarded as necessary to *produce* in God love towards men, but as necessary to his love being *manifested*. It is not looked upon as that which *renders* God placable, but as that which renders the *exercise* of his placability consistent with the other perfections of his nature. It does not *procure* the divine favor, but *makes way* for this favor being shown in the pardon of sin. There is a clear and broad distinction betwixt these two things, to which it is of the utmost importance to attend. This distinction is consistent with scripture, where the whole scheme of human salvation is referred to divine love as its origin; and it is as clearly implied in the doctrine under consideration, namely, that the work of Christ gives satisfaction to God for the sins of his people, for this necessarily supposes a previous willingness on the part of God to accept of satisfaction; and what is this previous good-will but love, or mercy, or grace? The true view of the matter is this, that divine love is the cause of the atonement, and not that atonement is the cause of the divine love. And when the subject is placed in this its just and proper light, so far from the atonement representing the Deity as unamiable, it must be regarded as itself the brightest display of the divine loving-kindness. Nothing can be conceived more expressive of the benevolence of God, than his sending his Son into the world to suffer and die for the guilty objects of his love. In the estimation of the inspired writers, the gift of his Son is ever regarded as the most perfect manifestation of the riches of God's grace. "For God so loved the world, that he gave his only-begotten Son, that whosoever believeth in him should not perish, but have everlasting life." "In this was manifested the love of God toward us, because that God sent his only-begotten Son into the world, that we might live through him."* When atonement is thus exhibited as the *effect* and not the *cause* of God's love and mercy, the objection in question is completely neutralized; for so far from representing the Supreme Being in an unfavorable light, it stands forth as the most brilliant and overpowering manifestation of his loving-kindness and grace—the pure emanation of infinite, eternal, and unchangeable love. And all such views of the doctrine as are inconsistent with Jehovah's original disposition to be merciful, or which represent him as changed, by the Saviour's sacrifice, from wrath and fury to kindness and grace, are either the misconceptions of friends or the misrepresentations of enemies, which are to be viewed with unmingled disapprobation and regret.

2. But this is not all. The objection proceeds on a mistaken assumption.

It assumes that God is ready to pardon sin without satisfaction, that retributive justice is no part of his character, and that, consequently, forgiveness is the result of a mere arbitrary resolve of will, with which law and government have nothing to do. But we must take leave to remind the objector that God is *just* as well as merciful. Rectitude is as essential a feature of the divine Being as love. If the Scriptures represent God in the light of a Father " in whom compassions flow," they no less distinctly reveal him as a

---

* John iii. 16. 1 John iv. 9.

Lawgiver "who will by no means clear the guilty." These views of the divine character must never be opposed to one another, but considered as alike essential, co-existent, co-operative, and harmonious. It is quite a mistake to regard God as acting at one time according to the one, and at another time according to the other; at one time according to mercy, and at another according to justice. He acts agreeably to both at all times. The exercise of the one never supposes the suspension of the other. When he punishes the guilty, it is not at the expense of mercy; when he pardons the transgressor, it is not at the expense of justice. Mercy must, therefore, proceed on a principle which is agreeable to justice. ⟨While mercy inclines him to forgive, justice must receive satisfation in order to forgiveness.⟩ Deny this, and you place in irreconcilable opposition two essential attributes of the divine nature. Admit this, and the objection under consideration falls to the ground; for the satisfaction which the doctrine of atonement supposes to be made by Christ is necessary, not indeed to awaken the feeling of mercy in the divine bosom, but to reconcile the merciful forgiveness of sin with the equitable demands of justice. If, then, justice or equity form any part of the character of God, if there be such a thing as a moral government in the universe over which God presides, that the pardon of sin should proceed on a principle which respects the claims of the divine character and government, can never represent the Supreme Being in an unfavorable light; unless it can be shown that the proper display of one feature of his character, involves the obliteration of another. The objection thus appears to proceed on a gross mistake regarding the nature of that connection which subsists between the love of God and the satisfaction of Christ. A connection there is, and a connection, too, of cause and effect. But in the mind of the objectors these are made to exchange places; the cause is put for the effect, and the effect for the cause; the love of God is represented as the effect, and the satisfaction of Christ as its cause: whereas the fact is quite the reverse; the love of God is the cause: and the satisfaction of Christ the effect. And when viewed in this light, which is that of God's word, the objection loses all its force.

II. The doctrine of atonement has been thought inconsistent with the divine immutability.

God is unchangeable. In his nature, perfections and will, he can undergo no alteration. This were to suppose him capable either of improvement or of deterioration, which suppositions alike involve a denial of his perfection. If he is capable of improvement, he was not before perfect. If he can undergo a deterioration, supposing him perfect before, he is perfect no longer. These suppositions are equally blasphemous and absurd; and consequently inapplicable to Him who says, "I am the Lord, I change not." Yet the atonement of Christ is supposed to effect such a change in the mind of God, that he is reconciled on account of it, to those with whom he was formerly displeased, and induced to love what he formerly hated.

This objection resolves itself into the former, and might be disposed of in the same way. Yet, as the form in which it is presented makes it to turn on the immutability rather than the amiableness of God, it requires a distinct consideration.

1. First of all, let it be remarked, that, if the orthodox employ language which *seems to imply* a change in God, this is nothing more than is done by the inspired writers themselves.

The phrase *God's being reconciled* may not, in so many exact terms, be found in the Bible; but, certainly, phrases of precisely equivalent import are to be found there in abundance. Is not his *anger* said to be *turned away?* "In that day thou shalt say, O Lord, I will praise thee: though thou wast angry with me, thine anger is turned away, and thou comfortest me."* Is he not spoken of as *keeping not his anger for ever?* "Go and proclaim these words towards the north, and say, Return thou backsliding Israel, saith the Lord, and I will not cause mine anger to fall

---

* Isaiah xii. 1.

upon you: for I am merciful, saith she Lord, and I will not keep anger for ever." "He retaineth not his anger for ever, because he delighteth in mercy."* Nay, is he not represented as being *pacified?* "That thou mayest remember and be confounded, and never open thy mouth any more because of thy shame, when I AM PACIFIED TOWARD THEE for all that thou hast done, saith the Lord God."† In these and similar passages, although the *word* " reconcile" is not used, the *idea* of reconciliation is surely expressed. It is to no purpose, then, that the enemies of atonement cite those passages in which man is said to be reconciled to God, as if it were impossible, at the same time, that God should be reconciled to man. Man is indeed reconciled to God, and this reconciliation, too, is effected by Christ. 'When we were enemies we were reconciled to God by the death of his Son. All things are of God, who hath reconciled us to himself by Jesus Christ.'‡ The orthodox believe that the atonement of Jesus has a bearing on man, a tendency to bring down the proud oppositon of the human heart, and to slay the enmity of the carnal mind against God. But they believe, also, that it has a bearing on God, because the Scriptures formerly quoted teach as much. And there is nothing in this incompatible with those other texts which suppose that it has a bearing on man. So far from there being anything inconsistent in admitting both ideas, it can even be shown, we think, that the latter supposes the former.

In scripture phraseology, when an offender is spoken of as being reconciled, it means his taking some steps to reconcile him whom he has offended. When the princes of the Philistines are wroth with David and say, "Wherewith should he reconcile himself to his master?"§ the meaning they intend to express, plainly is that he should find a difficulty in reconciling his master to himself. Such, also, is the import of the phrase in the well-known passage, " If thou bring thy gift to the altar, and there rememberest that thy

* Jer. iii. 12. Micah vii. 18. † Ezek. xvi. 63.
‡ Rom. v. 10. 2 Cor. v 18. § 1 Sam. xxix. 4.

brother hath aught against thee, leave there thy gift before the altar, and go thy way; first be reconciled to thy brother, and then come and offer thy gift."* This passage is most decisive. The person addressed is the *offender;* he has nothing against his brother, but his brother has something against him; yet is he exhorted to go and be reconciled to his brother, that is, to go and *reconcile his brother to himself.* This is the only meaning which the passage can bear, consistently with the terms employed. On the same principle, when man is required to be reconciled to God, may we not be warranted to conclude that the phrase implies that God is to be reconciled to man? When the facts of the case are considered, this inference is the more confirmed. God is the offended party, man is the offender; the reconciliation is effected by the blood or death of Christ, which is frequently represented in other places as offered to God; and the effect produced is equivalent to the non-imputation of trespasses which is certainly the prerogative of God alone. "God was in Christ, reconciling the world to himself, not imputing their trespasses unto them."†

How futile, thus, are all the attempts of Socinians to get rid of the scripture doctrine of God's being reconciled to men by Jesus Christ! The doctrine is plainly expressed in numerous parts of holy writ, and it is clearly implied even in those which are supposed to exclude it. Let them explain to us, therefore, on their theory, the texts of scripture in which language is used that seems to imply a change in God as well as in man. On the principle of atonement, these present no difficulty. Both sets of passages are easily interpreted, for God is supposed to be reconciled to man as well as man reconciled to God. On the Socinian hypothesis, however, which supposes that only man is reconciled to God, it is not easy to see how the one class of texts is to be understood at all. Betwixt the two, on the orthodox principle, there is no disagreement, but the most complete and delightful harmony·

* Matt. 23, 24.   † 2 Cor. v. 19.

on the principle of its opponents, the inconsistency is glaring and palpable.

2. Still, it may be thought, this does not get rid of the difficulty; it merely shifts it from our own shoulders to those of the sacred penmen.

And are we to suppose, on the authority of scripture too, that the atonement *does* effect a change on the immutable God? Far be the thought. The doctrine is not chargeable with anything so blasphemous. What we have affirmed is, that the texts in question *seemingly* imply a change in God. We have not said that they *really* imply such a thing. What, then, *do* they imply? To speak of a change in the nature, or attributes, or will of God, is blasphemous and absurd, as we have just now said. But it is neither blasphemous nor absurd to speak of a change in the mode of the divine administration. Now the *anger, wrath,* and *displeasure* of God, are not passions or affections of the divine nature resembling those which receive the same names in man. They are terms denoting the necessary opposition of the divine rectitude to such as have violated the holy law of the righteous Lord who loveth righteousness. They mark the relation into which iniquity brings such as are chargeable with it to the Lawgiver, and Judge of the universe. It is the language of *government*, not of *passion*. And what the atonement effects is, not a change in God the Lawgiver, but a change in the administration of his government; a change in the relation subsisting between his creatures and himself. Those whom he formerly treated in a way which is fitly represented to us by anger, indignation, and wrath, he, in consequence of what Christ has done, treats in a way which is fitly represented by love and complacency. But the change is *not in God*, it is in the *creature*, and in the *relation* in which the creature stands towards God. God does not love at one time what he hated at another. He does not, in respect of Christ's atonement, love what, irrespective of this atonement, he hated. No. He hates and loves the same things at all times. What does God hate? It is sin, and not the sinner; he cannot hate his creatures as such, but only as violators of his just and holy will. What does God love? Holiness, his moral image, which is reflected from men, not as mere creatures, but as *moral* creatures, as *new* creatures: not as sinners, but as saints. The change thus appears to be *not in God*. He is pleased and displeased with the same things at all times. He always hates sin—always loves holiness. The atonement does not make God love sin which he formerly hated, nor hate holiness which he formerly loved. The change which it effects is not in God who is the author of love, but in man who is the object of love. By means of Christ's death, man is brought out of a state of condemnation and depravity, which God could not but regard with repugnance, into a state of reconciliation and purity, which he cannot but look upon with complacency. The change, every one must perceive, is, in this case, not in God, but in man, or in the relation in which man stands to God. Whatever change the creature undergoes, God continues the same. The sun, the glorious fountain of light and beauty, is always the same in its nature and properties, although the earth may reflect its rays at one time and not another. But it were every whit as reasonable to ascribe the different appearances which the earth assumes by day and by night, to a change in the solar luminary, rather than to its own relative position with regard to that luminary, as to ascribe the state of man in consequence of Christ's atonement, to a change in God rather than in man himself. Thus do we dispose of the objection founded on the divine immutability.

III. It is further objected to the doctrine of atonement, that it is incompatible with the gracious nature of pardon.

The forgiveness of sin, say the objectors, is uniformly in scripture ascribed to grace. It is an act of free favor, of sovereign goodness. But on the supposition o. satisfaction being given for sin by Jesus Christ, the act can no longer be called an act of grace, it is an act of justice; and instead of its being merciful in God to pardon sin, it would be unjust in him to withhold forgiveness. Such is the objection with which we have now to deal. It is more specious, certainly, than some others, and, consequently a great favorite with the enemies of atonement. But the following observations may serve, it is hoped, to show its groundlessness.

1. The objection supposes justice and grace to be opposed to one another, not only in their nature, but in their exercise, so that both cannot respect the same object.

This supposition has already been refuted, and we must beg our readers to revert to what was before advanced in proof of the perfect harmony of these perfections of the divine nature.* In addition, we may here observe, that the inspired writers appear to have had no idea of any incongruity between justice and grace in the pardon of sin. On the contrary, they represent both as connected with forgiveness. What one apostle ascribes to grace, another refers to justice. Paul says, "We have redemption through his blood, the forgiveness of sins, according to the riches of his GRACE;"† while John, writing under the direction of the same Spirit, tells us, that "If we confess our sins, He is faithful and JUST to forgive us our sins, and to cleanse us from all unrighteousness."‡ It is worthy of remark, too, that in both these passages pardon is connected with atonement; in the former, mention being made of "redemption through the blood" of Christ, and in the context of the latter, reference being made to "the blood of Jesus Christ God's Son which cleanseth from all sin." This is agreeable to other parts of scripture; as, for example, when Paul, writing to the Romans, in one verse ascribes forgiveness through the redemption of Christ to *grace*, and in the very next speaks of it as a manifestation of *justice*. "Being justified freely by his GRACE, through the redemption that is in Christ Jesus; whom God hath set forth to be a propitiation, through faith in his blood, to declare his RIGHTEOUSNESS

---

* See p. 23.   † Eph. i. 7.   ‡ 1 John i. 9

for the remission of sins.'* Can anything more distinctly prove that the inspired writers had no notion whatever of an essential incompatibility between justice and grace, or between atonement and free favor?

2. The objection overlooks the origin of Christ's satisfaction.

It did not originate with man, but with God. Man did not find a surety for himself; it was God that found out the ransom. If another than God who pardons sin had provided the ground on which the pardon rests, there might have been room to deny the graciousness of the act. But as it is God that provides the Mediator, the work of the Surety, so far from interfering with the freeness of man's forgiveness, becomes the most illustrious proof and confirmation of divine grace. God manifests his grace in determining to pardon man; it is farther displayed in providing a legal ground on which pardon might proceed in consistency with justice; and it is again brought into view in accepting the satisfaction offered by the Surety, which he was not bound in absolute justice to do.

3. The objection also overlooks the circumstance, that although the satisfaction of Christ may be regarded as a legal purchase of pardon, the *bestowment* of pardon is altogether an act of grace as regards the persons on whom it is conferred.

It is free pardon at least to *men*. They have no claim; no satisfaction is made by them; they do nothing to procure for themselves forgiveness. If the pardon of sin is an act of justice at all, it is so only to Christ; to the sinner it is one of pure sovereign goodness. It flows through an equitable channel; it proceeds on a righteous foundation; the ground on which it rests is such as to meet every claim of divine justice; but, as regards the spring from which it issues and the objects on whom it terminates, it is wholly a display of superabounding mercy. "Being justified through the redemption that is in Jesus" is thus no way inconsistent with "being justified freely by God's grace.'

---

* Rom. iii. 24, 25.

"Fancy to yourself," says Dr. Wardlaw, "a band of traitors, apprehended, convicted, condemned, lying in irons under the sentence which their crimes have deserved. Suppose their prince, naturally benignant, desirous to extend mercy to them: but at the same time, wise and righteous, and mindful of the interests of the community, as well as benignant, solicitous to effect this in such a way as may at once secure the dignity and authority of his government, attach the hearts of the criminals to its administration and to himself, and impress all his subjects with the conviction that the remission of the penalty in the particular case implies no relaxation of the rigor of the law and the stability of its sanctions. Suppose that, in such circumstances, he should contrive some method by which these ends might be effectually answered; and that, having completed his scheme, and publicly announced its purpose, he should give his clemency its desired indulgence:— would the pardon now be less a matter of free favor or grace to the delinquents? Clearly not. The scheme does not render them one whit more deserving of it. It does not lessen their guilt: it rather shows its magnitude, by declaring it such as could not be passed by without some precautionary means for securing the honor of the prince and the respect due to his government; nay, it aggravates instead of extenuating, by showing the character of the prince and government against which the rebels had risen up, not a ruthless tyrant and an oppressive despotism, but a paternal ruler and an administration of equity and love. The pardon is to them, therefore, as much an act of mercy as ever:—and the character of the prince stands forth to more prominent view and to more rapturous admiration, as adorned with the twofold excellence of a gracious solicitude to show mercy, and at the same time a decided attachment to righteousness, and a determination for the good of his subjects, that its claims shall not be trifled with, but shall be maintained inviolate.— In like manner, the divine Ruler's adopting a plan for maintaining the honor of *his* character and government in the dispensation of forgiveness, does not, in the least degree, render that forgiveness less a matter of pure grace to those who receive it.—And, while it is pure grace, it is also rich;—rich indeed! that provided such an atonement!—and rich indeed! which, on the ground of the atonement so provided, blots out, to every sinner who partakes of it, so vast an amount of evil, and yet embraces among its favored objects a multitude which "no man can number, out of all kindreds, and peoples, and nations, and tongues!"*

4. These remarks may be deemed a sufficient reply to the objection. But, in refutation of the Socinian's favorite position, we may perhaps go farther still.

It may fairly be questioned, whether there could have been seen to be grace at all in the pardon of sin, had it not been for the atonement of Christ. Had God pardoned sin without satisfaction, our opponents think he would have given some satisfactory display of his grace. We are inclined to suppose, on the contrary, that, in such a case, there would have been no proof of grace at all. Make the supposition that God had pardoned sin without an atonement, and pardoned not only some but all the family of man, and what is the inference which intelligent and moral beings should have been disposed to draw from this act? That God is gracious, and that his grace is altogether without limits? We presume not. Would it not be a much more reasonable inference that sin, the violation of his law, was no evil, no *great* evil at least, not such an evil as it had been supposed to be, seeing it could be so easily passed over by a Being of absolute moral perfection? This we have no hesitation in saying, would be the more natural inference of the two. If even the awful view of sin's magnitude which the cross of Christ is fitted to give is found insufficient to prevent men from thinking lightly of it, it is not to be supposed that their sense of its turpitude would have been enhanced by the absence of an atonement. "So far then is it from being true, that the mercy of God would have been ready to forgive the sinner without

---

* Essays on Assurance and Pardon, pp. 199, 200

atonement had justice allowed it, and that it would have been highly honored by so doing, that the very existence of mercy can be proved only by the atonement. Remove that proof of it, and I may very safely challenge all the wisdom of human philosophy to prove that any such thing as mercy exists. I know not if this view of the matter be urged upon the attention of the church with sufficient frequency and prominence: but if it were, I can hardly think that so strange an objection to the atonement could ever have been conceived, as that which considers the atonement,—the only fact by which the very existence of mercy, and much more its infinite extent can be proved,—as a drawback upon the fulness and freeness of that mercy.'*

IV. Objection has often been made to the doctrine of atonement, on the ground that it supposes the innocent to suffer for the guilty; a thing which is regarded as inconsistent with reason, and with the goodness and justice of God.

The doctrine of atonement certainly involves the principle of substitution: whether that principle be liable to the objection alleged against it, is the thing to be considered. We have no wish to get rid of the difficulty by denying the fact; but as little are we disposed to suffer the admitted fact to lie under the weight of aspersions which are thrown upon it unjustly. Let us see, then, how the matter stands as to this point.

1. It must be admitted by all, that, under the moral government of God, the innocent do sometimes suffer for the guilty.

It is not pretended that cases exactly similar to that we are considering are of frequent occurrence in the providence of God. The contrary, indeed, is frankly admitted. The substitution of Christ is allowed to be altogether extraordinary—to be without a parallel in the divine proceedings with regard to moral creatures. Nothing like it, in all respects, has yet existed, or is

* Dods on the Incarnation of the Eternal Word, p. 120.

likely ever to exist again to the end of time. Yet cases sufficiently like to neutralize the objection in question are not of unfrequent occurrence. The innocent do often suffer for the guilty, and that too without such exalted purposes being served by it as in the case of Christ. Poverty, and pain, and disgrace, and disease are not seldom entailed on children, in consequence of the criminal indiscretions of their parents. This is what cannot be denied. It is not the same thing as the substitution of Christ; the suffering is of the nature of calamity rather than of punishment. Yet it is the innocent suffering for the guilty; and as this is the point on which the objection turns, we may call upon the objectors to explain this undeniable fact in divine providence, before we can admit their right to urge the principle of the fact against a doctrine of divine revelation. If the thing is unreasonable and and unjust in the one case, it cannot be less so in the other. Will they have the hardihood to affirm, that such occurrences in providence as have been mentioned, imply injustice in the administration of the moral government of our world? If they will, we have nothing more to do with them; we leave them to one from whom they will not find it so easy to escape. "He that reproveth God, let him answer it." But if they will not venture so far with regard to providence, we have just to tell them they have no right to make any such assertions in a matter of pure revelation. The difficulty, if it be a difficulty, is one which they cannot be permitted to urge as an insuperable objection in one case, while in a parallel case they feel it to be no difficulty at all.

And that the idea of the innocent suffering for the guilty is not so repugnant to the natural reason of man as the objectors allege, seems confirmed by the universal prevalence of expiatory sacrifices. Whether the practice of offering such sacrifices be of divine origin or not—a question which will fall to be considered at another stage of our argument—its universal adoption cannot be denied. This, be it remarked, is not a little in our favor, as the practice in question proceeds distinctly on the principle of the innocent suffering for the guilty. Whether you suppose this practice to have originated with man, or whether, as we are persuaded was the case, the suggestion proceeded from God, the fact is alike to our purpose. If it originated with man, the idea of substitution which it essentially involves must be anything but repugnant to the human mind. Supposing it to have originated with God, its having been eagerly and universally embraced by man when suggested conducts us to the same conclusion.

2. But the very same objection presses, with all its force, against the doctrine of our opponents.

They admit that Jesus Christ suffered for the benefit of mankind. They admit, too, that at least as regards the alleged grounds of his sufferings he was innocent. Few of them, indeed, have ventured even to " hint a doubt" with regard to his perfect immaculate purity; and none has gone the length to suppose he was the blasphemous usurper which his enemies alleged he was, as the ground of their inflictions upon him. Well, then, what is this but the innocent suffering for the guilty? In the one case he is supposed to suffer for our benefit; in the other, to suffer in our stead; in both he is understood to be innocent. The innocent, then, suffers *for the guilty*. There is, it is admitted, a distinction between what Socinians understand by Christ's suffering *for our benefit* and what the orthodox mean by his suffering *in our stead;* but the distinction is not of such a nature as to render suffering on the one supposition manifestly just, and on the other manifestly unjust If it be just in the one case, it is just in both: if it be unjust in one, it is so also in the other. Nay, inasmuch as suffering for our benefit, according to the sense of Socinians, is an end every way inferior to what the orthodox understand by suffering in our stead, if injustice is supposed to be involved in any degree in the latter supposition, in a much higher degree must it be involved in the former. The Socinian, then, by the objection in question stultifies himself. It is a two-edged weapon, which is capable of being turned with effect against his own cause. If it possess any weight, it falls with tenfold force on the system which he is pledged to support.

3. It is overlooked by the objectors, that, although Christ was *personally* innocent, he was viewed as *legally* guilty.

In *himself* he could put to the most impudent accuser the defiance—" Which of you convinceth me of sin ?" but as the surety and *substitute* of elect sinners, " the Lord laid on him the iniquity of us all—he made him to be sin for us, who knew no sin—he bare the sins of many." It was formerly explained, and we beg now to remind our readers of the explanation, that when Christ took the place of offending sinners, he not merely suffered their punishment, but bore their guilt, that is to say, was regarded by the holy law of God as under obligation to suffer. Apart from this obligation, as was remarked, his sufferings would have been nothing more than calamities; there could have been nothing *penal* in them, nothing of the nature of *punishment*, nothing possessing the character of a legal satisfaction. In order to this he behooved to be brought under an obligation to suffer, and, as he had no personal guilt by which this could take place, it was effected by the imputation of the guilt of others. " The Lord laid on him the iniquity of us all." This alters the case entirely. Guilt, not in the sense of *blameworthiness* but of *legal answerableness*, was his.* Innocent indeed he was in himself; and had he not been so he could not have stood as the substitute of others;

---

* "As the term *guilt* is liable to misconstruction, I have declined retaining it; though it was used in a sense quite, I trust, unobjectionable. We commonly employ this term both in the sense of LEGAL ANSWERABLENESS, (reatus,) and of BLAMEWORTHINESS, (culpa.)......In divinity, as well as in other sciences, it is necessary to attach to some terms a technical definiteness of signification, much more restrained than the ordinary acceptation of the same words. It were to be wished that, in all such cases, we had words appropriated only to the particular objects; but the usage of language (quem penes arbitrium est, et jus, et norma loquendi,) forbids such a wish. If scepticism or rashness should raise a cavil, we can only reply, that the cavil is unreasonable. No man ridicules mathematical terms because, in many instances, they are the words of common life employed in a very restricted signification."—*Smith on Sacrifice, &c.,* p. 284.

he must, in this case, have had to answer for himself: but, while free from all personal guilt, he was pleased to take upon him the guilt of his people, and in the character of their surety or substitute was it that he suffered the penalty of the law. The law held him guilty as standing in the room of the guilty, and in this character he suffered. Such a union subsisted betwixt Christ and his people as to lay foundation for a reciprocal proprietorship, in consequence of which, while he was "made sin for us," we are " made the righteousness of God in him." Nor let it be said, that this supposes God to have treated Christ as something different from what he was,—as guilty when he was not guilty, which would be essentially unjust. By no means. He was not personally guilty, and God did not treat him as personally guilty: but he chose to take upon him *our* guilt, and God treated him, not as one who had made himself guilty by personal transgression, but as one who was the representative of the guilty, standing in their place, and bearing their sins in his own body. Such was the light in which God viewed him; and, viewing him in this light, to inflict on him the sufferings due to human guilt involved no infringement of legal rectitude or justice.

4. It ought also to be considered how far the circumstance of Christ's suffering for guilty men under the sanction of divine authority, and by his own voluntary agreement, go to do away with the present objection.

An innocent person's being *compelled* to suffer for the guilty involves the highest injustice; but Christ *voluntarily* substituted himself in the room of his people;—he took upon him their sins; he bowed his neck to the yoke; he laid down his life, no one took it from him, but he laid it down of himself. It was a deliberate act, the result of solemn purpose, and not the sudden impulse of transient enthusiasm. He had a perfect right to dispose of himself as he thought fit, being under no antecedent obligation to law, but possessing an absolute independence, and being at perfect liberty to give his life a ransom for many. "I have power to lay it down," says he, " and I have power to take it again."—Nor was this wonderful act of voluntary condescension without the sanction of supreme authority. Although a private person, heroic and benevolent enough to offer himself as a substitute for the guilty, could be found, it is clear that, to the consequences of such surrender being perfectly just, the transaction must receive the sanction of the offended lawgiver. He alone has a right to say whether he will admit of the proposed commutation, as he only can judge whether such a procedure may be conducive to all the ends of justice. While, therefore, Christ "*gave himself* for our sins that he might redeem us from the present evil world," he did so " *according to the will of God* even our Father ;" and, when about to enter on the last awful scene of woe, he was heard to say, " As the Father gave me commandment, so I do; arise, let us go hence." The innocent suffering for the guilty involuntarily and without the countenance of legal sanction, may be allowed to be inconsistent with reason and with the goodness and justice of God ; but the same cannot surely be said of the innocent suffering for the guilty with the full approbation of supreme authority, and in a manner which is perfectly voluntary.

5. The futility of the objection will still farther appear, if it can be shown that, by the innocent suffering for the guilty, the ends to be subserved by punishment are more fully attained than by the suffering of the guilty for themselves, while at the same time, no injury is done either to the law or to the sufferer.

That no injury is done to the law or to the sufferer, in the present case, appears from what we have already adduced. It remains to be shown, that the ends to be accomplished by suffering the punishment of the law, are much more completely subserved by the substitutionary scheme than they could otherwise have been. " The matter may be illustrated thus,— A rebel is taken, tried, and condemned. As he is led out to punishment, the king's son,—the heir of his crown, steps forward and proposes to purchase the life and liberty of the rebel, by having the sentence transferred to himself, and consenting to undergo its infliction. His father consents, and his offer being accepted, the law has the same hold upon him that it had upon the rebel, while upon the latter it ceases to have any further claim. And though it be now his own son upon whom the sentence is to be inflicted, the king abates not one iota of its severity, but causes it to be carried into execution to its fullest extent. This shows on the part both of the father and the son, how highly they prize the safety of the rebel. It shows the unpardonable guilt of rebellion, that even the heir to the throne cannot deliver the rebel otherwise than by undergoing his sentence. It shows the majesty of the government, and the sanctity of the law in a much more striking manner than the death of the rebel himself could have done, when the king's son is spared nothing of what the rebel was doomed to bear.'*

If such be the case,—if by the method of a vicarious interposition rather than by suffering righteous vengeance to fall where it was personally due, the ends of God's holy government are attained, not only equally well, but unspeakably better; if the rectoral honor of the Eternal Sovereign is more inviolably preserved and exhibited; if sin is held up to the moral universe as more deserving of abhorrence and execration; if the designs of wisdom, justice, and mercy are more amply and effectually accomplished, who will presume to say that the Divine Being was not at liberty to adopt this method without subjecting his procedure to the charge of inconsistency and injustice? *Nay but, O man, who art thou that repliest against God?*

6. It ought, moreover, to be taken into consideration, that, in respect of the substitutionary sufferings of the Son of God, the case admits of such a compensative arrangement as to prevent all ultimate injury to the party concerned.

The idea here suggested deprives the objection before us of all force, and this idea is so happily stated

---

* Dods on Incarnation, &c., pp. 236, 237.

and illustrated by one of the greatest ornaments of our age, that I cannot resist presenting it in his own nervous and felicitous language. "However much we might be convinced." says Mr. Hall, "of the competence of vicarious suffering to accomplish the ends of justice, and whatever the benefits we may derive from it, a benevolent mind could never be reconciled to the sight of virtue of the highest order finally oppressed and consumed by its own energies; and the more intense the admiration excited, the more eager would be the desire of some compensatory arrangement, some expedient by which an ample retribution might be assigned to such heroic sacrifices. If the suffering of the substitute involved his destruction, what satisfaction could a generous and feeling mind derive from impunity procured at such a cost? When David, in an agony of thirst, longed for the water of Bethlehem, which some of his servants immediately procured for him with the extreme hazard of their lives, the monarch refused to taste it, exclaiming, *It is the price of blood!* but *poured it out before the Lord.* The felicity which flows from the irreparable misery of another, and more especially of one whose disinterested benevolence alone exposed him to it, will be faintly relished by him who is not immersed in selfishness. If there be any portions of history, whose perusal affords more pure and exquisite delight than others, they are those which present the spectacle of a conflicting and self-devoted virtue, after innumerable toils and dangers undergone in the cause, enjoying a dignified repose in the bosom of the country which its example has ennobled, and its valor saved. Such a spectacle gratifies the best propensities, satisfies the highest demands of our moral and social nature. It affords a delightful glimpse of the future and perfect economy of retributive justice. In the plan of human redemption this requisition is fully satisfied. While we accompany the Saviour through the successive stages of his mortal sojourning, marked by a corresponding succession of trials, each of which was more severe than the former, till the scene darkened, and the clouds of wrath from heaven and from earth, pregnant with materials which nothing but a div'ne hand could have collected, discharged themselves on him in a deluge of agony and of blood, under which he expired, we perceive at once the sufficiency, I had almost said, the redundancy, of his atonement. But surely deliverance even *from the wrath to come* would afford an imperfect enjoyment, if it were imbittered with the recollection that we were indebted for it to the irreparable destruction of our compassionate Redeemer. The consolation arising from *reconciliation with God* is subject to no such deduction. While we rejoice in the cross of Christ as the source of pardon, our satisfaction is heightened by beholding it succeeded by the crown; by seeing him that was *for a little while made lower than the angels, for the suffering of death, crowned with glory and honor, seated at the right hand of God, thence expecting till his enemies are made his footstool.*'*

7. There is one circumstance more which deserves to be taken into the account in replying to this objection. The substitution of Christ is a case which is absolutely peculiar.

Such a case could never be justified as a matter of ordinary or frequent occurrence. It could only be when something extraordinary called for its introduction, when such a combination of requirements met as could but seldom come together, that it would be warrantable to admit of the innocent being substituted in room of the guilty. Its frequent occurrence could not fail to have a most injurious influence in weakening the sense of moral obligation. That the bad should be pardoned at the expense of the good, the virtuous sacrificed that the wicked might be spared, and those who are a blessing to society cut off that such as are a curse might be perpetuated, are what no wise government could tolerate. The punishment of crime would, in this case, be so dissevered from the perpetration of crime, as to impair the motives to obedience

---

* Hall's Works, vol. i. pp. 514—517.

and take away all fear of offending against the law. The purposes of good government thus require that the principle of substitution shall be but rarely introduced. It cannot take place in the common course of justice; it must be an extraordinary interposition; not contrary to law, but above law; departing from the letter, but maintaining the spirit; and introduced by one who possesses the right of exerting a dispensing power, that is to say, by the lawgiver himself. Now the substitution of Christ is exactly of the nature required. It is an event quite *unique* in the administration of God's moral government. It is strictly and literally an extraordinary proceeding. We have no reason to conclude that the like ever existed before, or shall ever exist again. It stands forth an insulated and prominent fact in the economy of divine providence—" a single and solitary monument amidst the lapse of ages and the waste of worlds." Inspired history contains not a hint of any such transaction having ever before occurred on the theatre of the universe; nor does prophecy give us ground to expect that any thing similar is ever again to occur in the annals of eternity. It is the masterpiece of infinite wisdom—an unparallelled display of infinite goodness, calculated to engage the enraptured and eternal contemplation of every order of created intelligences.* *Christ hath* ONCE *suffered for sins. Christ was* ONCE *offered to bear the sins of many.* ONCE *in the end of the world did he appear to put away sin by the sacrifice of himself.*

V. We shall notice, only farther, the objection that the atonement of Christ was unnecessary.

It is supposed that God could as honorably acquit sinners *without* as *with* a satisfaction. It will not be necessary to dwell long in replying to this position, as we intend to devote the next section wholly to the investigation of the necessity of Christ's atonement. A few brief remarks may here suffice.

1. The objection is presumptuous.

---

* See Hall, vol. i. p. 516.

It is not for us, on the ground of mere abstract reasoning, to say what is absolutely necessary or not necessary in a case like the present. When we venture to say what God ought to do or ought not to do, what course it would be honorable, and what not honorable for him to pursue, we step quite beyond our limits; we set up our weak, erring, finite understandings as judges over the infinite mind of Jehovah. The only safe ground on which we can determine whether a certain line of procedure be necessary or honorable in God, is judging from what he has already revealed or done. To pronounce it antecedently unnecessary is thus to beg the question,—it is just to affirm that an atonement has not been made, nor any data given from which it can be inferred. This, however, is the very point in dispute, and must be determined by quite a different process from that of arrogantly pronouncing an atonement unnecessary.

2. But supposing, for the sake of argument, that the necessity of an atonement could not be shown from any thing that appears, it would not follow, even then, that we are at liberty to pronounce it absolutely unnecessary.

There may be reasons for its existence which we have never discovered, or which we are not qualified to comprehend. There may be purposes to be served by it which have never been made known to us, and which our unaided faculties are incapable of penetrating. Unless we can say that we are acquainted with every possible reason that can exist for such a course, unless we can affirm that we know every purpose which it is capable of serving, it must be obvious we have no right to pronounce it unnecessary; for amongst those things which are not known to us, there may be reasons numerous and sufficient why an atonement should be made. As well may a child object to the necessity of some intricate scheme of national policy, because it cannot perceive such necessity, when the only reason of its not perceiving it is its want of capacity to understand the subject. Let it not be supposed, from these remarks, to be our opinion that the reasons for a vicarious satisfaction to the law and justice of God, are either not revealed, or incapable of being understood. Far different is our conviction, as will appear in the sequel. But supposing it were so, we mean to say that the objection before us supposes an unwarrantable overleaping of the bounds of the human understanding.

3. The objection, too, supposes a most imperfect and restricted view of the nature of man's offence against God.

Inadequate views of sin are at the foundation of almost all the doctrinal and practical errors that exist in the world. Men are ready to regard it as something altogether different from what it is regarded by God. A thousand palliatives and excuses they can easily conceive for the commission of it, and, after it has been committed, they can talk of it in language which too plainly indicates the imperfection of their views. If sin were a mere insult offered to majesty, it might be overlooked, for dignity is often more consulted by passing by an offence, than by rigorously demanding satisfaction for every slight that is offered to it. If sin were a mere debt, it might have been remitted, as a creditor may, without any impropriety, suffer his debtor to go free. If sin were merely a thing to be abhorred, it might have been pardoned, simply on the person's showing, by his repentance, a disposition to abhor it. But it is something more than all this. It is the violation of a holy, just, and good law, an infraction of a moral constitution, in the maintenance of which the honor of God and the good of all his moral subjects are concerned. This alters the case materially, and renders it necessary, as we shall afterwards see, that steps be taken which would not otherwise have been required.

4. The objection, we shall only add, proceeds on a more imperfect view of the nature of human salvation.

Admitting that God might honorably pardon sin without a satisfaction, it should be remembered that the remission of sin is not the whole of salvation. The penal inflictions due to sin may be supposed to be remitted without the soul being saved. The salvation of the soul supposes deliverance from other evils, and the possession of other qualities, to which, after all, the virtue of an atoning sacrifice may be indispensable. " Were we even to concede," says Dr. Smith, with much acuteness and force, " that the Deity could remit the positive punishment of sin, by a determination of his gracious will; yet this would not effect the salvation of the sinner. This measure of gracious will (the supposition of which, however, I by no means think tenable) would be merely *the forbearing from certain positive acts* of righteous power, merely *waiving a right*, merely *declining to effectuate* that which, speaking analogically, as the Scriptures so often do, would be an insulated act in the procedure of the blessed God, alien from the ordinary tendency and character of his government, and which he would not execute without the greatest reluctance, " his strange work." But under a very different respect, in moral consideration, would come the arbitrary taking away of the natural and necessary consequences of sin. *These are not inflictions;* but they are events and states of things which *follow of themselves*, according to the general constitutions of the universe, the laws of intellectual and moral nature; constitutions and laws which are essential to the harmony and well-being of God's entire world. To intercept this course of things, which infinite wisdom and goodness have established, to prevent these effects from ensuing, when their proper causes have already occurred, is not a case of forbearing to act; it is the exact reverse, it is a case of acting. It would be an interference of the Deity to suspend the operation of his own laws, to cut off the connection between the cause and the effect, to change the course of nature; it would be to work a miracle."*

We have thus endeavored to state with fairness, and to examine with candor, the principal objections to the doctrine under review. If they have been, as we

---

* Disc. on Sac., &c., pp. 196, 197.

hope, satisfactorily refuted, an additional and important step of advancement has been made. We now not only see what atonement means, but are convinced that there exists no antecedent improbability that such an expedient should be introduced into the moral economy of God. No such antecedent improbability can be urged, either on the ground of reason or of the nature of salvation. We cannot, therefore, but bewail that deep depravity of man's understanding and will, which is manifested in his failing to perceive, or, perceiving it, refusing to admit the doctrine before us. Great indeed are the pride and presumption of human reason, which starts its little cavils against the great truths of revelation. We have need to be on our guard against the influence of objections which spring from a state of moral corruption common to all. Let us distrust ourselves, and, while we pity such as are led astray by gross and fatal errors, let us seek to enjoy the promised guidance of Him whose prerogative it is to lead into all truth. It belongs to God to bring good out of evil; and, although the existence of objections to divine truth is in itself to be deplored, the goodness and wisdom can never be too much admired which render this very evil a means of ultimate good. By leading to investigate the truth with greater care, by tending to quicken the understanding, by rousing to a more zealous defence of what is valuable, by producing stronger attachment to that for which we have had as it were to fight, and by inducing a firmer confidence in the truth itself as having stood the trial of the most searching scrutiny, the objections themselves may be turned to a profitable account. And how truly thankful ought those to be, who have been kept from error and established in the truth as it is in Jesus. If those who have escaped the temptations of the world through lust have reason to be grateful, those who have escaped the temptations of error through the prevalence of heretical opinion, have no less cause of gratitude. That mental error is safe and innocent, is much the same as saying that truth is a thing of no value; and neither the one sentiment nor the other can be held by those who have seriously pondered the import of those awful words—*that they all might be damned who believed not the truth.* And if error is in any case unsafe, and truth in any case valuable, it must be in a matter of such vital importance as tha now under discussion.

SECTION III.

NECESSITY OF CHRIST'S ATONEMENT.

The remarks at the conclusion of last section, on the objection that an atonement is unnecessary, are merely negative. They are designed to prove only that it cannot be shown to be unnecessary, without going the length of positively maintaining its necessity. We now advance a step higher, and shall endeavor to show that the atonement of Christ *is* necessary.

It cannot surely be requisite here to do more than remind the reader of the sense in which the term *necessity* is used. It is employed, not in an absolute, but relative sense. It is not supposed that the Deity was obliged, either by the perfections of his nature, or by the claims of his creatures, to furnish an atonement in order to the pardon of sin.—There was nothing in his own character that rendered it absolutely imperative to take any steps whatever towards the remission of iniquity: such a supposition goes to divest him entirely of grace or sovereignty in the exercise of forgiveness. Neither was it possible that the offenders against his moral government could, by anything they were capable of performing, lay him under an obligation to furnish them with a legal ground of deliverance from sin; this goes to invest a guilty creature with the power of controlling the divine Lawgiver, as well as to deprive the glorious provision of infinite mercy for the salvation of man of all claims to the character of free unmerited favor. The necessity of which we speak is not of this nature. It is a relative necessity that is affirmed with respect to Christ's atonement, a necessity springing from God's antecedent purpose to save sinners from the wrath to come, arising solely out of his own free purpose, determination, or promise. Having resolved that sin shall be pardoned, it becomes necessary that an atonement shall be made. The necessity, in one word, is not natural, but moral.

The moral necessity of an atonement supposes three things, all of which are understood as distinctly admitted in the subsequent reasoning. It supposes that man is a moral creature, the subject of a holy, just, and righteous law, which attaches eternal punishment to the violation of it :—It supposes that man has broken this law and become obnoxious to the punishment threatened :—It supposes, in fine, that God has determined to deliver some at least of such violators from the legal consequences of their transgression. These assumptions, it will not be expected, we should wait to prove. They are all understood as admitted by those with whom we are contending, and no advantage is taken of our opponents, when they are taken for granted. The first is involved in man's nature as a moral being: the second rests on the broad undeniable fact of the fall: the third is supposed in all reasoning about salvation. Let these admissions, then, be kept distinctly in view—let it be understood that God has determined to save guilty men from the punishment due to their sins; and we ask no more as a basis on which to construct our proof of the necessity of Christ's atonement.

I. The *perfections of God* rendered an atonement necessary to the remission of sin.

This might be argued even from the honor or majesty of God. His dignity as Creator of the ends of the earth, Preserver of man and beast, Lord of heaven and earth, and Lawgiver of the moral universe, is unspeakably great ; it is infinite. Sin is a dishonor done to this great Lord God ; a direct insult offered to the majesty of the skies; and, if pardoned without satisfaction, it is as much as to say that God may be insulted with impunity; that to offer the highest affront to the Great Supreme, to bid open defiance to infinite excellency, exposes to no hazard, involves no forfeiture of safety. What is this, but to unhinge the whole moral constitution of things, and to hold out a temptation to universal revolt? For if God may be insulted with impunity once, it may be oftener, it may be at all times; there can never be any infallible inducement to honor him; but license is proclaimed to all to treat him with sovereign and perpetual contempt. If such revolting consequences as these are to be reprobated and rejected with abhorrence, as they must be by all who have any remains of a moral sense, it follows, that, to the pardon of every sin, satisfaction must be given to the insulted majesty of God by an atonement.

The truth of Deity does not less imperatively call for such a provision. He is a God of *truth* and without iniquity, just and right is he. He is abundant in goodness and *truth*. The strength of Israel *will not lie*. He is a *God that cannot lie.** Now, let what God has spoken with regard to sin be here remembered. He has said—"Cursed is every one that continueth not in all things that are written in the law to do them—the soul that sinneth it shall die—the wages of sin is death—woe unto the wicked, it shall be ill with him—the Lord will by no means clear the guilty."† These are the true sayings of God. His veracity and faithfulness require that they be fulfilled. But if sin is pardoned without a satisfaction, fulfilled they are not; —the violation of the law is not cursed; death is not the wages of sin; it is not ill with the wicked; God *does* clear the guilty! And what is this but to impeach the truth of God—to make God a liar? Nor is there any way of reconciling such expressions with the fact of man's forgiveness, but by referring to him

---

* Deut. xxxii. 4. Exod. xxxiv. 6. 1 Sam. xv. 29. Tit. i. 2.
† Gal. iii. 10. Ezek. xviii. 4. Rom. vi. 23. Isa. iii. 11. Exod. xxxiv. 7.

who was "made a curse for us," who "tasted death for every one" of the redeemed, and whose substitutionary satisfaction is rendered necessary by the faithfulness of God to his own word.

More distinctly still, if possible, does this necessity appear from the divine holiness. The Lord our God is holy. He is free from every vestige of moral pollution; he delights in whatever is pure; he hates whatever is of an opposite character. Now, sin is opposed to the holiness of God; it is essentially impure, filthy, abominable. It follows that it is the object of his supreme detestation; he is of purer eyes than to behold evil, and cannot look on iniquity. But how can this be made to appear, without the punishment of sin? It is not enough that a penalty be annexed to transgressions, that a threat be appended to the violation of his law; if the penalty is not inflicted, if the threat is not executed, there is still room left to suppose that sin is not the abominable thing that was supposed; the blasphemous thought may nevertheless spring up in the bosom of moral creatures, that God, after all, approves of sin, and secretly connives at the commission of it. To vindicate the holiness of the divine character, the penalty annexed to disobedience must be executed. But its being executed on the *transgressor* is incompatible with the transgressor's being forgiven. To the pardon of sin, then, consistently with the purity of God, the punishment must fall on the sinner's substitute. In other words, the divine holiness proclaims the necessity of Christ's atonement. Thus, and thus alone, can the sinner be saved without sin being palliated, or the perfect moral purity of the Holy One being sullied.

To these add the requirements of divine justice. Justice consists in giving to every one his due—in rendering to every being what is right. It is much the same as equity or rectitude, and is an essential and unchangeable perfection of the divine nature. Of justice there are supposed to be four kinds:—general, commutative, distributive, and vindictive. The two last apply to our present subject. Distributive justice consists in giving every one his due, treating all according to their desert, acting towards the subjects of law agreeably to the terms of law. This requires that sin be punished according to its desert. The evil of sin is infinite. It must, therefore, receive an infinite punishment—infinite either in nature or in duration. A punishment which is infinite in nature cannot be borne by a finite creature; punishment infinite in duration is exclusive of all possible pardon; whence it follows, that if sin is to be punished agreeably to its desert, and yet sinners saved, it must meet this punishment in the person of one who can sustain an infliction which is infinite in nature; that is to say, the distributive justice of God renders necessary an atonement.

This is still more apparent from the vindictive o retributive justice of God. That opposition of the divine nature to sin, which leads to the annexation of a penalty to the breach of his law, the execution of which penalty is referable to distributive justice, is called the vindictive or retributive justice of God. The opposition of God's *law* to sin, is just the opposition of his *nature* to sin; his nature, not his will, is the ultimate standard of morality. His determination to punish sin is not *voluntary*, but *necessary*. He does not annex a punishment to sin because he *wills* to do so, but because his *nature* requires it. If the whole of such procedure could be resolved into mere volition, then it is not only supposable that God might not have determined to punish sin, but, which is blasphemous, that he might have determined to reward it. This is not more clearly deducible from the nature of a being of perfect moral excellence, than plainly taught in scripture. *He will by no means clear the guilty. The Lord is a jealous God, he will not forgive your transgressions nor your sins. Thou art not a God that hath pleasure in wickedness, neither shall evil dwell with thee. God is angry with the wicked every day. The Lord will take vengeance on his adversaries, and he reserveth wrath for his enemies. Who can stand before his indignation? and who can abide in the fierceness of his anger? Is God unrighteous*

who taketh vengeance? Our God is a consuming fire.*
We may confidently appeal to every unprejudiced mind whether such descriptions as these do not fully bear us out in the view we have taken of God's retributive justice. And if this view is correct, sin cannot go unpunished; it cannot be pardoned without a satisfaction; God cannot but take vengeance on iniquity: to do otherwise, would be to violate the perfection of his nature. Just he is, and just he ever must be; and there is only one way, that of an atoning sacrifice, by which he can be at once " a JUST God and a SAVIOUR." It is to no purpose to tell us that such language as we have quoted from the word of God is figurative, that it can never be understood as ascribing passions to God. This we fully admit; but if wrath in God is not an agitating passion, so much the worse for our opponents. It is a settled purpose or determination to oppose and to punish sin. Had it been a passion, it might have been supposed to cool, and, in process of time, to die away altogether; but being the fixed necessary opposition of his nature to evil, it is as incapable of change as the divine character itself.

We might even urge the goodness of God in proof of the necessity of Christ's atonement. This is the view of the Divine Being to which the enemies of the doctrine incessantly appeal. His goodness prompts him to consult the happiness and welfare of his creatures, especially his moral and intelligent creatures. It is the tendency of sin to destroy all happiness, and inflict all possible misery. *Natural* evil is the invariable effect of *moral* evil. It was sin that expelled angels from the abodes of bliss; that introduced sorrow and suffering and gloom into this lower world; and that lit up those flames of Tophet which are to inflict never-dying torment on the wicked in a future state of being. Does not goodness say, then, that everything should be done to check the progress and hinder the effects of such wide spreading evil? And is this to be done by inflicting on it its merited punishment,

---

* Exod. xxxiv. 7. Josh. xxiv. 19. Psalm v. 4; vii. 11. Nah. i. 2, 6. Rom. iii. 5. Heb. xii. 29.

or by suffering it to pass unnoticed and to operate unrestrained? Every man's reason must answer this question? Sin, to be put down, requires to be punished. It is not by pardoning it without satisfaction that it is ever to be prevented from spreading wretchedness and woe among every rank of God's moral creation. Mercy, not less than justice, demands, in order to pardon, that some one shall "drink the cup of the wine of the fierceness of the wrath of Almighty God. JUSTICE IS BUT GOODNESS DIRECTED BY WISDOM."*

II. The atonement of Christ was rendered necessary by the *nature of God's moral government.*

That God has placed moral creatures under a law or moral constitution, which is designed to promote the glory of the Lawgiver and the good of his subjects will, it is presumed, be fully admitted. To the accomplishment of these purposes, it must also be admitted, that this moral constitution requires to be upheld and obeyed, and everything done to prevent its violation. So far, all is clear, and can admit of no dispute. It merits consideration whether the notion of pardon without atonement be not directly subversive of the object in question, and destructive of the very principles of moral legislation.

It supposes a violation of the very letter of the law. The law says, "the soul that sinneth, it shall die;" but the theory in question says, the soul that sinneth shall not die. The law says, "Cursed is every one that continueth not in all things that are written in the law to do them;" but, according to the supposed theory, *not* every one, nay, *not any* one, shall be cursed. The law says, "Heaven and earth shall pass away, but one jot or one tittle of the law shall not pass until all be fulfilled;" but, says the theory we are considering, not only one jot or tittle, but the whole penal sanction of the law shall pass completely away.

It reflects on the nature of the law. If the breach of the law can be passed over without compensation, t is clearly supposed to have been originally too

* Stillingfleet.

strict, to have been over rigorous at first. This is much the same as to affirm that it was originally unjust, in opposition to the Scriptures, which declare that the law is holy, just, and good. What a perfect law once was, it must ever continue to be. If it was originally just, it must be always just; but pardon without satisfaction, says either that it was originally unjust, or that it is now so. If it was originally holy, it must be always holy; but if pardon must be dispensed without satisfaction, either originally it was not so, or it has ceased to be what it once was, as it can never be wrong to carry the sanction of a holy law into execution. If it was originally good, it must be always good; but pardon without satisfaction proceeds on the supposition that it would not consist with goodness or benevolence to fulfil the threatening of the law. This scheme militates, thus, against the nature of the law, and supposes the moral constitution under which man is placed to be different from what both reason and scripture lead us to conclude.

It supposes, moreover, a relaxation to take place of the law or moral government of God, such as a perfect constitution can never undergo. If sin is pardoned without an atonement, then the law, which requires perfect and perpetual obedience, and which denounces punishment on every deviation from its requirements, is clearly understood to have relaxed its rigor: its requisitions are supposed to have been modified and abridged in adaptation to what is called human frailty or infirmity. This is not only supposed in the theory of pardon, against which we are contending: it is openly avowed, and strenuously defended. But against such a relaxation of God's law, we have more than one thing to urge.

First of all, we say that it supposes the law to have been originally wrong, seeing it could either need or admit of a change; and this we cannot but regard as a direct impeachment, both of the wisdom and equity of the Legislator.

Secondly:—It supposes that man's indisposition to obey, (for his inability is wholly to be traced to want of will,) can nullify the obligation to obey,—a principle which, if admitted, would put an end to all legislation whatsoever, as the conclusion would be, that men were bound to obey, only so far as they chose.

Thirdly:—A law which does not require perfect obedience under pain of positive infliction, is absolutely no law at all; it is just a law which may be violated with impunity, the very propounding of which must be seen to be a burlesque on legislation.

Fourthly:—It is impossible to define the extent of relaxation requisite. No one has attempted to say to what extent the supposed relaxation has been carried. If the ability or inclination of the subject is to be the rule, the relaxation of the law must vary in every individual case of its application. And what is this but to throw everything loose, and to annihilate all standard of moral obligation?

Fifthly:—The laws which govern the moral world are fixed and unalterable, nay, more so than those which regulate the material world. The importance of maintaining the latter steady and inviolable, is readily admitted, and strongly urged. Is it not at least of equal importance—we think it could easily be shown to be of greater—that those of the intellectual and moral world be permanent and inflexible? Shall it be insisted upon that the laws which affect inanimate nature are to be considered incapable of a change, and yet maintained that those which connect the supreme moral Governor with his subjects, may fluctuate and vary indefinitely? The one supposes only a change in the divine *procedure*, and constitutes a *miracle;* the other supposes a change in the *nature* of God, and constitutes a grand moral *contradiction*.

In fine:—On the supposition in question, instead of the will of the creature being required to conform to the law of God, the law of God is required to conform to the will of the creature—which is not only a solecism in legislation, but a monstrous discrepancy in morals. We conclude, then, that, for all these reasons, the law of God cannot be relaxed: and if it cannot be relaxed, an atonement must be necessary to the pardon of sin.

Indeed, any other supposition tends directly to subvert all the purposes of God's moral government at large. Sin is an offence against the moral government of God; it is rebellion against the divine majesty; it strikes at the root of that authority on which repose all the order and happiness of the universe. It denies his right to the respect which is due to him as the head of the universe, the love which he deserves on account of his infinite excellencies, and the obedience which he has commanded as the sovere'gn Lord and Lawgiver.* To pardon it without satisfaction, then, is to hold out such a view of the supreme Lawgiver as cannot fail to encourage his moral creatures, both men and angels, to disobey; it is holding out a powerful temptation to revolt; it is letting his moral subjects of every class distinctly understand that they may hoist the flag of rebellion and defiance without fear. Only conceive of the hideous consequences that must necessarily succeed from such a line of procedure, and you will acquiesce at once in the opinion that the purposes of God's moral government at large render an atonement necessary. If sin is pardoned, it must be in a way by which the law is magnified and made honorable, and by one, too, whose business it is, not to destroy the law but to fulfil it. We are the more confirmed in this view of the matter, that the punishment of sin is necessary to prevent the repetition of it, and that to pardon it without satisfaction is equivalent to throwing down the barriers of morality, and setting open the flood-gates of iniquity; especially when we reflect how inadequately even the exhibition of the divine displeasure, which is made in the cross of Christ, restrains the growth of crime.

Such are our reasons for maintaining that the nature of the divine moral government renders atonement a necessary, indispensable provision to the pardon of sin. As sin is an infringement of the moral constitution su-

---

* Smith.

preme wisdom has appointed, it is calculated to introduce disturbance into the constituted moral order of the universe, and casts contempt on all the moral and legislative attributes of Deity, we hold it utterly impossible that the supreme moral Governor can connive at any one sin; for his doing so would inevitably lead to the subversion of the whole moral system of the universe. "As empirics in medicine, contented with a few facts imperfectly understood and ill-combined, deride the extensive search and the cautious inductions of the enlightened physician; and as the vulgar, looking only at appearances as they seem to them, reject and often hold in high contempt the demonstrated facts of natural philosophy; so those who disbelieve the atonement of Christ and its correlate doctrines, seem to me to form their sentiments from a very superficial consideration, hasty and incomplete views, and an unwarrantable confidence in first appearances; overlooking the great principles and general laws of a comprehensive moral system. Above all, I fear that they overlook the nature and obligations of obedience to the will of God, the rational grounds on which those obligations rest, and the true reasons of the demerit of sin."[*]

III. The necessity of an atonement may be argued from the *inefficacy of every other scheme* to secure the pardon of sin.

Penitence and future amendment, or repentance and good works, as they are commonly called, are chiefly brought forward as all that is necessary for this purpose. If these can be shown to be sufficient, it follows, of course, that the atonement of Christ is unnecessary, and consequently that no such atonement has ever been made. God does nothing in vain; and it is a law in all his operations that the greatest good is effected at the least possible expense. If the pardon of iniquity could have been rendered consistent with the perfections of his nature and the interests of his moral government, by the mere sorrow and reforma-

---

[*] Smith or Sacrifice, p. 288.

tion of the sinner, it is not to be conceived that he would ever subject his only begotten Son to the pain of crucifixion, the misery of satanic assault, and the unutterable anguish of divine wrath. It is important, then, to ascertain whether these be sufficient for such a purpose.

That repentance is necessary to pardon, and in the case of adults inseparably connected with it, is not disputed. But that it is *all* that is necessary, or that the connection is that of a meritorious ground or procuring cause, we unhesitatingly refuse; for these, amongst other reasons:

First:—No provision was made for repentance in the original moral constitution under which man was placed, and the necessity of maintaining which inviolate has already been shown. "In the day thou eatest thereof, thou shalt surely die—The soul that sinneth it shall die," is the language in which that constitution expressed its sanctions. There is no stipulation of repentance; not even a hint of such a thing being so much as admissible. It is never spoken of but in connection with a widely different constitution, in which, as we shall see, it springs from, rather than stands as a substitute for, atonement.

Secondly:—Penitence does not remove guilt, or the legal desert of punishment. It changes, indeed, the character of the sinner, but it leaves his liability to suffer the penalty of the law the same as before. No compensation whatever is made by it to the claims of justice; the guilt is lessened in no degree: it cannot, therefore, be enough to secure pardon, which is the remission of guilt.

Thirdly:—Penitence can never repair the consequences of sin. By sin the majesty of God is insulted; repentance has no effect in wiping off this reproach. By sin a debt is contracted to the divine law and justice; penitence makes no compensation for this debt. In case of the breach of human laws, repentance is never looked upon as making legal compensation or removing the consequences of guilt. It is never known among men that the thoughtless speculator who has involved himself in bankruptcy, on giving signs of repentance, receives a discharge from his creditors, and takes again the same honorable place which he formerly held in the commercial world. The intemperate voluptuary who has ruined his character, and fortune, and health, by his criminal indulgences, does not find these all retrieved on his barely repenting of his misconduct. It does not even happen that the penitent finds immediate and permanent relief from the painful reflections of self-dissatisfaction; and if not satisfied with himself for having repented, how dare he have the presumption to fancy that God will be satisfied with him for it? It is contrary to all our notions of rectitude that punishment should continue longer than criminality, that the consequences of guilt should be perpetuated after satisfaction for guilt has been given. But it consists with the facts of daily experience, that compunctions and other effects of criminality remain after men have repented; and, as these are the natural punishments of crime, their continuance after repentance demonstrates its utter incompetence to form a legal compensation.

Fourthly:—It does not appear that, without an atonement, there could ever exist such a thing as genuine repentance. That deep sense of guilt which is essential in every case of penitence, would seem to be otherwise incapable of being produced. If all that God had done had been to make known his readiness to receive repentant sinners, we have the best reason to conclude, from what we know of man, that instead of inclining him to repent, it would have tended rather to render him easy under his guilt, to harden his heart, and to encourage him to sin with a higher hand than ever. True mourning for sin is a thing unknown, excepting among those who have been taught " to look on Him whom they have pierced." Repentance is a state of soul which can only be produced at the foot of the cross. " He who receives the atonement weeps not to wash away his sins, but because they are washed away he weeps."

Fifthly —The sinner is as incapable, in himself, of

repentance, as of making an atonement. This important remark is so happily illustrated by an able theologian of our own day, that I cannot resist laying his remarks before the reader. "When it is said," remarks Mr. Dods, "that God is willing to pardon us upon our repentance, without any atonement, it is taken for granted that we can repent when we please. For, if repentance be something entirely out of our power, then, it can afford us no comfort to tell us, even if it were true, that repentance will purchase our pardon. For, besides that it seems just as difficult to perceive the connection between repentance and pardon, as to perceive the connection between atonement and pardon, I know not that even the most determined rationalism has ever promulgated a tenet more clearly absurd, or more decidedly opposed to all experience, than the tenet that a man can repent of himself, without being led to do so, and enabled to do so, by the Holy Spirit. Many a sinner is no doubt soothing himself to peace by the promise of a future repentance. But he neither knows as yet what repentance is, nor his own need of repentance, else he would build himself up in no such foolish delusion. For what does the sinner do, when he promises himself a future repentance? He just says, to-day, nothing shall induce me to abstain from indulging every appetite and every desire, nothing shall lead me to think of God at all, or to think of him without dread and aversion; nothing can make me delight to contemplate his perfections, or find any pleasure in drawing near to him: to-morrow, I will sit down and mourn, in the utmost anguish of spirit, those indulgences from which nothing will induce me to-day to abstain, and wish a thousand times that I had never yielded to them; nothing shall give me such delight as the contemplation of those glorious perfections which to-day I hate to think of; and I shall account nothing such a privilege as to draw near to that throne of grace before which nothing shall induce me to-day to bend the knee. This is exactly what the sinner says when he promises himself a future repentance. He promises that to-morrow he will hate with the most cordial detestation, that to which, to-day, he clings with the most ardent affection. He who says, to-day I am bowed down with all the weight of threescore years and ten, but to-morrow I am resolved that I shall flourish in all the vigor of unbroken youth, forms a resolution quite as rational, and quite as much within his power to accomplish, as he who says, to-morrow I will repent. He who says to himself, I will make to myself a new heaven and a new earth, makes a promise just as much within his power to accomplish, as he who says, I will make to myself a new heart and a new spirit. Repentance and renovation are not sacrifices which we give to God as the price of our justification; but gifts which God bestows upon us, and which God only can bestow, in consequence of our having been freely justified. That man has surely little reason to lay claim to the appellation of rational, who goes so directly in the face of common sense and of all experience, as to teach the sinner that he is capable of repenting, and that repentance will purchase his pardon; a tenet which, whether it be more deplorably absurd, or more fearfully fatal, I shall not take upon me to determine."*

Not less inefficacious is the scheme of future amendment. Good works can as little secure the pardon of sin as repentance; yet by such as deny the atonement, the worth of man's own doings is unblushingly taught. As in the case of repentance, it is not our intention to deny the importance of good works in the scheme of man's salvation; neither to dispute their connection with pardon. We are too well convinced of the "necessary uses" they are designed to subserve, with regard at once to believers themselves, to their fellow men and to God; and we are too well aware of their being the necessary fruits and indispensable evidences of a justified state, to let fall so much as a disparaging syllable respecting them. God forbid that we should for a moment forget or overlook, even in the heat of argumentation, the holy purpose and ten-

* Dods on Incarnation, pp. 158—160.

dency of the Gospel. But let good works be kept in their own place. We deny them the place of a *cause* in the salvation of man; their connection with pardon we hold to be *not* a connection with *merit*, as is supposed by those who maintain their efficacy to secure the pardon of sin. The reasons of this opinion are soon told.

In the first place, man can never do more at any one time than is his present duty, God having at all times a supreme right to all his services. He can never do more at any given time than it is his duty at that very time to fulfil. Being under obligation to the full extent of his ability, and throughout the whole period of his being, present obedience can do no more than fulfil present obligation. It follows that nothing man can ever do, can have the effect of meriting his release from the punishment due to former demerit. If it has merit at all, its merit is confined to the present, it cannot possibly be either retrospective or prospective. It can neither make amends for a past offence, nor purchase an indulgence for the future. As soon might the man who pays a debt which he contracted to-day, plead such payment as liquidating a debt which he contracted yesterday, or entitling him to contract another to-morrow without the intention of paying it. To maintain that past offences may be pardoned on the score of future amendment, is to adopt the anti-christian absurdity of supererogation. Nay, it is every whit as reasonable to suppose that past obedience should atone for future sins, (which is the principle of the Popish indulgences,) as to suppose that present obedience should atone for past sins; that is to say, neither can be maintained with the least claim to rationality.

In the next place there can be no works good in the sight of God but what flow from, and are connected with, the atonement. Good works can be performed only by those who are united to Christ by faith, that is, are in a justified state. Without faith it is impossible to please God. We are accepted in the Beloved. As an honest action can only be performed by an honest man, so a good work can only proceed from one who is himself good. The whole world is by nature guilty before God; there is none righteous, no, not one; in our flesh dwelleth no good thing; our best righteousnesses are as filthy rags in God's sight. None but such as are in Christ can serve God in newness of spirit, can yield him the obedience of faith; and to suppose any other kind of obedience to be acceptable, is to fancy that He who looks on the heart will be pleased with the performance without the principle, the shadow without the substance, the body without the spirit.

Moreover, the notion that good works are meritorious is expressly contradicted by scripture. On nothing is the Bible more full and explicit. The assertions are so express, that only the most inveterate prejudice can mistake their import or evade their force. Before the efficacy of good works to secure the pardon of sin can be held with any plausibility, its advocates would do well to have certain plain affirmations blotted from the records of divine truth. *By the deeds of the law there shall no flesh be justified in his sight. And if by grace, then is it no more of works; otherwise grace is no more grace; but if it be of works, then it is no more grace; otherwise work is no more work. As many as are of the works of the law are under the curse. Not of works, lest any man should boast.**

Such is the insufficiency of those other grounds of pardon which have been supposed to render atonement unnecessary, or, rather, have been proposed as substitutes for the atonement of Christ. If, by the previous remarks on this subject, we are warned against entertaining insulated views of the divine perfections, and defective notions of God's moral government, by that we have just been considering, are we put on our guard against trusting to repentance or future amendment of life, as a meritorious ground of forgiveness. What impious presumption do such thoughts imply! How perilous the state of those who rest their soul's eternal interests on the daring experi-

---

* Rom. iii. 20, xi. 6. Gal. iii. 10. Eph. ii. 9.

ment of supplanting the righteousness of God's own Son by worth of their own! God grant that we may have deeper impressions of the evil of sin, and humbler views of ourselves than such presumption supposes! The heathen themselves may well reprove such impiety; for the existence among them of expiatory sacrifices, indicates a universal sense of the inefficacy of other things to secure pardon to offenders, and of the necessity of something more than pardon and good works, to appease the anger of their divinities. The fact itself is highly instructive, and should put to shame those pretended Christians who would set aside altogether the plan of a propitiatory mediation.

IV. With the views already taken of the necessity of the atonement, agree the *assertions of holy writ*. The following are a specimen.

Luke xxiv. 26. " Ought not Christ to have suffered these things, and to enter into his glory?" The sufferings of the Redeemer are here spoken of by himself as being necessary. Such is the meaning of " Ought not ;" οὐχὶ ἔδει. The verb denotes necessity in the strict and proper sense of the term. *Necesse est, oportet, opus est*, ita, ut vel *necessitas absoluta* vel *relativa* indicetur?* The necessity is not absolute, but relative. It springs not from any personal sin on the part of Christ; but from God's sovereign and free determination to pardon the sins of those in whose room he stood, as well as from those scripture predictions in which his determination had been made known, and which required to be fulfilled.

Heb. ii. 10. " For it became him for whom are all things, and by whom are all things, in bringing many sons unto glory, to make the Captain of their salvation perfect through sufferings." Here we have an object proposed, " bringing many sons to glory," or the salvation of a number of the human family; the manner in which the object is accomplished, by " making the Captain of salvation perfect through sufferings," that

---

* Schleusner

is, by the sufferings of Christ, who is undoubtedly meant by the Captain of salvation;* and the necessity that exists for taking this method of effecting the end, "it became him for whom are all things, and by whom are all things." Necessity is the idea expressed by the original term—ἔπρεπε. It is *fit, decorous, becoming, proper.* The ground of this fitness is the character of God—"*it became him.*" There was a moral fitness or propriety arising from the nature, will, and government of God, that Christ should suffer, if men were to be saved. Any other way would not have been befitting the divine Being. A stronger necessity than what is founded on the nature of God, cannot be conceived; and such necessity we have here adduced by the inspired apostle for the sufferings or atonement of Christ.

Heb. viii. 3. "For every high priest is ordained to offer gifts and sacrifices: wherefore it is of necessity that this man have somewhat also to offer." The person spoken of as "this man," or this one, (τοῦτον,) *i. e.* this high priest, is Christ. What is said of him is, his having "somewhat to offer," some gift or sacrifice to present to God as an atonement for the sins of his people. And for this, there is stated to exist a strong necessity—"it is of necessity"—ἀναγκαῖον. The term expresses the strongest moral necessity, what cannot be dispensed with, indispensable. Not only to fulfil the type, to complete the office of high priest, but to satisfy the law and justice of God, on which account he assumed this office, was it necessary that Chris. should offer an atoning sacrifice.

Heb. ix. 22, 23. "And almost all things are by the law purged with blood; and without shedding of blood is no remission. It was, therefore, necessary that the patterns of things in the heavens should be purified with these; but the heavenly things themselves with better sacrifices than these." A grand general principle, in the moral economy, is here laid down—WITHOUT SHEDDING OF BLOOD IS NO REMISSION. The terms are most explicit; it is not *repentance*, it is not *amend-*

* ἀρχηγός is used in the New Testament only with reference to Christ. Acts iii. 15; v. 31. Heb. xii. 2.

ment, but the *shedding of blood,*—atonement,—without which there is no remission of the guilt or punishment of sin. It is spoken of, to be sure, in connection with the ceremonies of the typical law; but the remission of the temporal penalty, due to ceremonial offences, by means of typical blood, was prefigurative, if that dispensation had any meaning, of the irreconcilable opposition of the Divine holiness and justice to sin, and of the necessity of Christ's death to the remission of the eternal punishment due to the breach of God's moral law. Hence arose a necessity that there should be sacrifices of a typical nature to secure the privileges of the ceremonial economy. Whence it is inferred, that a sacrifice of superior intrinsic worth and relative value, was necessary to the enjoyment of communion with God here and of heavenly glory hereafter,—those high and glorious privileges of which the others were only shadows. The plural number—" better sacrifices "—presents no obstacle to the *one offering* of Christ being understood; when it is recollected that the plural for the singular is, in scripture, a not uncommon enallage, used to denote worth or dignity; and more particularly when it is considered that here the sacrifice of Christ stands in antithetical connection with the sacrifices of the law as that which fulfilled what these only typified.

SECTION IV.

PROOF OF CHRIST'S ATONEMENT—ANCIENT SACRIFICES.

We come now to a part of our subject which is of great importance. Hitherto we have been occupied with what may be reckoned preliminary matter. It was necessary to explain the nature of atonement; to show that the objections commonly urged against the principle are destitute of weight; and to evince the necessity that exists in the character and government of God for such an arrangement, in order to the bestowment of pardon on guilty men. But these do not prove the fact of an atonement. They suppose such a thing to exist, either actually or in the divine intention; but they afford no evidence of its existence. Had atonement been nothing more than a theory, all that has been said would have been necessary for its explanation and defence. But atonement is more than a theory; it is a FACT; a solemn, important, and undoubted fact, which is capable of being substantiated by the most complete and satisfactory scriptural evidence. This evidence is multifarious, ample, and diversified. Without pretending to exhibit the whole, or even any branch of it completely, the nature of our undertaking calls for such a digest as will require the diligent study and patient attention of the reader.

Let us, first of all, give our thoughts to the antiquity and universal prevalence of vicarious sacrifices, irrespective altogether of the Mosaic economy. This is a point of no small moment. If it can only be firmly established, as we presume there will be no difficulty in doing, the confirmation it affords of the fact in question is of the very strongest nature. It involves, however, a variety of points which require to be taken up separately and in order.

I. A primary consideration is due to the ANTIQUITY of sacrifices.

We speak now only of the fact, that the practice of offering sacrifices to God existed in the remotest ages of the world. The infliction of death on a living creature in the way of religious worship did not originate, as many suppose, with the Jews. When the Israelites entered the holy land, they found its aboriginal inhabitants addicted to the practice. Certain forms of it being expressly denounced in the law of Moses, is positive proof of its existence prior to the promulgation of that extraordinary document. In the records of heathen nations, also, as far back as they go traces of it are to be found; and the sacred history, which goes the farthest back of any records with which we are acquainted, contains abundant proof of the antiquity of sacrifices.

In the Book of Job, which is perhaps the oldest writing in existence, mention is made of sacrificing more than once. The patriarch himself followed the practice:—'And it was so, when the days of their feasting were gone about, that Job sent and sanctified them, and rose up early in the morning, and OFFERED BURNT-OFFERINGS according to the number of them all.'* The same thing was exemplified, under the sanction of a divine command, by Job's friends:— 'Therefore take unto you now,' said God, 'seven bullocks and seven rams, and go to my servant Job, and OFFER UP FOR YOURSELVES A BURNT-OFFERING, and my servant Job shall pray for you.........So Eliphaz the Temanite, and Bildad the Shuhite, and Zophar the Naamathite, went and DID ACCORDING AS THE LORD COMMANDED THEM.'† Abraham, if not belonging to a previous age, was at least contemporary with the man of Uz, and he also followed the same practice:—'And Abraham lifted up his eyes, and looked, and behold, behind him a ram caught in a thicket by his horns; and Abraham went and took the ram, and OFFERED HIM UP FOR A BURNT-OFFERING in the stead of his son.'‡ Nearly five hundred years earlier than this, we find Noah, the second father of our race, acting a similar part on an occasion of great solemnity and importance:—'And Noah builded an altar unto the Lord, and took of every clean beast, and of every clean fowl, and OFFERED BURNT-OFFERINGS on the altar.'§ Pushing our inquiry into still more remote antiquity, we meet with the practice, in the case of Abel, at a distance of not less than fifteen hundred years from the case last adduced:—'And Abel, he also brought of the firstlings of his flock, and of the fat thereof; and the Lord had respect unto Abel and to his OFFERING.'‖

Nor is even this the highest antiquity to which the

* Job i. 5. † Job xlii. 8, 9. ‡ Gen. xxii. 13.
§ Gen. viii. 20. ‖ Gen. iv. 4.

evidence of the existence of sacrifices can be carried. We are now, indeed, within little more than a hundred years of the creation of man. But, unless greatly mistaken, there is good reason to believe that the practice of sacrificing was coeval with the fall of man. We know not what else to make of the circumstance of our first parents being provided with garments of the skins of animals:—' Unto Adam also, and to his wife, did the Lord God make COATS OF SKIN, and clothed them.'* The animals whose skins furnished this primitive clothing, must have been dead, and the question is, how came they by their death?—Were they slain on purpose, merely to furnish garments for our first parents? This, to say the least of it, is extremely improbable, when we consider that there were so many other ways by which the same end could have been accomplished, without inflicting pain on sentient and innocent creatures. Can they be supposed to have died of themselves? This is barely possible, but not at all probable. They had just lately been created in perfection, and that in so short a time they should have died a natural death is a most violent supposition. Could they have been slain for food? This, too, is an unreasonable presumption. It does not appear that animal food was in use till after the flood. The first grant of animals for meat, which we find on record, is that given to Noah after the deluge. To man, at first, we read only of the herb of the field and the fruit of the tree yielding seed being given for meat.† How, then, we repeat the question, could those animals have died whose skins were the clothing of our first parents? And the only answer that accords with reason, or with the facts of the case, is, that they were slain for sacrifices. The impossibility of satisfactorily accounting otherwise for their death, taken in conjunction with the mention made of animal sacrifices immediately afterwards, gives to this supposition the weight of the very highest presumption, if not

---

* Gen. iii. 21.
† See Magee on Atonement, vol. ii. p. 31. Smith on Sac., p. 230.

the force of absolute demonstration.* And thus are we entitled to claim for the practice of sacrificing the highest possible antiquity. The most ancient records, both sacred and profane, furnish evidence in point. The farthest back that we can carry our inquiries, even with the assistance of divine revelation, we meet with traces of the practice in question. It is as old nearly as creation : it is coeval with man.

II. Connect with this the UNIVERSAL PREVALENCE of sacrifices.

Of this fact there can be as little doubt as of that of which we have just been speaking. The one, indeed, serves to account for the other. The antiquity of the practice explains its universality. Having its origin at a time when the inhabitants of the earth were few in number, its adoption by all who were then living can easily be conceived; and this again satisfactorily accounts for its being spread by them among their more numerous descendants. The families of Adam and of Noah comprehended, at the respective periods of their existence, all the inhabitants of the earth. At these periods, the practice in question, existing in these families, may be said to have been universally prevalent; and in every period since, both ancient and modern, it has been found to exist among all those who have not adopted the Christian religion. Its prevalence is strictly universal. Among antediluvians and postdiluvians; among the Greeks and Romans, Phenicians and Carthaginians, Gauls and Britons, of former ages; as well as, in modern times, in Africa, India, and the islands of the South seas, the practice is known to prevail. In proof of this, appeal may be made to the history, poetry, and languages of the different nations, as well as to writers of our own day who have made the customs and manners of distant tribes the subject of their researches. Pliny, speaking of sacrifices, says, 'All the world have agreed in them, although enemies or strangers to one another.' The writings of Homer and Virgil, of Ovid, Horace, and Juvenal, abound with allusions of this nature. And

---

* Magee, vol. ii. p. 230.

what is more decisive still, the language of every people on earth contains terms which express the idea of sacrifice; a circumstance which cannot otherwise be accounted for than by supposing that this idea entered deeply into their sentiments and customs. The Greek and Latin languages contain many such words, which have been transfused into those of modern times, and especially our own. We need only remind the learned reader of such verbs as ἁγιάζω, καθαίρω, and ἱλάσκω, in the Greek; and *pio, expio, lustro,* &c., in the Latin tongue.* As for the continuance of the practice down to the present time, the writings of modern travellers, antiquaries, and missionaries, afford the most ample and incontestable evidence.†

III. Now, it is important to ascertain what was the NATURE of those sacrifices which we have found to prevail from the remotest ages of antiquity, and among every people under heaven.

What idea did those by whom they were offered attach to them? Did they involve the notion of atonement? That they should have done so is necessary to our argument; but this has been stoutly and pertinaciously denied. It has been affirmed by certain learned Socinians, that neither Jews nor heathens had any idea of a proper atonement, but were equally strangers to the notion of expiatory sacrifice.‡ It will readily be granted that *all* the sacrifices of antiquity were not of an expiatory nature; but that *some* of them were of this description admits, we apprehend, of the clearest proof.

The ancient sacrifices seem to have been of three kinds. Some very impetratory, or designed to express the desire of the offerer to obtain some favor of Deity. Others were eucharistical, or designed to express thankfulness for favors received. And others again were expiatory, or designed to obtain the forgiveness of sins of which the offerer acknowledged himself guilty. But even those which have been al-

* See Hill's Lect. on Div., vol. ii. p. 467.
† Magee on Atonement, vol. i. p. 96.
‡ Theo. Repos., vol. i. p. 409; cited by Dr. Magee, vol. i. p. 258.

lowed to have a respect to the removal of sin, have not been understood by all to involve the idea of atonement or vicarious suffering Other theories have been contrived with a view to explain their nature. They have been considered by some in the light of *gifts*, or as of the nature of a voluntary fine or bribe, offered by the culprit with a view to buy him off from punishment and purchase the favor of God.* By others they have been represented in the light of *federal rites*, expressive of the renewal of that friendship with God which had been broken off by the violation of his law, as eating and drinking together were the known and ordinary symbols of reconciliation.† Another theory is, that they are to be regarded as a sort of *symbolical language*, denoting either gratitude or contrition, according as they are eucharistical or expiatory.‡ These theories, though supported by such names as those of Spencer, and Sykes, and Warburton, are manifestly defective, and come far short of explaining the ancient sacrifices either of the heathen or of the patriarchs.

· That the ancient *heathen* sacrifices were of an atoning nature—that they involved the idea, not merely of contrition for sin, but of satisfaction to God by substitutionary suffering, appears from the language in which they are spoken of by the writers of antiquity. This language clearly denotes that the guilty were spared on account of the punishment borne by the guiltless. Homer, Hesiod, and Plutarch, among the Greeks; and Virgil, Horace, Juvenal, Cæsar, Ovid, Livy, &c., among the Latins, have all been adduced as witnesses on this particular point.§ The testimonies are indeed innumerable, as those conversant with the ancient authors are aware. And the earlier the times from which they are collected, they are always the more numerous and striking. The very name given to the second month in our year originated in what itself affords strong confirmation of the fact; that being the

---

* See Magee, vol. ii. p. 18.   † Ibid. vol. ii. p. 21.
‡ Ibid. vol. ii. p. 18.
§ Ibid. vol. i. p. 124—128; Hill's Lect., vol. ii. p. 405; Smith on Sacrifices, p. 234.

last month in the ancient Roman calendar, when it was customary to make atonement for the sins of the soul by sacrifices which were called *Februa* or expiations.* 'Thus,' as has been well observed, 'strongly and universally did men recognize that their crimes insured the vengeance of superior powers, except its course was stayed by the atonement of sacrifices, often in a high degree difficult, costly, and terrific. As, amidst the errors of idolatry, it is easy to perceive the indelible effects of the primitive belief and worship of the only God; so, under this mass of corruption, we obviously see the foundation of original truth.'

Of the vicarious nature of the ancient *patriarchal* sacrifices, the evidence is not less decisive. The learned theories before mentioned cannot explain the early sacrifices of scripture. The sacrifices of our first parents and of Abel, for example, cannot be looked upon as mere gifts, for this palpable reason, that the distinction of private property, which is supposed in a gift, had not then an existence. Neither can they be regarded as federal rites merely, inasmuch as there is no evidence that the practice of partaking of the sacrifice was introduced till a much later period; and even supposing its existence, it is an unwarrantable presumption to maintain that this participation constituted the whole essence of the sacrifice, instead of being a mere adventitious circumstance connected with it. With as little propriety can they be reckoned as only a species of symbolical language, there being no good ground for supposing that the language given to man at first was so defective as to require such a supplement. That they were, indeed, vicarious in their nature, best accords with their substance being animal. All other purposes but that of substitutionary suffering might have been equally well served, if not better, by vegetable productions. The preference given to the offering of Abel over that of Cain corroborates this view, the fruit of the ground being as suitable as a gift

---

* This circumstance is referred to by Cicero, by Ovid, and by Pliny. The passages are quoted by Dr. Pye Smith in one of his supplementary notes. Disc. on Sac., p. 236.

or as an expression of gratitude as a firstling of a flock. The ground of preference may be supposed to have been the state of Abel's mind, he being said to have acted in faith; and this is no doubt true; but we have reason to believe that the state of his mind directed him in the choice of the kind of offering that would be acceptable to God, and that had Cain also been in a right frame of soul he would never have thought an inanimate substance to be a suitable offering to an offended Deity.

With regard to the sacrifice of *Noah*, several things concur to show that it was of an atoning nature. The term 'burnt-offering,' which is employed with reference to it, is the term which is commonly used, in other parts of scripture, to denote an expiatory sacrifice. Besides, with respect to the acceptance of the offering, Jehovah is said to have 'smelled a sweet savor,' or a *savor of rest*, as it is given in the margin of our Bible--or *an odor of placability*, as the Syriac version has it;—a phrase which implies the appeasing of one who is offended. And then the answer which God is said to have given to Noah supposes that the sacrifice was of such a nature as to procure the withdrawment of divine wrath :—'I will not again curse the ground any more for man's sake ; neither will I again smite any more everything living, as I have done.'*

The same thing may be said of the sacrifices mentioned in the book of *Job*. It is clear that they were *sacrifices* FOR *sin*. Job assigned this reason for offering those which he presented on behalf of his children: 'It may be that my sons have sinned and have cursed God in their hearts.' The reason given by the Almighty for requiring sacrifices of Job's friends turns on the same thing :—' Lest I deal with you after your folly, in that ye have not spoken of me the thing that is right.' And unless we can regard the animals sacrificed in the light of a fine, or bribe, or gift, in consideration of which the Almighty, like a corrupt judge, agrees to remit the sin, we must look upon them as

---

* Gen. viii. 21.

real propitiatory offerings. But this we cannot do, for God expressly disclaims any gift presumptuously offered him for the mere purpose of deprecating his displeasure. *There is no iniquity with the Lord our God, nor respect of persons, nor* TAKING OF GIFTS.*

IV. We have now seen that sacrificing existed from the most remote antiquity; that the practice was universally prevalent; and that these ancient and universal sacrifices were of a strictly piacular or vicarious nature. And the point next to be considered respects THE ORIGIN of these ancient and universal sacrifices.

They must have had some adequate origin, and that origin must be either human or divine. To account for the practice, on the principle of a human origination, many theories have been formed, and much discussion has been expended; but the only satisfactory explanation of the singular fact is to be found, we presume, in the principle that sacrifice was originally instituted by God with reference to the atonement of Christ; the heathen sacrifices being so many imitations of the primitive practice, a knowledge of which was obtained by tradition, though greatly corrupted by cruel and frivolous inventions of man. This view of the subject admits of being extensively argued.

1. The divine origin of primitive sacrifice may be argued from its being impossible otherwise to account for its existence.

It cannot be regarded as a dictate of *reason;* for reason can discover nothing either acceptable to God or fitted to remove the guilt of sin, in the destruction of an innocent creature; but rather the contrary, as such an act of cruelty seems more calculated to increase than to take away guilt, and an injury done to one of God's works seems fitter to incur than to appease his displeasure. It cannot have originated in *natural instinct;* for there is no appetite in man which can be supposed to be gratified by shedding the blood and burning the flesh of an unoffending animal. As little

---

* 2 Chron. xix. 7. For a full and learned view of the sacrifices of Noah and Job, the reader is referred to a Treatise on the Origin of Expiatory Sacrifice, by Mr. Faber. London, 1827.

can it be supposed to have originated in *priestcraft*. In primitive times no distinct order of priesthood existed; the sacred functions were performed by the head of the family, who could have no pecuniary inducement to introduce expensive religious rites; and even in later times, the sacrifices were provided at the expense of the offerers, and were no source of emolument whatever to any order of men. There is just one other supposition, and this is not less unsatisfactory than those to which we have already referred, namely, that the practice originated in *superstition*. But superstition is the corruption of true religion, and supposes something similar in the latter, on which it is based, and from which it takes its rise. Without true religion there could be no superstition, just as without sincerity there could be no hypocrisy; without a genuine currency there could be no counterfeit coin; without truth there could be no falsehood; without a proper use there could be no abuse. Superstition can never, thus, of itself, account for the existence of sacrifice. Besides, superstition is apt to be endlessly diversified in its forms, while the practice in question is uniform throughout the whole range of its existence, which we have seen to be universal. Admitting that superstition might have accounted for its existence among a single people, it could not without a miracle, be supposed to have given rise to the same uniform practice in every nation of the world.

It thus appears that no mere human principle can account for the origin of primitive sacrifice. But the practice existed from the greatest antiquity, and prevailed over the whole earth. There is no disputing this fact. And as no effect can exist without an adequate cause, the fact in question must have originated in something sufficient to give it existence: and if this is not reason, nor natural instinct, nor priestcraft, nor superstition, what, pray, can it be, but the sovereign authority of God? 'How any practice,' says Dr. Patrick Delany, in his admirable dissertation on this subject, 'how any practice could obtain in the world, o which mankind were neither urged by the interest

and subtilty of any set of men, nor by any dictate of
reason, nor by any instinct or demand of nature, nor
by any interest of any kind; but quite the contrary, in
direct contradiction to every principle of reason, and
nature, and interest; (for the destruction of innocent
creatures is against reason, against nature, and against
interest:) I say, how such a practice could prevail, and
prevail universally, is impossible to be accounted for,
but from some powerful and irresistible influence of
example, or injunction of authority. And what example
could have such influence, except that of *Adam*,
or what authority could have such power, except that
of *God*, is to me, I own, utterly inconceivable....Where
any practice is universal, it must demonstrably have
some universal cause. And that can be no other in
the case before us, but either *God*, the founder of the
world, or *Adam*, the founder of the human race; from
whom it was derived to all his posterity.....But sacrifice
was such a practice, as, unless enjoined by the
authority of God, must of necessity be detrimental;
without any prospect of pleasure, or profit, or advantage
of any kind. And therefore, unless Adam was
worse than an idiot, it was impossible he could enjoin
on his posterity such a practice, from any other motive
than divine authority; or, if he had, it is unimaginable
why they should universally obey him, from any other
motive; unless they also were idiots for two thousand
years successively. Nay, this is not all; for it will
follow that the Egyptians, and Greeks, and Romans,
were likewise worse than idiots in their turn; that the
whole heathen world were brutes and monsters for
two thousand years more, in the practice of this very
rite; nay, they actually are so to this day. In a word,
either this rite had some foundation in true religion,
which swayed the whole world to the practice of it for
four thousand years, and yet sways the heathen part of
it to this day; or else this boasted principle of reason,
which could suffer men to go on in a train of such absurdity
and barbarity, for four thousand years, nay, for
six thousand years together, is a very bad and insufficient
guide. One of these positions is indisputably

.rue; if the latter is admitted, then revelation was absolutely necessary, to reform and to instruct the world, at the time that Jesus Christ came into it; if the former, then sacrifices were of divine institution. Let the adversaries of revelation take which side of this dilemma they like best."*

To the same purpose writes Mr. Faber, with admirable clearness and force, in reference to the universal accordance of the pagan world in the rite of sacrifice: "Clearly, the common origin of which we are in quest, must be far more ancient than the time of Moses; and perhaps it will not be easy to give any satisfactory account of it, if we stop short of that second father of mankind, whom the traditions of the Gentiles themselves describe as the earliest postdiluvian sacrificer. Let Noah be propounded as the common origin of the doctrine and the practice to ALL his posterity; and the riddle of pagan UNIFORMITY will be forthwith read; let Noah be rejected, as this common origin; and the riddle of pagan UNIFORMITY must then be left for a more satisfactory solution to those who advocate Mr. Davison's opinion. But if Noah be admitted as the common origin of the doctrine and the practice to ALL his posterity, the necessary conclusion will, I fear, be fatal to the system now under discussion. Noah could not *communicate* what he himself did not *possess*. Hence, if Noah communicated the doctrine and the practice to all his posterity, Noah must assuredly have been *well acquainted* both with the doctrine and with the practice. But in what manner did the doctrine and the practice become known to that great patriarch? Was it from a special revelation, made to himself or to his remote ancestors? Or was it from the wayward operation of a presumptuous and unauthorized superstition? The character of the just man,

---

* A circumstance strongly corroborative of the above conclusion is, that persons who had not the light of revelation, have found it impossible to account, on rational principles, for the existence of animal sacrifices, at the same time that they admit their universal prevalence. Pythagoras, Plato, Theophrastus, and Porphyry, have been adduced as instances to this purpose by Mr. Faber. See Treatise on Origin of Expiatory Sacrifice, p. 23, note.

who was perfect in his generations, and who walked with God, forbids, I think, the latter part of the alternative. Mr. Davison himself allows, that the doctrine and the practice could not emanate from the light of nature or from the principles of reason. It remains only, that Noah received them from revelation either mediate or immediate."* Thus clearly does it appear that on no other principle than that of a divine origin can the existence of primitive sacrifices be explained.

2. The ready acceptance of the ancient sacrifices recorded in scripture furnishes another proof of the point in hand.

The fact on which this argument rests is easily established. Nothing is clearer than that the earliest sacrifices of which we read were immediately accepted by God, without the slightest hesitation or delay. That the sacrifices of Job's friends were acceptable, appears, not merely from their being divinely prescribed, but from the recorded promise and its fulfilment, which stand connected with them. Annexed to the prescription we read:—"And my servant Job shall pray for you, and him will I *accept;*" and annexed to the compliance:—"The Lord also *accepted* Job." The whole account of Abraham's sacrifice, too, supposes its acceptance; but for which we should not have read of the act being immediately followed by the remarkable promise made to him on the occasion, nor had the patriarch had reason, in grateful commemoration of the divine goodness, to call the name of the place *Jehovah-jireh*. With respect to that of Noah, we are expressly informed, "The Lord smelled a sweet savor,"—a mode of phraseology which, as before remarked, strongly denotes the idea of acceptance. And as to Abel's offering, it is distinctly recorded, "The Lord had *respect* to Abel, and to his offering."

What was the mode in which the acceptance of these sacrifices was signified is a matter of inferior moment. The fact of acceptability is the chief consideration; although, if we suppose, with the Christian fathers and the Jewish doctors, that this was intimated

* Treatise on Origin of Expiatory Sacrifice, pp. 51, 52.

by the offering being consumed with fire, the fact is thus rendered more striking and impressive. We are sure that such was the mode of signifying the divine acceptance of the sacrifices under the law :—"And there came a fire out from before the Lord, and consumed upon the altar the burnt-offering and the fat."* Hence to *turn* a sacrifice *to ashes* is the Hebrew for to *accept* it, as may be seen by comparing the common version with the marginal reading of Psalm xx. 3: "Remember all thy offering, *accept* (turn to ashes) thy burnt-sacrifice." It is therefore a highly plausible supposition, that the acceptance of the early sacrifices was accompanied with this very significant token, which might be regarded as an infallible sign of their divine institution. Be this as it may, of the fact of their acceptance, whatever was the mode in which it was intimated, there can be no doubt; and for this it will be difficult to account, excepting on the principle of their being divinely instituted. *In vain do they worship me*, says God, *teaching for doctrines the commandments of men.* Had sacrifice been a human invention, it must have been an essentially and palpably superstitious act of will-worship, altogether uncommanded and gratuitous. In this case it could not be pleasing to God, but, on the principle first laid down, must have been, as an act of worship, utterly useless and vain. It is thus that the clearly established fact, of the unscrupulous and complacent acceptance of the early sacrifices by God, stands forth as an invincible proof, if not an actual demonstration, of the divine appointment of this primitive mode of worship.

3. This will become still more apparent if we confine our attention to Abel's sacrifice alone.

There are several things recorded concerning it which proceed on the supposition of its being divinely authorized. There is, first of all, something worthy of notice in the easy, familiar way in which the fact is introduced in the sacred narrative :—"And in process of time it came to pass." There is nothing here of the

* Lev. ix. 23. See also Judges vi. 21; 1 Kings xviii. 38; 1 Chron. xxi. 26; 2 Chron. vii. 1.

air of novelty It is no new occurrence. It is brought forward as quite an ordinary affair; which is all perfectly natural, if we suppose the rite to have been previously instituted and observed; but which it will be difficult to explain if this is denied. This inference is still more confirmed by the marginal reading:—"And it came to pass *in the end of the days*," (מקץ ימים) or as some of our most learned critics* translate the words, *at the close of the appointed season.*

There is, next, the consideration that it was an *animal* sacrifice. The very substance of it goes far to prove that it was agreeable to a divine institution. While it is admitted, that natural reason might suggest the propriety of offering to God eucharistic oblations, it is plain, for reasons formerly adduced, that these would consist of vegetable productions. It is absurd to suppose, that the destruction of an innocent animal should be, in itself, acceptable to God. Nothing but *duty*, as is observed by Delany, could make it acceptable, and nothing but the *command* of God could make it a duty. So much convinced of this have been some of those who have opposed the divine origin of primitive sacrifice, that they have found it necessary to deny that what Abel offered was an animal at all. Grotius, and such as have adopted his views, have maintained that it was the wool and the milk of the flock that were presented by Abel to the Lord, and not the flesh of the animals. To this opinion, so fanciful, and so contrary withal to the facts of the case, as well as to the whole tenor of the sacrificial rite, it would not be necessary to advert, were it not that it shows decidedly how difficult it is found to account for the existence of animal sacrifices on the principle of their being a human invention, and how far, consequently, the bare circumstance of Abel's bringing the *firstlings of his flock* proves that he was complying with a previously existing divine institution.†

Again: the language, "If thou doest well, shalt thou not be accepted?" implies plainly enough, that Abel, in

---

* Kennicot and others.
† See the wild sentiment of Grotius overthrown, Magee, vol. ii. p. 203.

the matter of his offering, *did well.* He did what was right, what was agreeable to the will of God, what was sure to meet the divine approbation. But it is only when we act in obedience to divine authority that we can be said to *do well.* This applies in a special manner to acts of worship. Obedience, even without sacrifice, may be graciously approved; but sacrifice without obedience never can. *To obey is better than sacrifice, and to hearken than the fat of rams.* We therefore feel entitled to conclude, that as Abel, in presenting his offering to the Lord, *did well,* he must have done it in obedience to a divine command.

It is, further, said that Abel offered "a more excellent sacrifice"* than Cain: or, as the original words might be rendered, *a much more sacrifice,* that is, an offering which partook more of the nature of a sacrifice than that of his brother. But this language seems to suppose the existence of some original divine institution, which is regarded as the standard to which reference is made in drawing the comparison.

But what puts the matter at rest, regarding the sacrifice of Abel, is its being said to have been offered in *faith.* "By *faith* Abel offered unto God a more excellent sacrifice than Cain." Of the nature of the patriarch's faith, the context leaves us no room to doubt. It was faith in divine revelation; in promises which received their fulfilment in Messiah; in an express command of God. Such, at least, was the faith of the other worthies with whom Abel is associated in the eleventh chapter of the Epistle to the Hebrews, and we have no right to conclude that *his* was different in its nature from *theirs.* Noah in building the ark, and Abraham in leaving his country, and Moses in rescuing the Israelites, acted in obedience to commands of God distinctly interposed, and in so doing they are said to have acted "by faith." From this are we not entitled to infer, that what Abel did *by faith,* was also done in compliance with a divine command? Now, what Abel did was offering a sacrifice. Sacrifice must, therefore, have been a divine institution. This crowns

* Πλείονα θυσίαν. Heb. xi. 4.

the whole with regard to the sacrifice of Abel. Commentators have differed with respect to the point on which the preference given to Abel's sacrifice turned; some fixing on the matter, others on the quality, of the respective offerings, others on the previous moral character of the offerers, and others again on the state of mind in which they were presented. But all these fail to account for the fact apart from that faith of which we have been speaking, and which, indeed, itself gives rise to all the other distinctions. The offerings of Cain and Abel were different, to be sure, in substance, in quality, in the previous character and immediate state of mind of the offerers. But whence arose those differences, but from the one being a believer and the other not? Had Cain possessed Abel's faith, he would have presented Abel's sacrifice; his moral character must necessarily have been different from what it was; and his state of mind at the time, instead of being that of a self-righteous infidel, who trusted to his own merit for acceptance, should have been characterized by an humble reliance on that all-sufficient atonement, of which the very act he was performing was prefigurative.

4. The expostulation of God with Cain gives additional confirmation to the argument in favor of the divine origin of primitive sacrifice.

According to the common version, that expostulation runs in the following terms:—"If thou doest well, shalt thou not be accepted? and if thou doest not well, sin lieth at the door." To this translation it may fairly be objected that it conveys no very satisfactory meaning; that it fails to explain the distinction that was made between the offerings of the two brothers; and that it represents the Almighty as speaking in a manner unsuited to infinite wisdom and dignity. Sin lying, or couching like an animal, at the door, is, at the best, but uncouth phraseology. But this is not the worst of it; for by retaining this translation the sense of the passage is rendered grossly tautological. Sin's lying at a person's door, we understand to express that the person is a sinner. According to this, all that the clause in question expresses is this miserable truism If *thou doest not well, thou art a sinner*, i. e. If *thou art a sinner, thou art a sinner*. But the word translated *sin* (חַטָּאת) is that which is commonly rendered elsewhere *sin-offering*, and accordingly the passage may, with manifest propriety, be translated thus:— "*If thou doest well*, shalt thou not be accepted? *And if thou doest not well*, a SIN-OFFERING COUCHETH BEFORE THE DOOR." In support of this rendering much might be said; but to enter into the subject at large would require more critical discussion than it accords with the plan of the present undertaking to introduce. It may be observed, however, that it was long ago proposed by Lightfoot, and has since been adopted by Kennicot, Faber, and other learned writers on the subject of sacrifice. The principal term, we have just said, is that which is employed in other parts of scripture, and particularly in the writings of Moses, to denote an expiatory sacrifice. Examples to this effect are numerous.* And, in support of the propriety of this rendering in the case in question, there is a peculiarity of grammatical construction which every scholar will admit to have great weight.† Nor is this translation liable to any objection of a formidable nature, especially if the final clause of the expostulation

---

* Exod. xxix. 14; xxx. 10. Lev. iv. 3, 21, 24, 29; iv. 25. 2 Kings xii. 16. Ezek. xlv. 23. Hos. iv. 8.

† "There is yet another circumstance of some weight which is remarked by *Parkhurst*, and is also noticed by *Castalio, Dathe*, and *Rosenmuller*, although they have not drawn from it the natural inference; namely, that חטאת, which is feminine, is here connected with a word of the masculine gender, רבץ; which, as Parkhurst judiciously observes, is perfectly consistent, on the supposition that חטאת denotes a sin-offering; for then, according to a construction common in Hebrew, which refers the adjective not to the word but to the thing understood by it, the masculine רבץ is here combined with the animal (a male) which was to be the sin-offering. In conformity with this reasoning, it will be found, that חטאת, in other parts of scripture where it is used for a *sin-offering*, is, though feminine itself, connected with a masculine adjunct. See Exod. xxix. 14; Lev. iv. 21, 24; v. 9, and other places of Leviticus, where the masculine pronoun הוא is used instead of the feminine היא. But in Gen. xviii. 20, xx. 9, Exod. xxxii. 21, 30, and other places, where the word occurs in its original signification of *sin*, it has constantly the adjective connected in the *feminine*."—Magee, vol. ii. p. 236, 237. See also Faber, p. 129.

be so rendered as to mark its reference to the sin-offering and not to Abel. Instead of "*Unto thee shall be* HIS *desire and thou shalt rule over* HIM," read, "*Unto thee is* ITS *desire,* and *thou shalt rule over* IT," as expressive of Cain's having full power over the animal which he was to use as a burnt-offering. Viewed in this light, the passage amounts to a *command* addressed by the Almighty himself to Cain, directing him, in case of sin, to take the necessary step of presenting a sin-offering. The command, too, from the manner in which it is introduced, supposes the rite of sacrifice to have been previously appointed; as what he is commanded to perform seems plainly to have been an antecedent duty, and to have been known to him as such. But as an *offering for sin* could not have been appointed before the existence of sin, it follows that the appointment must have taken place some time between the fall of Adam and the offerings of Cain and Abel. And, as it is reasonable to conclude that God, with whom the appointment originated, would introduce it just when it became necessary, we are thus led to trace the divine origin of sacrifice to the very period of the fall.*

There are two objections commonly urged against the divine institution of sacrifice, which it becomes us, in candor, to weigh.

The first is the alleged silence of the sacred writers on the subject. They are not silent with regard to the *fact;* instances of sacrifice are recorded; but whether these occurred in virtue of an existing divine institution, or in consequence of a mere spontaneous impulse on the part of the offerer, is not stated. Now, in reply to this, it might be deemed sufficient to say, that for such silence it is possible to account without supposing the non-existence of that of which we are speaking. The very commonness and notoriety of the observance at the time when the Pentateuch was written might account for the omission of the original command.

---

* See the subject of this paragraph most conclusively argued in the able Treatise of Mr. Faber, so often referred to, pp. 85—138. Also Magee, vol. ii. p. 229.

The succinct brevity of the sacred narrative rendered it impossible that every minute circumstance could find a place in it. Nor is the divine institution of sacrifices the only thing that has been omitted. There are other things, belonging to the same period, of which no mention is made in the narrative, but of which we read in other parts of scripture. It may be sufficient to remind the reader, as instances, of the fall of angels, the prophecy of Enoch, and the preaching of Noah, of which we read in the New Testament, but of none of which have we the slightest intimation in the narrative of the periods when they occurred. An example still more in point is that of the institution of the Sabbath. Indeed, it has been supposed by those who advocate the human origin of primitive sacrifice, to be a circumstance greatly in their favor, that the sacred historian is careful to record the divine original of a day of sabbatical rest, while of the rite of sacrifice he makes no similar record. But how stands the fact? There is mention made, in the narrative, of the *fact* that God rested on the seventh day from all his work which he had made, and that God blessed the seventh day and sanctified it. But there is nothing said of the *institution* of a seventh day of rest in so many words; we have no express *command* enjoining the observance of such a day. We legitimately *infer* from the recorded facts that there must have been such a command. And this is just what we do in the case of sacrifice. There are facts stated of the early observance of the rite, with manifest marks of divine approbation; there is no explicit intimation of its having been originally enjoined by God; but, without an express intimation to this effect, we are enabled, from what is recorded, to infer that there must have existed such an institution. The two instances are in these respects on a level, and if the silence of scripture on the subject of sacrifice is to be held as a valid argument against its divine original, so also must the silence of scripture on the subject of the Sabbath be held as a valid argument against *its* divine original. But we are not to dictate to God, as to the method in which he shall make known any part of his will to man. There are other ways of conveying a truth besides that of a formal scholastic enunciation. Many of the most important truths of our holy religion want this formality; and, by those who admit these truths, it ought to be reckoned no objection to the divine origin of sacrifice that the scriptures contain no precise intimation of the fact.

Another objection to the divine origin of primitive sacrifice has been founded on those passages of scripture in which sacrifices seem to be disowned by God. Such are those passages in the Psalms in which He is said *not to desire sacrifice, nor to delight in burnt-offering;* and a parallel passage in the prophecies of Jeremiah.* In reply to this objection it is easy to see that the expressions in question cannot be taken literally, as in this case they would contradict the whole of what is contained in Leviticus and Deuteronomy respecting the appointment of sacrifices. They must therefore be understood, like similar expressions in other parts of scripture, in a comparative sense; and then their meaning will be, that God desires not sacrifices, unless they be accompanied with those inward principles and that outward behavior without which they cannot be acceptable to Him. It is thus that God, by the prophet Isaiah, addresses the people of Israel, on account of their wickedness:—"To what purpose is the multitude of your sacrifices? Bring no more vain oblations, incense is an abomination unto me; the new moons and Sabbaths, the calling of assemblies, I cannot away with—*Your hands are full of blood.*"† In this light the language under consideration is in accordance with that of the wise man:—"*The sacrifice of the wicked is an abomination to the Lord.*" Or the meaning may be, that other things are preferred to sacrifices, although the latter are not excluded. The language of exclusion is often employed when only the preference of one thing to another is meant. "*I will have mercy and* NOT *sacrifice,*" means, *I prefer mercy to sacrifice.* "*Labor* NOT *for the meat that per-*

* Psalm xl. 6; l. 9; li. 16. Jer. vii. 22, 23.
† Isaiah i. 11, 15. See also Isaiah lxvi. 3; Amos v. 21, 25.

isheth, but for the meat which endureth to everlasting life," cannot be understood as condemning a diligent attention to business, but as commending attention to spiritual things in *preference* to those which perish by the using. On the same principle must we explain the words of the apostle, "*Adam was* NOT *deceived, but the woman,*" as meaning that the man was not *first* in transgression. The whole then that can be legitimately inferred from those passages on which the objection in question is founded, is, that Jehovah *prefers* the dutiful obedience of his creatures to the mere performance of ritual services; not that the latter is *not* acceptable to him, but that the former is *more* acceptable; in short, that "*to obey is* BETTER *than sacrifice, to hearken than the fat of rams.*"

V. Having now seen the divine origin of sacrifice established, we hope, beyond all reasonable doubt, it remains to complete our argument in behalf of the atonement of Jesus Christ, that we consider what was the USE or DESIGN of this institution.

Every institution of God must have an end worthy of himself and appropriate to the appointed means. Nor does it seem possible to conceive, consistently with the wisdom and goodness of God, that the institution of sacrifice could have any design short of being a prefigurative memorial of the way in which he had determined to save the life of man which had been forfeited by sin. By transgression, the human race had forfeited the life they possessed, and all right to its continuance. Of this there could not be a more striking representation than was given in requiring a living creature to be sacrificed on occasion of every offence; while the symbol still farther intimated, in an equally striking manner, God's willingness to accept of the life of a substitute for that of the actual offender. The institution of sacrifice thus taught man at once the evil of sin, the punishment sin deserved, and the way by which he might escape this merited consequence. Death by sin, and life by substitution, were as clearly pointed out, as can well be conceived possible, in symbolical language. Both the *fall* and the *recovery* of man, the death introduced by sin and the death by which sin was to be taken away, were thus strikingly portrayed. And, as it is impossible to conceive that the life of an irrational animal could be deemed an adequate compensation for the life of a moral creature, it is clear that the institution must have been regarded as prefigurative of a greater and more excellent sacrifice afterwards to be offered up. A promise of a great deliverer had, indeed, been conveyed to our guilty progenitors; and nothing is more natural than to suppose that sacrifice was appointed as a memorial of the deliverance which he was to effect.

"If we admit," says one of the ablest advocates of the doctrine, "that the scheme of redemption by the death of the only begotten Son of God was determined from the beginning; that is, if we admit, that when God had ordained the deliverance of man, he had ordained the means; if we admit that Christ was *the Lamb slain from the foundation of the world;* what memorial could be devised more apposite than that of animal sacrifice?—exemplifying by the slaying of the victim the death which had been denounced against man's disobedience:—thus exhibiting the awful lesson of that death which was the wages of sin, and at the same time representing that death which was actually to be undergone by the Redeemer of mankind:—and hereby connecting in one view the two great cardinal events in the history of man, the FALL and the RECOVERY: the death denounced against sin, and the death appointed for that Holy One, who was to lay down his life to deliver man from the consequences of sin. The institution of animal sacrifice seems then to have been peculiarly significant, as containing all the elements of religious knowledge: and the adoption of this rite, with sincere and pious feelings, would at the same time imply an humble sense of the unworthiness of the offerer; a confession that death, which was inflicted on the victim, was the desert of those sins which had arisen from man's transgression; and a full reliance on the promises of deliverance, joined to an acquiescence in the means appointed for its accomplishment. It this view of the matter be just," adds he, "there is nothing improbable even in the supposition that that part of the signification of the rite which related to the sacrifice of Christ, might have been in some degree made known from the beginning."* Why the learned author should have felt any hesitation on this point, we must confess ourselves at a loss to perceive. It was Jesus Christ who was from the beginning the alone object of saving faith, and as an ignorant belief can never be looked upon as entitled to this character, man must have had from the beginning some knowledge of the reference of the sacrificial rite to Him who was to appear in the end as the propitiation for our sins. Without such a reference the rite itself must have been an unmeaning, useless, burdensome ceremony; and, without some such knowledge, the observance of it must have been anything but a reasonable service—must have been, on the contrary, a piece of heartless drudgery.

Nor, taking this view of the matter, can we reckon it as at all a fanciful supposition, that the very first promise of a Saviour given to man was accompanied with the significant ratification of a sacrifice, setting forth that bruising of the heel of the woman's seed by which the serpent's head was to be bruised. And it is not a little interesting to remark, how, on this supposition, the first blood which stained the earth was that of a sacrifice, and the first idea which the forefathers of our race would have of death was derived from that of a victim slain to prefigure Him who was afterwards to abolish death and bring life and incorruption to light by his Gospel. "How much," says Dr. Pye Smith, with great beauty and eloquence, "how much must the impression on the heart have been increased, when the *first* sacrifice was offered: when the parents of our race, recent from their guilty fall, were abased by the divine rebuke, driven from their blissful seat, and filled with dismay at the threatening of DEATH! A threatening piercing through their souls, but of the nature and effects of which they could form

* Magee, vol. ii. pp. 51, 52.

none but vague ideas. But when directed by stern authority, to apply some instrument of death to the lamb which, with endearing innocence, had sported around them,—an act of whose effects they as yet knew nothing,—they heard its unexpected cries, they beheld the appalling sight of streaming blood, and struggling agonies, and life's last throes,—they gazed upon the breathless body, and they were told THIS IS DEATH: how stricken must they have been with horror, such as no description could ever paint! When, farther, they had to go through all the other process of the sacrifice, their hands reluctant, and their hearts broken, and all their soul crushed down by the sad consciousness that these horrid things were the fruit of their sin, and yet contained the hope of their deliverance,—who can imagine the extremity of their feelings?"*

Now let us collect together in a single sentence the different points of the argument thus elaborated. Sacrifices have existed from the remotest ages of the world, and prevailed among every people under heaven;—these sacrifices have been, without all controversy, of an expiatory and vicarious nature; it is found impossible to account for their existence but on the principle of their being derived from an original divine institution;—of such an institution, we can conceive of no design worthy of God, short of its being to prefigure the death of the Lord Jesus Christ;—but, as the type and antitype must resemble each other in their most essential and significant features, the typical sacrifices of ancient divine institution being vicarious and expiatory must be held demonstrative of the atoning nature of the Saviour's death.

Such is the first argument in support of the doctrine of atonement—an argument which prejudice may resist and ignorance despise, but which it will not be easy, either by learning, or reasoning, or scripture, to overturn.

How inexcusable, then, are such as deny the atone-

* Disc. on Sac., pp. 9, 10.

ment of Jesus Christ! Blind, insolent, and rash, they arraign the wisdom of God, for which conduct they are reproved by the heathen themselves. Though reason could never have devised the plan of substitution, the vicarious nature of pagan sacrifices is a proof that there is something in God's method of redemption, when revealed, which unsophisticated reason cannot gainsay or resist. The testimony hence derived in favor of our doctrine is, thus, universal as the practice of the rite of which we have been speaking; and every sacrifice of the heathen may be regarded in this way, as pointing directly to the one perfect sacrifice of the Son of God. The errors and superstitions which are mingled up and incorporated with these offerings, cannot but awaken, in the breast of the true Christian, a feeling of pity for those who are without the sacred writings, and of gratitude for this inestimable boon. It is impossible to reflect on the high antiquity of the sacrificial institute, without thinking of the divine goodness manifested in giving to man at so early a period the knowledge of atonement. This doctrine, so essential to his hopes as a sinner, was coeval with the fall, so that the very first human transgressor was made acquainted with the way by which the fatal consequences of guilt might be for ever averted. Nor is the wisdom of God less apparent in thus preparing the world for the universal reception of the only true religion. Wherever Christianity can be carried, the people must be so far prepared to acquiesce in its grand essential principle of salvation by an atoning sacrifice. Every part of the Gentile world is familiar with the idea of substitution, and the very terms which this principle suggests the use of, are to be found incorporated in almost every language on earth. Without this, the prospect of the universal spread of the Christian faith must have been, humanly speaking, much more hopeless, as the difficulty of bringing men to understand its nature must have been greatly increased.

SECTION V.

PROOF—LEVITICAL SACRIFICES.

The distinction put on Abraham and his posterity by their being selected as the depositaries of certain peculiar privileges, is a striking circumstance in the providential development of God's purposes of grace. It forms an era in the history of the species, and more particularly of the church. It pleased God to separate the family in question from the rest of mankind; to appoint them laws peculiar to themselves; and so to situate them that they should have every opportunity of punctually observing the institutions of Jehovah. The prescription of these laws occurred about two thousand five hundred years from the creation of the world, and about fifteen hundred years before the advent of Christ. The laws themselves embraced everything respecting the civil and religious interests of the people; and among those of a religious nature, the law of sacrifice held a prominent place.

This was not the first time that the rite in question was mentioned. We have seen that it was known to the church long before. And, indeed, the manner in which it is introduced, in the Levitical code, is no small confirmation of the view we have given, in the preceding section, of the divine origin of primitive sacrifice. It is not brought forward as a new thing, on which the authority of God is stamped for the first time. New regulations respecting the *mode* and the *occasion* of the *rite* are laid down, but the *rite* itself is not made the subject of any authoritative enactment. It is taken for granted that the rite exists, and that its divine authority is acknowledged and well understood. "*Speak unto the children of Israel, and say unto them: If any man of you bring an offering unto the Lord, ye shall bring your offering of the cattle, even of the* *herd and of the flock.*"* Such is the manner in which the Levitical institutes regarding sacrifice are introduced; and it must be admitted to furnish a striking corroboration of the views of those who believe that the ordinance was not then appointed for the first time.

It is not meant by these observations, to insinuate a doubt with respect to the divine authority of the sacrifices which existed under the law. That regulations were prescribed by Jehovah respecting the substance of which these sacrifices should consist, the qualifications they were required to possess, the mode in which they should be offered, and the occasions on which they were to be presented, is quite sufficient evidence that the rite itself possessed the sanction of divine authority. We are thus enabled to appeal to the nature and design of the Levitical sacrifices as a second argument in favor of the doctrine of Christ's atonement. This position, like that of which we have already disposed, admits of ample illustration. To perceive its force, it will be requisite to attend, in proper order, to these distinct statements:—that sacrifices were sanctioned by God as a part of the religious service of the Hebrews—that many of these sacrifices were unquestionably expiatory and vicarious in their nature—that they were in themselves incompetent to remove moral guilt—that they were designed to prefigure the sacrifice of Christ, and were actually fulfilled in him. If these statements are successfully established, it will not be possible to resist the inference that the death of the Son of God was a real and proper atonement for sin.

I. Sacrifices formed an essential part of the divinely authorized religious services of the Jews.

There can be no dispute on this point. The law was given on the first day of the first month of the second year after the deliverance from Egypt; and the same year, on the arrival of the children of Israel at Kadesh-barnea, the Levitical priesthood was instituted, and every regulation connected with it laid down. No one who believes the Bible to be true, and

* Lev. 1. 2.

who takes the trouble to peruse the books of Exodus and Leviticus, can call in question the divine authority of the Jewish sacrifices. These sacrifices, however, were of various kinds. They are generally divided into bloody and unbloody. The latter were, strictly speaking, rather offerings than sacrifices; they consisted solely of vegetable substances, such as meal, bread, corn, oil, and frankincense; and were not admissible as sin-offerings, excepting in the case of persons so very poor as to be unable to provide an offering of two young pigeons or turtle doves. The bloody sacrifices again were partly stated and partly occasional. The *occasional* sacrifices were of four kinds:—*Burnt-offerings*, or holocausts, which were free-will offerings, devoted to God by the spontaneous act of the offerers;*—*Peace-offerings*, which were presented in token of reconciliation to the Lord, either in the way of petition or of thanksgiving:†—*Sin-offerings*, which were required for sins of ignorance, or sins contracted wilfully;‡—and *Tresspass-offerings*, which were to be presented when a person was in doubt whether he had violated the law or not.§ The *stated* sacrifices were some of them daily; some weekly; some monthly and some yearly. The daily sacrifices were to be offered morning and evening.‖ The weekly sacrifices were to be presented on the Sabbath day, when the daily sacrifices were doubled.¶ The monthly sacrifices occurred on occasion of the new moon.** And there were four occasions on which annual sacrifices were appointed to be offered;—at the feast of the passover, at the feast of pentecost, at the feast of tabernacles, and on the day of expiation.†† All these sacrifices had the express sanction of God, as any one may easily satisfy himself, by looking into the laws divinely prescribed respecting them, recorded in the books of Exodus, Leviticus, and Numbers.

II. It is not pretended that the Jewish sacrifices

---

* Lev. i. 1, 10, 14; vi. 1—6. † Lev. iii. 1—6.
‡ Lev. iv. 2—19. § Lev, vii. 1—10.
‖ Lev. vi. 8—19. ¶ Num. xxviii. 9, 10. ** Num. xxviii. 11—14.
†† See Horne's Introd. vol. iii. pp. 226—284. Also Dr. Winer's Bible Dict. cited by Dr. P. Smith. Disc. p. 239, &c.

were, without exception, propitiatory; but certainly many of them were vicarious and expiatory in their nature.

It is freely admitted that the unbloody offerings at the feasts of pentecost and tabernacles, were only eucharistical, commemorative, or impetratory; but it is presumed that all the bloody sacrifices were of the description above specified, involving a transference of guilt and substitution of punishment. With regard to the *burnt-offering* we read;—" If his offering be a burnt sacrifice of the herd, let him offer a male without blemish—and he shall PUT HIS HAND ON THE HEAD of the burnt-offering; and it shall be accepted FOR him, to make ATONEMENT FOR him."* With regard to the *peace-offering*:—" If his oblation be sacrifices of peace-offering........he shall LAY HIS HAND UPON THE HEAD of his offering, and kill it at the door of the tabernacle of the congregation."† With regard to the *sin-offering*:—" If the whole congregation of Israel sin through ignorance........then the congregation shall offer a young bullock for the sin........and the elders of the congregation shall LAY THEIR HANDS UPON THE HEAD of the bullock before the Lord........and the priest shall make an ATONEMENT for them, and it shall be forgiven them."‡ With regard to the *trespass-offering*:—" As the sin-offering is, so is the trespass-offering; there is one law for them: the priest that maketh ATONEMENT therewith shall have it."§ With regard to at least one of the sacrifices appointed to be offered on the occasion of the passover, we read:—" And one goat for a sin-offering, to make an ATONEMENT for you."|| With regard to that on the day of expiation there is no room to doubt:—" Also on the tenth day of this seventh month there shall be a DAY OF ATONEMENT; it shall be an holy convocation unto you; and ye shall afflict your souls, and offer an offering made by fire unto the Lord. And ye shall do no work in that same day; for it is a DAY OF ATONEMENT, to MAKE AN ATONEMENT FOR YOU before the Lord your God."¶ Many more

---

* Lev. i. 3, 4. † Lev. iii. 1, 2. ‡ Lev. iv. 13—20.
§ Lev. vii. 7. || Num. xxviii. 22. ¶ Lev. xxiii. 27, 28.

passages might be added, in which similar language is employed; but these may be deemed sufficient to establish the position, that the bloody sacrifices of the Jews were vicarious in their nature and import.

We are aware of the objections that have been started against this view of the legal sacrifices; but they have all received the most triumphant refutation.* Indeed, let any one calmly consider the circumstances connected with the act of sacrificing:—the selection of the victim; the relation of the animal to the person for whom it was offered; its substitution in his stead; his confessing over it all his iniquities; the imposition of hands on the head of the victim; its being actually slain and offered to God; let any impartial person candidly consider these circumstances, and say whether he can resist the inference that the sacrifice was regarded as a piacular substitute for the individual by whom it was brought to the altar.

The ceremony of the scape-goat in particular, merits attention in this connection. This sacred solemnity belonged to the annual day of expiation. It consisted in presenting to the Lord two goats, one of which was slain, and the other sent away alive into the wilderness. The two animals together made but one offering, as the language of the statute expresses more than once;—" He shall take of the congregation of the children of Israel two kids of the goats for a SIN-OFFERING. Aaron shall bring the goat upon which the Lord's lot fell, and offer him for a sin-offering; but the goat on which the lot fell to be the scape-goat, shall be presented alive before the Lord, to make an atonement WITH HIM (*i. e.* together with the other goat) and to let him go for a scape-goat into the wilderness."† Each contributed to the atonement, and both were essential to the perfection of the ceremony. Now, the imposition of hands on the animals, and the confession of sins which accompanied it, point out unequivocally that the sins of the people were understood to be transferred to the victim, and, by means of this substitute, expiated or taken away. "And Aaron shall

* Magee, vol. i. pp. 354—366. † Lev. xvi. 5, 9, 10.

lay both his hands upon the head of the live goat, and confess over him all the iniquities of the children of Israel, and all their transgressions in all their sins, PUTTING THEM UPON THE HEAD of the goat, and shall send him away by the hand of a fit man into the wilderness. And the goat shall BEAR UPON HIM ALL THEIR INIQUITIES unto a land not inhabited."*

III. Let it now be remarked that the Jewish sacrifices were not, in themselves, sufficient to take away sin, that is, to atone for moral guilt.

That they were offered in cases of moral offence admits of the most satisfactory proof. We are aware that a contrary opinion has been strenuously maintained. It has been supposed that it was only in cases of ceremonial offence, of breaches of the ceremonial law, or of sins of ignorance to which no moral character could properly attach, that sacrifices were admissible. Not to say that sins of ignorance may involve moral guilt, as ignorance itself is often criminal; not to insist that breaches of the ceremonial law might well be considered as involving moral turpitude from the state of mind which they indicated; not to remark that once in the year, at least, atonement was to be made for ALL the iniquities of the children of Israel, and of course for moral as well as ceremonial offences; not to build on these things, it is sufficient to observe that sacrifices were required in cases of fraud, injustice, perjury, debauchery—all of them direct violations of the moral law, which it was impossible to commit without such a state of mind being implied as could not but be highly criminal in the view of a holy and just God.

It is true, there were certain moral offences of an aggravated nature, such as idolatry, adultery, murder and blasphemy, for which no sacrifice was appointed, or permitted to be offered. But the reason of this was, not that sacrifices were inadmissible in cases of moral delinquency, but that the offences in question subjected the offenders to death, and consequently did **not** admit of exemption from the outward penalty at-

Lev. xvi. 21, 22.

tached to all offences of the law, and which exemption always resulted from the offering of an acceptable sacrifice. Nor from the circumstance of a sacrifice being inadmissible is it to be supposed that these offences were unpardonable. They were capital offences against the state, and therefore no sacrifice, tending to reinstate the offender in his place in society, was to be offered. But the guilty person might still lift a penitential prayer to the throne of mercy, and, through the propitiation of Christ, might obtain the full forgiveness of his iniquity, be restored to the favor of God, and be admitted to his presence forever.* Independently of this, however, it is clear that the legal sacrifices had a respect to moral guilt, being offered on occasion of breaches of the moral law.

Now, what we wish to be observed is, their utter inefficacy, in themselves, to expiate moral transgression. "Which was a figure for the time then present," says the writer of the epistle to the Hebrews, "in which were offered both gifts and sacrifices, *that could not make him that did the service perfect, as pertaining to the conscience.*"† The conscience of the offerer told of guilt which they could not atone, of pollution which they could not remove, of wrath from which they could not protect. "The law being a shadow of good things to come, and not the very image of the things, can *never with those sacrifices*, which they offered year by year continually, *make the comers thereunto perfect.*"‡ That moral perfection which consists in justification, sanctification, peace with and access to God, they could never effect, from an inherent unfitness for such a purpose. "FOR IT IS NOT POSSIBLE THAT THE BLOOD OF BULLS AND OF GOATS SHOULD TAKE AWAY SINS."§ The reason of this inefficaciousness of the legal sacrifices was, not simply that they were not

---

* "Quod si pro quibusdam peccatis ultroneis gravioribus nullum legitur institutum sacrificium, qualia erant homicidium, idololatriæ, adulterium, et similia quæ בְּיָד רָמָה elata manu et per superbiam fiebant, ideo hoc factum est, quia puniri ea Deus voluit supplicio capitali, atque adeo peccantes non opus habuerunt hoc remedio, cum eorum mors fuerit instar expiationis cujusdam publicæ."— *Turretin*, vol. ii. p. 470.
† Heb. ix. 9. ‡ Heb. x. 1. § Heb. x. 4.

appointed by God for the purpose in question. It is true, they were not appointed for such an end. But the inspired apostle carries the reason much higher—they *could not have been so appointed* by a wise and perfect God, because inherently inadequate to fulfil any such design. It was NOT POSSIBLE that the blood of bulls and of goats should take away sin. They did not comport with the majesty of Him against whom the sin was committed, the great God of heaven and earth, whom the death of a beast could never appease. They gave no proper expression of the divine displeasure at sin; the holy repugnance of God's nature at iniquity, and his righteous determination to punish it, could not be thus unequivocally announced; if something more had not been required to procure remission, it could never have appeared that sin was exceedingly sinful. They gave no adequate exhibition of the inviolable rectitude and authority of God's moral government or law; for if such was all that was requisite to secure exemption from the penalty annexed to its violation, no inference could be more legitimate than that its requirements were originally too strict, its sanctions originally too severe, and that it might be violated with comparative impunity. They bore no proper relation to the sinner, either in point of nature or legal obligation; the animals which composed them were in respect of nature greatly inferior to man, and in no sense under that law, the breach of which occasioned the guilt. And they possessed no value at all proportioned to the life that had been forfeited, and which required to be redeemed; that was the life of an intelligent, moral, immortal creature, but the sacrifice was only an irrational, perishing beast. For these and similar reasons, the sacrifices of the law could not take away sin. Lebanon was not sufficient to burn, nor the beasts thereof sufficient for a sin-offering; and it might well be asked, Will the Lord be pleased with thousands of rams, or with thousands of rivers of oil?

It does not follow from this, that the Jewish sacrifices were useless. Because they did not serve a purpose for which they were never designed, it would be rash surely to infer that they served no purpose at all. They served all the purposes for which they were appointed. They taught the evil of sin and its desert of death. "In those sacrifices there was a remembrance made of sins every year." They were offerings of memorial bringing iniquity to remembrance. And they not only reminded men of their sins, but strikingly intimated that these sins were remembered also by God; that something more was necessary to cover them from the eye of omniscient justice; that something else was required before they could assure themselves that HE would no more remember them. They also procured the remission of those temporal penalties which attached to the iniquities of the people of Israel. From the theocratic nature of the constitution, every violation of the laws possessed a double character. As an offence against the statute law, it had a civil character, and exposed to temporal pains; as an offence against the moral law, it had a moral character, and exposed to spiritual pains. The sacrifices seem to have procured a remission of the temporal pains, whatever might be the inward feeling and exercise of the offerer, and to have restored him to his status in the commonwealth. And this is all the use which many conceive the legal offerings to have served. But we presume they served a farther and much higher end—an end connected with the remission of moral guilt. Though inadequate, in themselves, to procure such remission, they were capable of prefiguring that which could. Though unable to atone for a single moral transgression, they could point distinctly forward to that one offering by which Christ was afterwards to perfect forever them that are sanctified. This was their great and chief use; and when offered by those whose faith clearly embraced and whose hearts cordially approved this ultimate reference, it is not too much to believe that they were connected with the remission of those spiritual pains to which the contraction of moral guilt exposed the offender.

IV. It is, thus, incumbent on us, in the prosecution of our argument, to show that the Jewish sacrifices were designed to prefigure Christ, and were actually fulfilled in h m.

From this, it is presumed, all their value and efficacy arose. Without such a reference, it is impossible to account for their appointment by a wise and beneficent God. To them the remark is equally applicable as to the patriarchal sacrifices, that, excepting on the principle of being prefigurative of Christ, they appear useless and unmeaning, a culpable waste of animal life and valuable property, and an intolerable yoke of burdensome exaction. This itself affords strong presumptive evidence of their ultimate design; but the direct proof is neither scanty nor obscure.

If we look into the writings of the prophets, we find them speaking of the legal sacrifices, in such connection with that of the Messiah, as plainly to intimate the fulfilment of the former in the latter. "Sacrifice and offering," says David, "thou didst not desire; mine ears hast thou opened: burnt-offering and sin-offering hast thou not required. Then said I, Lo, I come: in the volume of the book it is written of me, I delight to do thy will, O my God; yea, thy law is within my heart."* That this prediction refers to Messiah is obvious from the use to which it is applied in the epistle to the Hebrews. "Wherefore, when he cometh into the world, he saith, Sacrifice and offering," &c.† It is to the Son of God, in regard of his incarnation, that the inspired writer refers when he speaks of *his coming into the world;* on which occasion he is represented as having used the language in question. This language could not be used by David, or any other member of the Jewish church, of whom sacrifice and offering were peremptorily required; neither is it necessary to suppose that it was employed literally, in so many words, by the Messiah at his advent in the flesh; it is sufficient to understand it as expressive generally of what was then his great design or intention. And what is it that he expresses? The speech consists of four clauses, each of which, according to the poetical structure of the psalm, makes a line of tetrastich or stanza of four

* Psalm xl. 6—8. † Heb. x. 5—7.

lines, the first corresponding to the third, and the second to the fourth; thus:

> "Sacrifice and offering thou didst not desire;
> Mine ears hast thou opened;
> Burnt-offering and sin-offering hast thou not required.
> Then said I, Lo, I come," &c.

Now, " sacrifice and offering," " burnt-offering and sin-offering," must be understood as meaning the whole sacrificial rites of the law. Of these it is affirmed, that God "did not desire—did not require" them; which cannot mean absolutely that they were not required, for this is contrary to the whole tenor of the law. Nor can it mean merely that God had no pleasure in these sacrifices when improperly presented, for this does not comport with the scope of the passage. But it plainly enough intimates, that they were not required by God as a real atonement for sin; that for such a purpose they were quite inadequate; that God could take no delight, could feel no satisfaction or complacency in them in this view; that, in short, for such a purpose they were never appointed, and could not be accepted by the moral Governor of the world.

But, on the other hand, he says, "Mine ears hast thou opened," (or "a body hast thou prepared me,") and " Lo, I come, in the volume of the book," &c. Whichever reading of the former clause we adopt, whether that of the Hebrew text, or that of the Septuagint translation which is adopted by Paul, the meaning is the same; it denotes the entire devotedness of Christ to the will of his Father in offering himself as a proper sacrifice for sin,—his full acquiescence in this as the grand purpose of his incarnation. Such also is the import of the corresponding clause, " In the volume of the book," &c. The book of the law, the pentateuch, the only volume extant when the psalm was penned, taught in general that a higher sacrifice was requisite to accomplish the will of God, and contained several particular and distinct predictions respecting the Messiah himself. A body, or human nature, was provided, in which he might accomplish what the Levitical sacrifices could not effect, might do that which Jehovah willed, and in which he could take full pleasure; and this the personage by whom the language is spoken fulfilled, most readily cheerfully, and piously, without the least reluctance or aversion.

Such is plainly enough the import of this famous passage. In this way it invincibly asserts the prefigurative reference of the sacrifices of the law to that of Christ: and if any shadow of doubt should remain of the correctness of this view, let it be dissipated for ever by the testimony of the inspired writer who thus expounds its meaning:—" Above, when he said, sacrifice, and offering, and burnt-offering, and offering for sin, thou wouldst not," &c.—" HE TAKETH AWAY THE FIRST THAT HE MAY ESTABLISH THE SECOND." That is, he abolishes the legal sacrifices first spoken of, as insufficient for the purpose of a real atonement; and confirms or ratifies the work of Christ, second spoken of, as all-efficacious and perfect.* It is not easy to

---

* It has been remarked above, that whichever reading we adopt of the second line of the passage now explained, it comes to the same thing. It may be proper to set down in a note the various methods resorted to for the purpose of reconciling these readings, the one of which occurs in the Psalm itself, and the other in the quotation from it in the epistle to the Hebrews.

1. It has been supposed that the clause is unimportant, and has no proper bearing on the object for which the apostle makes the quotation; and that, therefore, quoting, as was then the custom, from the Septuagint, he does not take the trouble to correct, but takes it just as he finds it. But if we are right in our interpretation of the passage, the clause *is* important, and independently of this, it is not to be thought that an inspired writer would lend his support to an error, supposing the rendering of the LXX. to be wrong.

2. It has been thought that the apostle merely brings an *argumentum ad hominem* against the Jews, with whom he is reasoning. They acknowledged the Septuagint translation, and it was enough for his purpose to confute them from what they admitted as authoritative. But it does not comport with the ideas we form of the perfect integrity of an inspired writer, to suppose him bringing forward as scripture what was not so, even although it was so understood by those with whom he is contending. It was not for victory that he contended, but for the purpose of awakening conviction on the ground of truth. At least, if he so argued we should expect him to apprise us of it, which is not done in the case under consideration.

3. It has also been imagined, that the writer of the epistle to the Hebrews does not profess to quote literally, but to give the sense of the passage from which he quotes—that he quotes, not *ad literam*, but *ad sensum*. Now, this is frequently done: and it is not a little in favor of this view, that the two expressions are strictly the same in meaning. "Mine

see how the idea could have been more strongly expressed, that Christ was actually to fulfil what the legal offerings were intrinsically incapable of accomplishing, and thus to supersede these sacrificial observances completely and forever.

The prophet Daniel may also be adduced as a witness. His celebrated prediction, in the ninth chapter of his book, plainly teaches, that when Messiah the prince should be cut off, for the purpose of finishing transgression and bringing in everlasting righteousness, the sacrifice and the oblation, which had previously existed among the people of Israel, should be abolished. From this it is a natural and irresistible inference, that the Jewish sacrifices were symbolical representations of the sacrifice of Christ. "Seventy weeks are determined upon thy people, and upon thy holy city, to finish the transgression, to make an end of sins, to make reconciliation for iniquity.......and after threescore and two weeks shall Messiah be cut off, but not for himself.......and he shall confirm the covenant with many, and in the midst of the week he shall cause the sacrifice and the oblation to cease."*

If we turn to the New Testament, we shall find no lack of evidence to prove that the sacrifices of the

ears thou hast opened," whether referring to the ancient law respecting servants (Exod. xxi. 5), or to the common mode of expressing willing obedience (Is. l. 5), denotes perfect submissiveness. And the other clause, "A body hast thou prepared me," means just the same thing; bodies being often used for servants or slaves, as in Rev. xviii. 13, where, in the inventory of Babylon's merchandise, we find " horses, and chariots, and slaves, (σώματα, bodies) and souls of men," (*See Schleusner in loco.*) The Messiah, as an obedient servant, devoted himself to the will and service of God.

4. It has been farther suggested, that an emendation of the Hebrew text might easily remove the difficulty. For אזנים, *mine ears*, substitute אז גוה, *then a body*. The letters in both cases bear a strong resemblance to each other; and it is not at all impossible, nor even improbable, that, in the course of transcription, the one might have been substituted for the other. This suggestion was first made by Dr. Kennicott, and is adopted by Owen, Pye Smith, and M'Lean; but we do not find it so much as alluded to by Professor Stuart in his critical commentary on the Hebrews.

Those who wish to pursue this inquiry farther, may consult the authors just referred to, and also Carpenter's Scripture Difficulties, where they will find a learned dissertation on the passage; pp. 536—458.

* Dan. ix. 24—27.

legal dispensation had a designed reference to Christ. His person and his death are spoken of in such terms as to leave no room to doubt on the subject. John the Baptist says, "Behold the Lamb of God that taketh away the sin of the world."* Christ himself tells us, that "the Son of Man came to give his life A RANSOM for many."† Paul speaks of Christ having " given himself for us AN OFFERING AND A SACRIFICE to God for a sweet-smelling savor."‡ Throughout the epistle to the Hebrews, this apostle speaks of Jesus as a *priest*—a *high priest*—a *sacrifice;* as *offering himself to God,* —*bearing the sins of many*—and *offering one sacrifice for sins.* From such expressions the inference is plain—an inference which we are not left to draw of ourselves, the Spirit of God having given it in so many words, that CHRIST IS THE END OF THE LAW for righteousness, and the law a schoolmaster to bring us to Christ.§

Indeed, the striking analogy subsisting betwixt the legal sacrifices and that of Christ, strongly corroborates the view that the latter is the substance, reality, and antitype of the former. With regard to sacrifices in general, the selection of the victim, the properties it required to possess, its substitution in room of the offerer, its death, and its presentation to God on the altar, are circumstances all of which are most exactly fulfilled in the eternal appointment, the spotless purity, the actual substitution, and the final crucifixion of the incarnate Redeemer. The minute distinctions that have been industriously traced between the sin-offerings of the law and the death of the Messiah, affect not in the least the inference deducible from the above analogy, as these differences arise solely from the necessary superiority of the antitype as compared with the type.—In the case of the annual expiation, the points of resemblance are still more numerous and striking. Here, the exclusive nature of Christ's office as our great High Priest, his making atonement for the whole chosen of God, and his entrance into the highest

---

* John i. 29   † Matt. xx. 28.
‡ Eph. v. 2.   § Rom. x. 4.   Gal. iii. 24.

heavens, not without blood, there to minister on their behalf in the immediate presence of the Most High, were distinctly shadowed forth.

But the Jewish rite which, above all, prefigured the sacrifice of Christ, is the passover. It has been questioned, indeed, whether the paschal lamb partook of the nature of a sacrifice at all: and others besides Socinians have held the opinion, that it was solely of a festal nature. Those who wish to examine the question minutely, can consult the document to which reference is made in the margin.* It may be sufficient here to observe, that there seems to be abundant reason to conclude, that the paschal lamb was a real sacrifice. Indeed, it is expressly so called, again and again:—" It is the *sacrifice of the Lord's passover*, who passed over the houses of the children of Israel in Egypt—Thou shalt not offer the blood of my sacrifice with leaven; neither shall *the sacrifice of the feast of the passover* be left unto the morning—Thou shalt *sacrifice the passover* unto the Lord thy God—Thou mayest not *sacrifice the passover* within any of thy gates; but at the place which the Lord thy God shall choose to place his name in, there thou shalt *sacrifice the passover* at even."† Besides, *priests* were employed in slaying the paschal lamb: "Moreover, Josiah kept a passover unto the Lord in Jerusalem, and they killed the passover on the fourteenth day of the first month. And he set the PRIESTS in their charges, and encouraged them to the service of the house of the Lord; and said unto the Levites—*so kill the passover*, and sanctify yourselves, and prepare your brethren. So the service was prepared, and the PRIESTS stood in their place, and the Levites in their courses, according to the King's commandment, and THEY KILLED THE PASSOVER, AND THE PRIESTS SPRINKLED THE BLOOD FROM THEIR HANDS."‡ The *sprinkling of the blood* by the priests is related elsewhere:—" Then they killed the

---

* Magee (vol. i. pp. 297—321) maintains the sacrificial character of the paschal lamb. The opposite view is held by Mr. Orme in his treatise on the Lord's Supper, pp. 13, 14.
† Exod. xii. 27; xxiv. 24. Deut. xvi. 2, 5, 6.
‡ 2 Chron xxxv. 1—11.

passover—the *priests sprinkled the blood* which they received of the hand of the Levites."* Moreover, the paschal lamb was to be offered only in the *tabernacle* or *temple*, the place appointed for sacrifice:—" Thou mayest not sacrifice the passover within any of thy gates, but at the place which the Lord thy God shall choose to place his name in."† On these grounds do we regard ourselves as warranted to view the passover in the light of a true and proper sacrifice; and the analogy betwixt it and Christ is too marked and particular to admit of a doubt that the one was designed to prefigure the other.

The paschal lamb itself, both in its natural qualities and particular circumstances, strikingly portrayed the person of the Redeemer. The proverbial *meekness* and *unresisting patience* of the animal, rendered it a fit representative of Him who was " led as a sheep to the slaughter, and like a lamb dumb before his shearers, so he opened not his mouth." Its being *without spot and blemish*, pointed directly to him who was " holy, harmless, undefiled, and separate from sinners." Its being *taken out from the flock*, agrees with his being chosen from among men, a possessor of the nature of those for whom he was to die. Its being *set apart some time before*, tipyfied his eternal dedication in the covenant of peace. Not less striking is the analogy in the matter of its *suffering and death*. The roasting of the paschal lamb with fire, points not obscurely to the nature and intensity of those sufferings which the Son of God endured from men, and devils, and his heavenly Father, and which drew from him the agonizing complaint, " My heart is like wax; it is *melted* in the midst of my bowels." Even the *form* in which it is said to have been roasted bore a striking resemblance to the death of the *cross*. Justin Martyr, who flourished in the beginning of the second century, tells us, in his conference with Trypho the Jew, that the animal was transfixed longitudinally with one spit, and horizontally with another which passed through the fore-legs, thus giving it the exact form of a person.

* 2 Chron. xxx. 15, 16.   † Deut. xvi. 5, 6.

under crucifixion. To some this may seem a trifling circumstance. But the fact, at least, is abundantly singular: and, as it cannot be doubted, we are not at liberty to overlook so striking a coincidence, believing that nothing is unworthy of notice which it has seemed good to Him who is sovereign in all his ways to connect with the prefiguration of the death of his Son. The *time*, too, when the paschal offering was slain, namely, betwixt the evenings, corresponds to that when the crucifixion of Christ took place. And the *advantages* resulting from the one resemble the blessings connected with the other:—protection, redemption, and salvation. Considering this manifold analogy, we can no longer wonder that the apostle should have said, "EVEN CHRIST OUR PASSOVER IS SACRIFICED FOR US."*

The analogy in the case of the scape-goat is not less remarkable; but we shall not wait to specify the particulars. Enough has been adduced for the sake of our argument. There is only one circumstance to which we would advert here, namely, the memorable and undoubted fact, that immediately after the death of Christ, the Jewish sacrifices were completely abolished, and have never been restored. In a short period, the Levitical genealogies fell into inextricable confusion, so that it became impossible for any one to substantiate his right to the sacerdotal office; and it was not long till the sacred structure, within whose precincts alone legitimate sacrifice could be offered, was irretrievably demolished, and every attempt to rebuild it has been met with the frown of an incensed Providence. It is now impossible, without a miracle, to offer a single sacrifice agreeably to the prescriptions of the legal economy. The institution has fully answered its purpose in pointing forward to Christ, and, as has been well remarked, "by the finger of Omnipotence its expiration is recorded on the everlasting columns of historic truth."

To prevent cavil, it may be proper, before concluding this department, to take notice of some things that

---

* 1 Cor. v. 7.

have been urged in opposition to the view on which the argument it contains is built. That the sacrifices of the law were designed to prefigure Christ is essential to this argument, and this, we think, has been proved in the foregoing pages. Yet it is fair to remark, that other views have been taken of the nature and design of these rites. which, if they could only be substantiated, would go far to overturn the above reasoning. It may help to strengthen our position, if we allow ourselves time to examine a little more closely these views.

It has been alleged by some, that the legal sacrifices were appointed simply in accommodation to the heathenish taste acquired by the Israelites while in Egypt. No supposition can be more repugnant to all right conceptions regarding the divine character. The inclinations of man are naturally corrupt; and to suppose them a rule of procedure to the Deity, or a standard to fix the forms of religious worship, is altogether monstrous and absurd. Besides, in the present case, the supposition is at variance with facts. So far from the Jewish worship being formed on the model of the Egyptian rites, in order to meet the perverted taste which the people had contracted in the land of their captivity, we know that they were led about in the wilderness forty years, till the generation who came out of Egypt had perished, without being permitted to enter that country where their religious rites could be observed in perfection. The generation who entered Canaan were uncontaminated with the pagan ceremonies of which their fathers were witnesses; and, lest they should become corrupted with any species of false worship, they were required to extirpate completely the race of idolators who were previously in possession of the land that had been assigned them by God. Nay, in the book of statutes with which they were furnished, express warning was given against imitating the conduct or practising the rites of any heathen nation whatever, with special reference to Egypt and Canaan. "Speak unto the children of Israel," said Jehovah to Moses, "and say unto them, I am the Lord your God. AFTER THE DOINGS OF THE LAND OF EGYPT WHEREIN YE DWELT, SHALL YE NOT DO; and AFTER THE DOINGS OF THE LAND OF CANAAN, whither I bring you, SHALL YE NOT DO; neither shall ye walk in THEIR ORDINANCES. Ye shall do MY judgments, and keep MINE ordinances, to walk therein; I am the Lord your God."* How can it be thought, after this, that the Levitical rites were formed on the model of the Egyptian ceremonies? Or what language can more decidedly express the marked opposition that existed betwixt the ordinances of the heathen and the Lord's ordinances? In addition to these things it may be observed, that it is more reasonable to suppose the Levitical economy was formed with the view of preserving the Israelites from idolatry, than that it was itself an imitation of an idolatrous system.

Others, again, suppose that the sacrifices of the Jews were mere emblems of holiness, or memorials of divine placability, and not types of a better sacrifice at all. That they served these purposes, along with others, might perhaps be safely granted; but that such was their sole use and design cannot be so easily conceded. It must occur to every sober thinker on the subject, that for these purposes they were not indispensably requisite, there being other methods of expressing the same things. Moreover, it must be admitted, that a great deal more was signified by them. Nor is it unworthy of notice, that neither the holiness nor the placability of God, as we have seen in another department of the subject, can be shown to consist with the pardon of sin, on any other principle than that of an atonement. And it is not a little unfortunate for the supporters of this opinion, that the cases in which symbols of the holiness and placability of God were most necessary, such as murder and adultery, did not admit of sacrifices being offered at all.

It has, also, been maintained, in opposition to the view we have taken of the Levitical economy, that it was not the sacrifices which made atonement, but the appearance of the high priest in the holy of holies

* Lev. xviii. 2—4.

From this it is inferred, that the death of Christ constituted no part of his sacerdotal work, the whole of which, it is alleged, was performed in heaven. It is sufficient, in reply, to remark, that the appearance of the high priest in the inner sanctuary presupposed the offering of a sacrifice. Unless a sacrifice had been previously offered on the brazen altar, he could not enter within the veil, at least his entering could serve no purpose whatever; the blood of the burnt-offering had to be carried by him into the holy place and sprinkled upon the mercy-seat. The one was as much a part of his priestly functions as the other; and if the latter prefigured Christ in any part of his sacerdotal service, so also did the former; to separate them is to put asunder what God has joined together.

But the view which is most commonly taken by the modern enemies of Christ's atonement, is, that although the sacrifices of the law were real and proper sacrifices, so far from being types of Christ, the sacrificial language used respecting him in the New Testament is employed only figuratively, in allusion to the customs and practices of the Jews, with a view to conciliate that people to the Christian religion. It is wonderful that this position should ever have been maintained, considering how contradictory it is to scripture and to reason. The very same terms are so often applied to the sacrifices of the law and to that of Christ, that, if the latter is not a real and proper sacrifice, the language of scripture seems fitted to mislead rather than instruct. Indeed, the object of the whole epistle to the Hebrews seems to be lost sight of by those who hold the opinion we are now considering. The design of this part of scripture evidently is, to remove the objections of the Jews to the Christian economy, by showing that everything which was possessed under the law is enjoyed in equal, nay greater, perfection under the Gospel;—that Christianity has its high priest, and its sacrifice, and its sanctuary, as well as Judaism. And are we to suppose that the privileges and blessings of the new dispensation, which the apostle describes by such language, are merely figurative,—

shadowy emblems and not substantial realities; and that all his powerful reasoning, to secure the attachment of the Jews to the religion of Jesus, is built on a deception, and consists only of a well-managed trick in which a disingenuous use is made of the language of accommodation? Is it not infinitely more worthy of the character of an inspired writer to believe, that he affirms, what undoubtedly his words are calculated and designed to convey, that the import of the legal ceremonies is completely fulfilled in the Lord Jesus Christ? The theory in question reverses the scriptural order of relation between the rites of the law and the privileges of the Gospel. In innumerable instances are the former spoken of as types, figures, shadows, of which the antitype, the reality, the substance is affirmed to be Christ. But, if the sacrifice of Christ was only figurative, this order is inverted; the sacrifice, sanctuary, and high priest of the new dispensation are the shadows of which those under the law are the substance. Nothing more can require to be said to expose the unsoundness of the view on which we are animadverting. Yet we cannot help remarking, how much more reasonable and natural it is to suppose, as the Jewish religion undoubtedly possesses a less degree of perfection than the Christian that the language employed under the former should derive its complexion from what was to exist under the latter, than the reverse. It is surely more likely that the less perfect system should look forward to the more perfect, than that the more perfect should go back to the less perfect. It appears a more rational mode of proceeding, to construct a scaffolding with reference to the form and dimensions of a contemplated building, than to shape the building agreeably to a scaffolding which happened to exist before. In like manner, it is more reasonable to view the sacrificial language in use under the law as taking its rise from the reality of that sacrifice which was afterwards to exist, than to suppose that such language is employed with reference to the latter only in accommodation to the modes of speaking in use under a more imperfect economy. In short, it were much nearer the truth to maintain, that *the only real and proper sacrifice is that of Christ, and that all others were only figures of it.* This is the substance; the rest were shadows. "Which are a SHADOW of things to come," says Paul when treating of the Levitical rites, "but THE BODY IS OF CHRIST."

The futility of all other views of the Jewish economy, thus confirms the sentiment before expressed, of its figurative reference to Christ—the only view which satisfactorily explains its usages, or comports with the wisdom of its divine Author; and which infallibly conducts, as we shall see, to an irrefragable argument in favor of the doctrine of atonement.

V. We are now prepared to deduce, from the preceding evidence, an argument in favor of the atoning nature of Christ's death.

The sacrifices of the law, we have seen, were expiatory and vicarious;—these expiatory and vicarious sacrifices were designed prefigurations of the death of the Lord Jesus Christ;—THEREFORE, the death of the Lord Jesus Christ was expiatory and vicarious too. Such is our argument. If the premises are admitted, the inference cannot be refused. The type and the antitype must correspond in every essential point. Nothing was so characteristic of the typical sacrifices as their propitiatory nature: and, if the antitype possess not this quality, the whole typical economy is nullified. In this case the sacrifices of the law were useless, nay, worse than useless; they were positively hurtful; they were fitted to mislead more than to assist the ancient worshipper. They taught him, as plainly as symbolical language could teach, to look forward to a sacrifice which should be a real substitute for the sins of men. If, therefore, we hold that the death and sacrifice of Christ were destitute of everything atoning in their nature, we must be prepared to admit that the entire Levitical economy was a divinely established system of delusion—a grave imposture palmed upon a whole nation by the express appointment of God. The admission of the doctrine of Christ's atoning sacrifice can alone save us from this blasphemous assumption. On this principle, the legal dispensation admits of an easy solution; it appears to be not simply harmless but useful, highly useful, and every way worthy of its righteous and beneficent Author.

It is not possible to conclude this section, without recommending to our readers the diligent study of the Levitical institutes, particularly those respecting sacrifice. This we would enjoin, not as matter of vain curiosity, but of profitable and delightful instruction. Without this, the beauty and force of many parts of the New Testament scriptures must be lost. An acquaintance with the laws respecting the daily oblations, the paschal lamb, the scape goat, and such like, cannot fail to afford valuable assistance in understanding the most important doctrines of the Christian faith. The spiritual reader, as he peruses the pages of the law, will never be without sufficient matter to remind him of the Great High Priest, who is passed into the heavens, the Lamb of God which taketh away the sin of the world, the Lord Jesus Christ by whom we have received the atonement. When burdened with sin, he will learn to put his hand by faith on the head of the blessed Surety, by whom all his iniquities may be carried to the land of forgetfulness. From the bleeding victim of Calvary, his thoughts will be conducted to the heavenly sanctuary, where the true Priest appears in the presence of God for us, not without blood.

In connection with the institutes of the law, let the epistle to the Hebrews be made the subject of devout investigation. The latter records the fulfilment of the former. This masterpiece of skilful reasoning is adapted not to Jews only. but to all who need a priest, a sacrifice, a Saviour. Every sinner of the family of man will find here what is suited to his case, if he has only the wisdom to perceive and the grace to improve it. The dignity of the Christian high priest, the worth of his sacrifice, the efficacy of his intercessions, are here set forth in the most lucid and impressive style; and nowhere can the sin-burdened soul, panting for salvation, go, with such prospects of finding relief, as to this incomparable composition, an acquaintance with which will do more to establish the faith, and comfort the heart, and direct the conduct of an humble inquirer, than all that has been written since the days of the apostles. Happy they who read, believe, and apply. Wherefore, holy brethren, partakers of the heavenly calling, consider the Apostle and High Priest of our profession, Christ Jesus. We have such an High Priest, who is set on the right hand of the throne of the Majesty in the heavens; a minister of the sanctuary, and of the true tabernacle which the Lord pitched and not man.

SECTION VI.

PROOF—PROPHECY.

The glorious person of whose work we are now treating is He of whom Moses in the law and *the prophets* did write, Jesus of Nazareth the son of Joseph. From the legal institutes we naturally pass to prophetic intimations, in proof of Christ's atonement. In proceeding thus, we advance into still clearer light. The evidence adduced, it will be remarked, is not merely cumulative, each successive proof being only an addition to the *number* of arguments; but progressive, each being, in its own nature, stronger than that by which it is preceded, inasmuch as it is drawn from a source in which the light is more perfect, the evidence more direct, and the reasoning less open to dispute. The light derived from the *law* is brighter than that derived from the *ancient and universal practice* of mankind; and the light derived from *prophecy* is brighter still than that furnished by the *law*. If, on the one hand, the law may be regarded as a key to unlock the more difficult words of prophecy; on the other, prophecy may be looked upon as an exposition, an inspired exposition, of the law. Prophecy lifts the veil which had previously concealed the mystery of man's redemption, and rescues it from the shade of these ceremonial rites, through which, comparatively speaking, it could be but faintly discerned.

The mystery of redemption forming the proper subject of a revelation from heaven, it was to be expected that the prophecy which came not in old time by the will of man, but which holy men of God spake as they were moved by the Holy Ghost, should treat distinctly of this matter. This expectation is justified by fact, and by the assertions of the New Testament. The apostles not only declared that "the spirit of Christ, which was in the prophets, testified beforehand the *sufferings of Christ* and the glory that should follow," but protested that, in their public ministrations, they "said none other things than those which the *prophets* and Moses did say should come, that Christ should suffer."* Nay Jesus himself, in conversation respecting his sufferings with two of his disciples after his resurrection, made express reference, more than once, to the writings of the prophets on this very subject:—"O fools, and slow of heart to believe all that *the prophets* have spoken! Ought not Christ to have suffered these things, and to enter into his glory? and beginning at Moses and ALL THE PROPHETS, he expounded unto them in all the Scriptures the things concerning himself—These are the words which I spake unto you while I was yet with you, that all things must be fulfilled which were written in the law of Moses and *in the prophets*, and in the psalms concerning me. Then opened he their understanding, that they might understand the Scriptures, and said unto them, thus it is written, and thus it behooved Christ to *suffer*."†

The passages in the prophecies which treat of the sufferings of Christ are innumerable. Indeed, "God hath showed, by the mouth of ALL the prophets, that Christ should suffer. But, instead of going over the whole of the prophetical testimonies, it will serve our

* 1 Pet. i. 11. Acts xxvi. 23, 24.   † Luke xxiv. 25—27, 44—46.

purpose better to confine our attention to two, in which not merely the *fact*, but the *nature* and the *reason*, of the Messiah's sufferings, are stated with great fulness, clearness, and force.

Isaiah liii.

The first of these is the distinguished description of the sufferings and death of Christ given by Isaiah in his fifty-third chapter, which has been justly called one of the brightest constellations in the prophetic hemisphere.

1. The prophecy, which commences at the thirteenth verse of the preceding chapter, notwithstanding the objections of certain enemies of the truth, bears an obvious reference to the Messiah.

The Targum or Chaldee paraphrase of Jonathan Ben Uzziel supports this view, as well as other early Jewish expositors; not to speak of the earliest Christian fathers. Indeed the testimony of the New Testament writers is too decided on this point, to admit of any room for doubt, in the minds of all humble and candid interpreters of the word of God. Matthew quotes, with reference to Jesus of Nazareth, the fourth verse of this chapter:—"Himself took our infirmities and bare our sicknesses."* Mark and Luke refer, with the same view, to the twelfth verse:—"And he was numbered with the transgressors."† John, speaking of the unbelief of the people with regard to the miracles of Christ, finds in it a fulfilment of the first verse:—"Lord, who hath believed our report? and to whom hath the arm of the Lord been revealed?"‡ In the Acts of the Apostles, that beautiful part of the prophecy which speaks of the Messiah being led as a sheep to the slaughter, is represented as the text from which Philip preached to the eunuch concerning Christ:—"Then Philip began at the same scripture and preached unto him Jesus."§ And Peter, in his first epistle, has obviously a view to the prediction of Isaiah, when he speaks

---

* Matt. viii. 17. † Mark xv. 29. Luke xii. 37.
‡ John xii. 38. § Acts viii. 35.

of Christ thus:—"Who did no sin, neither was guile found in his mouth. Who his own self bare our sins in his own body on the tree—by whose stripes we are healed."* These testimonies will be sufficient to convince all who regard Christ and his apostles as correct interpreters of the Old Testament scriptures, that this prophecy of Isaiah refers to the Messiah. That this should ever have been called in question, by any who claim the Christian name, might have excited surprise, had we not known, that, in every age, there have been those who have resisted the clearest evidence in support of the most vital and important Gospel truth.

The grounds on which it has been denied that this prediction refers to the sufferings of the Messiah are most untenable. No small stress has been laid by some on the want of all allusion to it, in illustration of the doctrine of substitution, in the writings of Paul. The fact is singular enough, it must be acknowledged; but the inference deduced from it is far from being conclusive. We are not at liberty to say from what source the infinitely wise God should draw his confirmations or illustrations of the precious truths he is pleased to make known to us by his Spirit. Our duty is to receive and improve what he has seen meet to give; without complaining, either that he has not given us more, or that that which he *has* given is not different from what it is. The application of the language of some parts of this remarkable portion of revealed truth has been thought to proceed on the principle of accommodation. Without denying that such a use is ever made, in the New Testament scriptures, of the language of the Old, it is sufficient at present to remark, how preposterous it is to resort to this method of interpretation in a case like the present, where the passages quoted are expressly declared by the inspired writers to have a reference to the Messiah.†

---

* 1 Peter ii. 22, 24.

† Other objections to the application of Isaiah's prophecy to Christ have been started by Neologians. Such as take an interest in these matters will find them all stated and refuted in a very able note by Dr. I'ye Smith. Disc. on Sac., pp 260—271.

II. This prediction treats of the SUFFERINGS of the Messiah.

These are set forth with a plenitude and variety of expression, which it is deeply interesting and highly instructive to mark and consider. The terms and phrases made use of for this purpose are truly worthy of notice, and a consideration of these lies directly within the line of our argument. It may also serve a good end, to note the translations given of the original of these respective expressions, by some of our most distinguished modern biblical scholars, even such as do not accord in sentiment with the doctrine which it is our object to establish.* The following classification of terms and phrases may help to give us some idea of the amount of evidence which the prophecy contains, to the extent of Messiah's sufferings:—

1. "Despised and rejected of men." v. 3. אִישִׁים נִבְזֶה וַחֲדַל. *Despised, nor accounted in the number of men.* (Lowth.)—*Despised and neglected by men.* (Dr. P. Smith.)—*Contemptible! the most feeble of men!* (Michaelis.)—*Disdained is he, scorned among men.* (Seiler.)—*Disdained was he, and deserted by men.* (Gesenius.)—*The most despised and rejected of men.* (Rosenmueller.)

2. "A man of sorrows and acquainted with grief." v. 3. אִישׁ מַכְאֹבוֹת וִידוּעַ חֹלִי. Lowth adopts the common version. *A man of sorrows and familiar with sufferings.* (P. Smith.)—*Full of sufferings, and recognized only by his wounds.* (Mich.)—*The man of sorrows, known by his sufferings.* (Seil.)—*Sorrow-laden and marked with disease.* (Gesen.)—*A man afflicted with sorrows eminently marked with disease.* (Rosen.)

3. "Stricken, smitten of God, and afflicted." v. 4. נָגוּעַ מֻכֵּה אֱלֹהִים וּמְעֻנֶּה. *Judicially stricken, smitten of God, and afflicted.* (Lowth.)—*Stricken, smitten, by God, and devoted to affliction.* (P. Smith.)—*Marked out by the stroke of God and thrown down.* (Mich.) —*By God punished, smitten, and tormented.* (Seil.) —*Punished by God, smitten and distressed by God.*

* These translations are given at length by Dr. Smith, in the Note last referred to.

(Gesen.)—*Ruin-stricken, smitten of God, and afflicted.* (Rosen.)

4. "Wounded." מְחֹלָל. v. 5. Lowth, Michaelis, Gesenius, and Rosenmueller, adopt the common version.—*Pierced.* (P. Smith.)—*Pierced through.* (Seil.)

5. "Bruised." v. 5. מְדֻכָּא. *Smitten.* (Lowth and Seiler.)—*Crushed.* (P. Smith.)—*Broken.* (Mich.)—*Smitten down.* (Gesen.)—*Bruised.* (Rosen.)

6. "Chastisement." v. 5. מוּסַר. Lowth, Smith, and Rosenmueller follow the common version.—*Punishment.* (Mich., Seil., and Gesen.)

7. "Stripes." v. 5. חֲבֻרָה. *Bruises.* (Lowth and Mich.)—*Bloody stripes.* (P. Smith.)—*Wounded.* (Seil.)—*Wounds.* (Gesen.)—*Wheals.* (Rosen.)

8. "He was oppressed." v. 7. נִגַּשׂ. *It was exacted.* (Lowth and Seil.)—*It is exacted.* (P. Smith.) —*He came to it.* (Mich.)—*Ill treated was he.* (Gesen.)—*Cruelly treated.* (Rosen.)

9. "He was cut off out of the land of the living." v. 8. נִגְזַר מֵאֶרֶץ חַיִּים. Smith and Rosen. adopt the common version.—*Cut off from the land of the living.* (Lowth.)—*Torn out of the land of the living.* (Mich.) —*Out of the land of the living he is torn away.* (Seil.) —*Taken away out of the land of the living.* (Gesen.)

10. "Travail of soul." v. 11. עֲמַל נַפְשׁוֹ. The common version is adopted by Lowth.—*The effects of his soul's pains.* (P. Smith.)—*Severe toil.* (Mich.)— *Labor.* (Seil.)—*Sorrows.* (Rosen.)

11. "He hath poured out his soul unto death." v. 12. אֲשֶׁר הֶעֱרָה לַמָּוֶת. Lowth adopts the common version.—*He yieldeth his life to death.* (P. Smith.)— *He poured out his life's blood unto death.* (Mich. and Seil.)—*He gave up his life unto death.* (Gesen.)— *He poured out his life unto death.* (Rosen.)

III. We have now seen that this singular prediction refers to the Messiah, and to the Messiah as suffering. THE PUNITIVE character of his sufferings, as here set forth, is the next thing to which we solicit attention.

We have before adverted to the distinction between *suffering on account of sin and suffering disconnected from guilt,* the latter being what is called *calamity,* the former *punishment.** Now the sufferings of **Messiah**, as they are here exhibited, were of the former description,—not calamitous, but punitive. He suffered *for sin;* whether his own, or that of others, remains to be seen; meanwhile, we beg attention to those expressions in the prediction which distinctly mark the *punitive* character of Messiah's sufferings. They are the following:—

1. "He hath *borne* griefs." v. 4. נשׂא. "He shall *bear* iniquities." v. 11. יסבל. "He *bare* the sin." v. 12. נשׂא. The original word, in the first and last of these verses, is the same; and, in their rendering of it, there is a close agreement among all the critics formerly referred to. In the second passage, the original word is different, although our translation and that of most of the other critics, are the same. Dr. Smith, however, renders it "take away," and Rosenmueller renders it "made atonement." That Messiah took away the sins of his people, by making atonement for them, we, of course, believe to be true, and to be taught in this part of Scripture; although, perhaps, it admits of being questioned, whether this be the exact import of the phrases we are now considering. It is the opinion of many learned men, that the original terms denote, not so much the *removal* of sin as the *sustaining* of guilt; not so much the *bearing of it away,* as the *bearing of its weight;* not so much Christ's being the means of *taking sin from others,* as his actually *lying under its load,* or being subjected to its awful pressure *himself.* They thus point our attention to the *result* of his sufferings, rather than to the *manner* in which those sufferings effected their result. The enemies of the doctrine for which we are contending, are anxious to restrict their meaning to the result; but that they mark the manner of bringing about the result, seems capable of being satisfactorily established. The reference to the Jewish ceremony of the scapegoat, which was understood to "bear upon him all the iniquities" of the children of Israel "unto a land not inhabited,"† is supposed to be strongly in favor of the

* See p. 17. † Lev. xvi. 22.

former view but, if another circumstance connected with this rite is duly considered, it will be seen to be not less strongly corroborative of the latter, for the high priest was to confess over the animal all the iniquities of the children of Israel, "PUTTING THEM UPON THE HEAD OF THE GOAT," and this as a preparatory step to his being "sent away by the hand of a fit man into the wilderness."*

It is also worthy of notice, that these original terms, when they occur in connection with *sins* or *iniquities*, never signify to bear *away*, but to *bear a burden;* to *sustain a load;* to *bear the punishment* of sin, the *suffering* due to iniquity. Hence the doctrine of this prediction is, that the load of guilt, the burden of punishment, was borne by the Messiah, that is, that his sufferings were punitive.†

2. "The *chastisement* of peace was upon him." v. 5. מוּסַר. Lowth, Rosenmueller, and P. Smith, agree with the common version. Michaelis, Seiler, and Gesenius employ the word *punishment*. Each of these supposes sin or guilt, and consequently determines the view of Messiah's sufferings we are now attempting to set forth.

3. "He was wounded for *transgressions*—bruised for *iniquities*." v. 5. The critics employ different words here, but always such as convey the idea of crime or moral turpitude.

4. "He bare *sin*." v. 12. The same remark applies to this expression.

5. "Thou shalt make his soul a *sin-offering*." v. 10. אָשָׁם. A *propitiatory sacrifice*. (Lowth.)—*A sacrifice for sin*. (Smith.)—*A trespass-offering*. (Mich., Seil., Gesen.)—*An atoning sacrifice*. (Rosen.) This requires no comment.

Thus ample is the evidence of the punitive character of Messiah's sufferings. These sufferings were not mere calamities, then, or afflictions which came upon the person without any reference to guilt, but partook

---

* Lev. xvi. 21.
† For a very full, elaborate, and learned criticism on the words in question, see Magee, vol. i. pp. 408—463.

directly of the nature of a punishment or penalty, judicially inflicted, somehow or other, on account of moral transgression.

IV. It remains to examine whether the guilt, for which Messiah suffered a legal punishment, was his own; and on this point, the evidence is no less full, which this prediction supplies, of the SUBSTITUTIONARY character of the punishment the Messiah endured.

1. "He had done *no violence*, neither was *any deceit* in his mouth." v. 9. *No wrong, neither any guile.* (Lowth.)—*No injustice, no guile.* (Smith.)—*No unrighteousness, no deceit.* (Mich.)—*No wrong, neither any deceit.* (Seil.)—*No injustice, and no deceit.* (Gesen.)—*Nor violence, nor deceit.* (Rosen.) Language strongly affirmative of the *personal innocence* of the sufferer.

2. "He hath borne OUR griefs, and carried OUR sorrows." "He was wounded for OUR transgressions; bruised for OUR iniquities; the chastisement of OUR peace was upon him." v. 4, 5. Language as strongly implying that the guilt for which he suffered was that of *others*.

3. "The Lord hath laid on *him* the iniquity of *us* all." v. 6. "*He* shall bear *their* iniquities." v. 11. "*He* bare the sin of *many*." v. 12. Language in which the *substitution* of one for another is not merely supposed, but most distinctly expressed.

Some of these phrases have an undoubted reference to the ancient ceremony of the scape-goat. Let us, by an effort of imagination, suppose ourselves witnessing this expressive rite. The animals are selected. The sins of the people of Israel are typically transferred. The priest pronounces the imprecation of vengeance due to these sins. The whole congregation stand round in silent awe. As the one goat is immolated and laid on the altar, a prophet of the Lord, wrapt in holy visions, pronounces these words, "He was wounded for our transgressions." And, as the other animal bounds from the view into the land of oblivion, the same sacred person exclaims under the same divine influence, "Surely he hath borne our griefs and carried our sorrows." Would there be one, we ask, in all the solemnized assembly, who could fail to perceive that the person to whom the prediction referred was pointed out as a real vicarious sacrifice?

Such is the testimony of this remarkable passage of holy writ to the doctrine of Christ's atonement. The more it is examined, the more decided will the evidence it affords appear. The doctrine is interwoven with its very texture, so as not to be separated from it but by a process which must effect the destruction of the fabric itself. While the prophecy holds a place in the volume of inspiration, it will not be possible to rob the church of this precious truth. "If the Scriptures," to adopt the words of Dr. Smith, "are of any use to mankind; if they convey any definite sentiments, if we can at all rely on the meaning of the words, if the strength and variety of phrase here employed by the wisdom of inspiration can avail to inform and impress our minds,—WE MUST believe that the Messiah would devote himself as a voluntary SACRIFICE, a real and effectual EXPIATION, suffering the heaviest woes, and all the bitterness of DEATH, in concurrence with the gracious intentions of Jehovah, and for the salvation of rebellious men."*

The other prophecy to which we refer is

DANIEL ix. 24—27.

The reference of this splendid prediction to the *Messiah* is admitted on all hands. Indeed the express mention made in it of "Messiah the Prince" precludes all doubt on this point. And its fulfilment in Jesus of Nazareth is not less plainly established, by the agreement of the description with his general character and history, and by the seventy weeks, when dated from the seventh year of Artaxerxes Longimanus, terminating in the year of his crucifixion.

The *death* of the Messiah is obviously meant by his being "cut off;" phraseology which implies a painful violent, and untimely death at the hands of others.

* Disc. on Sac., pp. 31, 32.

The character under which he should die, namely, as a *substitutionary sacrifice* for the sins of others, is distinctly marked by a variety of impressive language. The sacrificial nature of his death is, first of all, clearly implied in the circumstance that immediately on its taking place *the sacrifice and oblation should cease:* thus pointing him out as the great antitypical sacrifice, the offering of which necessarily put an end to every other. To this circumstance there is supposed by some to be a reference in the clause, "to make an end of sins," v. 24, or "sin-offerings," as the word may signify.—There, is next, the very remarkable clause, "but not for himself," in which his death is most explicitly taken off the ground of personal demerit.—While the expiatory and propitiatory nature of his sacrifice is directly affirmed, in its object being declared to be "to finish transgression, to make reconciliation for iniquity, and to bring in everlasting righteousness." v. 24.

It is unnecessary to go more at length into this part of scripture; or even to dwell longer on this department of proof. These passages of Isaiah and Daniel are sufficient to show, that evidence in support of our doctrine is not wanting in the writings of those prophets who were prompted, by the divine Spirit, to testify beforehand the sufferings of Christ and the glory that should follow. So conclusive, indeed, is the testimony thus supplied, that after duly considering its amount, we can only express our wonder at the wilful blindness or lamentable perversity of mind by which its force is resisted.

SECTION VII.

PROOF—THE SUFFERINGS OF CHRIST.

The circumstance on which we are now to found is matter of fact. The sufferings of Jesus Christ are recorded in indubitable history. The argument derivable from this source, is of a stronger nature than any of the preceding. History is so much more plain and distinct than prophecy, that the evidence it affords must be higher than that which is derived from the latter.

The facts regarding the sufferings of the Son of God are not affected by the sentiments that are entertained respecting the nature and design of these sufferings. The doctrinal opinions of men may differ, but historical truths must ever remain one and unalterable. There is no room for diversity here; whoever admits the canonical authority of the writings of the evangelists, must give credit to the statements they contain these are subjects of *belief*, not of *opinion*. And how stands the matter of fact with regard to the sufferings of Emanuel? It will be admitted by all who believe the New Testament history, that in their nature, variety, intensity, and continuance, these sufferings were of no ordinary character.

His whole life was a scene of suffering. From his birth to his death, from the cradle to the cross, from the manger at Bethlehem to the tomb of Joseph, sorrow and suffering seem to have marked him as their own. While yet a babe in his mother's arms, he was driven into exile, to escape the fury of those who sought his life; when but a youth, he was doomed to follow a servile employment, that he might procure the means of bodily subsistence; and when he became a man, he was successively reproached, persecuted, accused, condemned, and crucified. At every period of his abode on earth we meet with the same general features of suffering; we see them in the weeping infant, the pensive youth, the man of sorrows, and the bleeding victim of Calvary. He seems to have been marked out as the object of bitter hatred, the moment he entered our world; to have been followed throughout with deadly malice; and to have been at last hunted down with implacable revenge. The cup of woe, put to his lips at his birth, was never removed till he wrung out its bitter dregs on the cross. Called to dip his feet, so soon as he was born, in the troubled waters of affliction, wave after wave continued ever after to lash with undiminished strength, deep calling unto deep, till the billows of death overwhelmed him, and cast his exanimate body on the desolate shore.

Every variety of suffering was compressed into his life of woe. He suffered *poverty* in all its rigor; being born in a stable and cradled in a manger, being ofttimes dependent on the charity of others for a precarious support, having no property that he could call his own, and being in many cases worse situated than the inferior orders of creation:—"Foxes have holes, and birds of the air have nests; but the Son of man hath not where to lay his head." He suffered *reproach* in all its bitterness; which to one, conscious of perfect innocence, as he was, and possessing the keenest moral sensibility, must have been inconceivably severe. The most malignant accusations, the vilest aspersions, the most cutting sarcasms, were directed against his person, character, and sufferings; and he who had done no violence, neither was guile found in his mouth, had to submit to be taunted as a glutton, a wine-bibber, a deceiver, a blasphemer, a Samaritan, a devil, nay the Prince of devils. He suffered *temptation* in all its malignity. The prince of darkness assailed him with all his ingenuity and power, and let loose upon him his legions, with their infernal suggestions, and wicked purposes, and cruel aims, surrounding him as strong bulls of Bashan, and gaping on him with their mouths like ravening and roaring lions. He suffered the indignity of an *unjust trial;* being rudely apprehended, dragged unceremoniously to the bar, falsely accused, subjected to the testimony of suborned witnesses, and finally condemned without a shadow of proof. He suffered *crucifixion* with all its ignominy and pain, being subjected to the previous scourging; bearing the cross on his lacerated body; having the bolts driven with ferocity into his hands and feet; having the whole joints of his body dissevered by the upright beam being let fall with a sudden jerk into its place in the ground; being left to linger out a wretched existence amid the taunts, and jeers, and insults of an unfeeling mob; and having his heart pierced through with the spear of the infuriated soldier, whose demoniac wickedness impelled him to seek infamous distinction by an act of gratuitous barbarity. He suffered, above all, the *wrath* of God. It pleased the Father to bruise him. His agony in the garden and on the cross cannot otherwise be accounted for. When he came into the place called Gethsemane, "he began to be *sorrowful* and *very heavy*,"*—"he began to be *sore amazed*,"†—he said "My soul is *exceeding sorrowful*, even unto death,"‡—"being in an *agony*, he prayed more earnestly, and his *sweat* was, as it were, *great drops of blood* falling down to the ground,"§— in the climax of his anguish, falling on the ground, thrice did he pray, "O my Father, if it be possible, let this cup pass from me"—" he offered up prayers and supplications with strong crying and tears."‖ And, when hanging on the cross, he gave utterance to the bitter, piercing, piteous cry of felt desertion, "My God, my God, why hast thou forsaken me?" In all this description, the translation falls as far short of the original language, as the energetic original falls short of the awful reality; no words being adequate to express that fearful amount of mingled terror, and amazement, and horror, which then seized, with all its intensity, on the holy soul of the devoted sufferer. Without any visible cause, his sufferings were awfully intense, as the bitter tears which he wept, and the deep sighs which he heaved, and the loud groans which he uttered, and the bloody drops which he sweat, and the heart-rending exclamation to which he gave vent, do all most abundantly testify. "I am poured out like water, and all my bones are out of joint: my heart is like wax; it is melted in the midst of my bowels. My strength is dried up like a potsherd; and my tongue cleaveth to my jaws; and thou hast brought me into the dust of death."

---

* Matt. xxvi. 37. ἤρξατο λυπεῖσθαι καὶ ἀδημονεῖν.
† Mark xiv. 33. ἤρξατο ἐκθαμβεῖσθαι.
‡ Matt. xxvi. 38. Mark xiv. 34. περίλυπός ἐστιν ἡ ψυχή μου ἕως θανάτου.
§ Luke xxii. 44. ἐν ἀγωνία. ‖ Heb. v. 7.

Such are the facts of the case. They are recorded plainly on the page of inspired history. It is no exaggerated description, no overcharged picture we have given of the sufferings of the Man of sorrows. The recital may fall below, but it certainly does not go beyond, the matter of fact. And now comes the question, Can these facts, respecting the Saviour's sufferings, be accounted for without an atonement? Let us see.

The sufferings of Jesus of Nazareth cannot be explained on the simple principle of retributive justice. He was perfectly pure and innocent in himself. Not only was his life unmarked by any atrocious wickedness demanding a peculiar severity of punishment, but he was so free from the slightest stain of sin as not to have had "one recollection tinged with remorse." If it be denied that he suffered as the substitute of guilty men, it concerns such as hold this opinion to show, how, in consistency with the equity of God, he could have been subjected to a single pang of that accumulated woe which came upon him to the uttermost, much less to the whole amount of this fearful suffering. The ordinary course of equitable retribution fails to account for a single drop of that full and bitter cup of wrath, which he drank to the very dregs.

The same reason, namely, the innocence of the sufferer, precludes the supposition that the sufferings were simply corrective,—chastisements, severe in themselves, kindly meant for the good of him who was their subject. In the case of one who was holy, harmless, undefiled, and separate from sinners, one who had no sin, of what could his sufferings be corrective? for what could they be chastisements? God corrects man for iniquity; but Jesus had no iniquity. If his children forsake his law and walk not in his judgments, God visits their transgression with the rod and their iniquity with stripes; but he of whom we now speak "did always those things that pleased the Father." Even the daring theory which represents the Redeemer as a *peccable* mortal will not avail here; as it is not the liability to transgress, but actual transgression, which calls for correction; not the possibility of going astray, but actual deviation from the right path, which calls for chastisement.

Nor will it do to assert that the sufferings and death of Christ were necessary to confirm the truth of his doctrines in general, as if this were the only purpose served by them. This is all that many will admit. He suffered and died, say they, as a martyr. That his sufferings and death prove his sincerity, is readily granted, and thus far they may be said to involve the idea of martyrdom. But it merits consideration here, that to prove the sincerity of belief in a doctrine is one thing, and to prove the truth of the doctrine believed in, is quite another thing. Sufferings and death on its behalf may do the former; but they cannot do the latter. The sufferings of Christ could never have proved his doctrine true, had it been false. They cannot then be said, properly speaking, to *confirm its truth*, so much as to confirm *the sincerity of his belief*. But the death of Christ is what *makes* his doctrine true. The doctrines of the Gospel derive their *truth* itself, rather than the *confirmation* of their truth, from the death of Christ; and had Jesus not suffered and died, there could never have been such a system of doctrinal truth as the Gospel exhibits. Incarnation—atonement—resurrection—the Spirit's influence, would all have been nonentities. The tendency, then, of the theory which explains the fact of Christ's suffering on the principle of its being confirmatory merely of his doctrine, is virtually to annihilate the priesthood of Christ, and all the peculiarities of the Gospel. According to this, he is to be looked upon only as a *Teacher*, a Prophet, an Instructor:—a teacher, too, of nothing more than the simple principles of deism. The divine Being is thus robbed of all legal satisfaction in the salvation of sinful men; the language of scripture in general on the subject of salvation is converted into unmeaning, unintelligible jargon; while the epistle to the Hebrews in particular becomes a forced and unnatural allegory. Where, in this case, is the propriety of so much being said about the sacrifice, and blood, and cross of Christ? Why is he so often and so emphatically called a *Saviour,* if all that his death effected was merely to seal the truth of what he taught? Nay, where, this being the whole, was the necessity at all for his becoming man? Could not the truths of revelation have been established without so formidable an expedient as this? Was there so great a lack of external and internal evidence, as to render such a step indispensable? Were the doctrines, in which it was thought necessary that the world should be instructed, possessed of so little intrinsic reasonableness? Were prophecy and miracles so destitute of all power to convince, that nothing would suffice, but that the Son of God must leave the heavenly glory, assume the likeness of sinful flesh, tabernacle with men upon the earth, submit to every form of bodily pain and mental anguish, and finally die the accursed death of a malefactor; and all for no higher purpose than to give credibility to a system of divine truth? Before this can be received as the true explanation of Christ's sufferings, it must be shown,—which never can be shown,—that there was no possibility of establishing the truth of the Gospel without them. Nay more, it must be proved that the Gospel truth could not have been confirmed without the whole amount of suffering to which he was subjected. For, admitting that suffering and death *were* necessary for the purpose, it will be difficult to show that such severity, variety, and intensity of suffering, were indispensable. But, unless it is maintained that had one pang of all that he endured been spared, there would not have been sufficient ground to believe the Gospel, the theory fails satisfactorily to account for the sufferings of Christ.

It may be said, that, if the death of Christ was not necessary to confirm the truth of his doctrine in general, it was indispensable to put us in possession of that of his resurrection in particular. True; without his death there could not be such a thing as his resurrection. But, while we believe the doctrine of Christ's resurrection from the dead to be a most important and essential part of Christianity, it is surely going too far to say that his death had no other or higher design than to put us in possession of this tenet. According to this he died only that he might rise again. To be sure, that he might rise it was necessary he should die: but it is not the simple fact of his death or of his resurrection, which gives to either its importance. Had not the purpose and design of his death been what we conceive them to have been, his resurrection would have been void of all that importance which attaches to it in the Christian system. It is as the testimony of God to the value of his sacrifice, and as the pledge and security of his people being raised, that the resurrection of Christ possesses so high a claim on our regard; and both of these views, it will be perceived, it derives from the atoning character of his previous death. But, this reasoning apart, it must be obvious to all, that, admitting the death of Christ to have been necessary to his resurrection, had this been all that was necessary, nothing more than the simple fact of his death would have been required. The simplest form in which this could have occurred would have served all the purpose. It would have sufficed to have died in ease and in honor. The magnitude and severity of his previous sufferings, the agony, and torture, and ignominy, and bitterness of death by crucifixion, are thus all accounted for, and inexplicably gratuitous. Being uncalled for by the necessity of the case supposed, they are still unexplained on the principles of divine equity, and some other view is necessary to be taken of them.

Nor will the theory of example supply the desideratum. Much stress has been laid on this, as if the whole design of Christ's sufferings and death was to set mankind a pattern of fortitude, and resignation, and patient endurance. On the supposition that he made atonement for sin, he certainly did set such an example; but not otherwise. Put the case that he suffered not as a legal substitute for sinners, and what an example have we before us! The innocent subjected to the most cruel and excruciating sufferings! Perfect obedience rewarded with the most terrible punishments! The greatest holiness doomed to the greatest anguish!—an example which we hesitate not to pronounce frightful, disgusting, detestable, and impossible under the moral government of a righteous God. Put the case that Christ suffered not the wrath of God for our sins, and we scruple not to say that he failed to set us the example supposed. His mental agony, the anguish of his soul, the fearful bitterness of his cries and his prayers, the bloody sweat of the garden, and the piteous exclamation of the cross, are, on this supposition, out of all proportion to the intensity of the external causes which we observe in operation. The desertion of his friends, and the cruelty of his enemies, might surely have been borne with more equanimity of soul. Many martyrs have been treated with greater external severity, and yet have manifested under it all more apparent magnanimity and comfort, and have expired in triumphant anticipation of heavenly glory: whereas Jesus died amid the horrid darkness of desertion, and complaining, in accents of inconceivable bitterness, of being forsaken by God. Who will say, after this, that he died only to set mankind an example of patience and resignation? Neither should it escape notice, that, if the whole design of Christ's sufferings was to exhibit an example, it was impossible that those who lived in preceding ages could be benefited by it. It will be admitted that the work of Christ had a retrospective virtue; the law was only a shadow of good things to come, of which the substance was Christ; the patriarchs beheld his day afar off and rejoiced. But to the efficacy of an example it is essential that it exist prior to the benefit which it confers. Its influence cannot be retrospective; it cannot be the subject of beneficial anticipation. It may also be observed here, that the theory we are now examining tends to preclude all but adults from the benefit of Christ's sufferings and death. If these were simply exemplary, it follows, of course, that only such as are capable of imitating, can derive advantage from them. Thus infants can reap no benefit from the sufferings of Christ;

and all who die before they are qualified to study the example exhibited in his history, must necessarily perish:—a conclusion which would go directly to destroy the dearest hopes of bereaved Christian parents, did not such know assuredly that it is in direct contradiction to the testimony of him who said, "Suffer the little children to come unto me, and forbid them not, for of such is the kingdom of God."

Such are the theories to which the enemies of the doctrine of atonement have had recourse, with the view of accounting for the sufferings of Christ. How entirely they fail, the preceding observations may help us to judge. They leave the facts of the case, in all their peculiar features, wrapt in inextricable mystery. The solution of the difficulty is to be found in the doctrine of Christ's atonement. Admit this, and all is clear. Considering that he bore our iniquities. that he suffered the wrath of God, that he was exposed to all the direful consequences of God's manifested displeasure at guilt, that he drank the bitter cup of penal woe, in short, that he gave his soul an offering for sin—considering this, the mystery of his intensest sufferings is explained; the bitter anguish, and bloody sweat, and awful desertion, and final cry, give us no difficulty; all is natural, and easy, and consistent. On every other supposition, however, the whole is involved in impenetrable clouds. Can we hesitate, then, what view of the subject to adopt? Truly we must say CHRIST SUFFERED FOR SINS, THE JUST FOR THE UNJUST, THAT HE MIGHT BRING US TO GOD!

SECTION VIII.

PROOF—THE APOSTOLICAL WRITINGS

The evidence we are now to bring forward is not inferential, like that formerly adduced. It is direct, conveyed in plain didactic statements; statements, indeed, so plain, numerous, and unequivocal, as not to be mistaken without the most obstinate resistance of the light. In this department the evidence is so abundant, scattered over so wide a field, and so diversified withal, that it is not possible to convey a definite idea of it, without having recourse to a process of classification.

There are, first of all, those passages in which express mention is made of *atonement* or *reconciliation*, as effected by Christ. In our version, the former term occurs but once in the New Testament :—" We also joy in God through our Lord Jesus Christ, by whom we have now received THE ATONEMENT (τὴν καταλλαγὴν.)"* But the original word occurs in other passages :—" And all things are of God, who hath *reconsiled* (καταλλάξαντος) us to himself by Jesus Christ, and hath given to us the ministry of *reconciliation* (τῆς καταλλαγῆς); to wit, that God was in Christ *reconciling* (καταλλάσσων) the world unto himself, not imputing their trespasses unto them ; and hath committed to us the word of *reconciliation* (τῆς καταλλαγῆς)."† Of the proper import of this term, we have before given our opinion. We have seen that *reconciliation* and *atonement* are synonymous, and that to confine the effect expressed by these terms to man, is contrary altogether to the scripture usage of them, as well as to a consistent interpretation of the passages in which they occur. That salvation implies the removal of man's moral enmity to God is frankly admitted : but this is not in-

* Rom. v. 11. † Cor. v. 18, 19.

consistent with firmly maintaining that it also necessarily supposes and requires the removal of God's legal enmity to man. The party offended must be reconciled as well as the offender, before any real or permanent friendship can be effected; and this we contend is what the language we have quoted above is designed to express. The reconciliation or atonement spoken of, is said to be effected by the death of Christ, whereas the removal of the enmity of man's heart is more properly the work of the Holy Spirit. It is also represented as something synonymous with the non-imputation of trespasses, which itself is decisive of the sense in which it is to be understood; for, while the imputation of guilt presents a *legal* barrier to reconciliation on the part of God, it interposes no *moral* barrier on the part of man. Besides, the phraseology of the first of the texts is itself sufficient to determine the point:—"by whom we have now *received* the atonement." To speak of a person's receiving the boon of reconciliation to God, in the sense of the removal of all legal offence, is intelligible enough; but to speak of his *receiving* the *laying aside of his own enmity to God* is, to say the least, uncouth and unnatural phraseology.

Allied to these, and to much the same purpose, are those texts which ascribe *propitiation* to the work of Christ:—Whom God hath set forth to be a propitiation (ἱλαστήριον) through faith in his blood."* "Jesus Christ the righteous—he is the propitiation (ἱλασμός) for our sins."† "Herein is love, not that we loved God, but that he loved us, and sent his Son to be the propitiation (ἱλασμόν) for our sins."‡ The corresponding verb is also used:—"God be merciful (ἱλάσθητι) to me, a sinner."§ "A merciful and faithful high-priest in things pertaining to God, to make reconciliation for (ἱλάσκεσθαι—to propitiate) the sins of the people."‖ The use of these terms by the Septuagint translators of the Old Testament, to denote the mercy-seat, and the taking away of wrath by means of sacrifice, has al-

* Rom. iii. 25. † 1 John ii. 2. ‡ 1 John iv. 10
§ Luke xviii. 13. ‖ Heb. ii. 17.

ready been mentioned. Nor does this application rest solely on their authority, for the writer of the epistle to the Hebrews gives it his high sanction, when, treating of the furniture of the ancient tabernacle, he speaks of "the cherubims of glory overshadowing the mercy-seat (τὸ ἱλαστήριον)."* The mercy-seat sprinkled with the blood of the sacrifice, was that to which the pious Israelite looked when imploring the pardon of sin. Over it hovered the Shekinah, or symbol of the divine presence, with reference to which Jehovah, as propitiated by sacrifice, was understood to dwell between the cherubim, and to commune with his guilty children from above the mercy-seat. Can anything more satisfactorily determine the sense in which we are to understand the work of Christ? His death is that by which the wrath of God is appeased; by which Deity is propitiated; the grand propitiatory, with reference to which alone it is, either that God can regard man with benignity, or that man can ever approach God in the hope of being accepted.

To the same purpose are all those passages before cited, in which *ransom* and *redemption* are spoken of in connection with the work of Christ. These terms are correlative in their import, the former denoting the sum paid for the emancipation of a prisoner or captive, the latter marking the deliverance or escape which is thus effected. The use of them with reference to man's salvation, of which we shall adduce instances immediately, shows that this salvation is brought about by the interposition of a substitute who procures the liberation of the prisoner by paying his debts, or the emancipation of the captive by tendering his ransom. Men by their sins are brought under obligations to the law and justice of God, which God can neither gratuitously fall from demanding, nor men of themselves ever implement, for reasons that have been already assigned. To the law of God they are debtors; they are the prisoners of divine justice. Their salvation is not a simple discharge without compensation—not a mere manumission without price

* Heb. ix. 5.

Neither is the salvation of guilty men an act of power only, effected by the interposition of an arm full of might to secure their escape. Gratuitous favor and almighty power are both, doubtless, concerned in it; the grace of God being perfectly free as regards the persons saved, who themselves give no price for the redemption of their souls; and the omnipotence of Christ being exerted on the footing of his legal purchase to rescue them from the thraldom of sin. But there is more than grace and power. There is a price paid, a ransom laid down—a price, a ransom, every way equivalent to the redemption for which it is offered. In proof of these assertions, observe the following texts:—" The Son of Man came—to give his life a ransom (λύτρον) for many."* " Justified freely by his grace through the redemption (διὰ τῆς ἀπολυτρώσεως) that is in Christ Jesus."† " In whom we have redemption (ἀπολύτρωσιν) through his blood."‡ " Who gave himself a ransom (ἀντίλυτρον) for all."§ " Who gave himself for us that he might redeem (λυτρώσηται) us from all iniquity."|| " Ye know that ye were not redeemed (ἐλυτρώθητε) with silver and gold, but with the precious blood of Christ."¶ These passages,— and there are many more to the same purpose,— abundantly show that the salvation of sinners is effected by a process of *commutation*, that it is something for which an adequate price is paid without the payment of which it could not have taken place. It is vain to attempt to throw ridicule on this view of the subject, by representing the idea of a pecuniary compensation as too sordid and degrading a principle for the divine Being to act upon; for the truth is, that commutative equity is involved in the essence of true righteousness. Neither will it avail our opponents to assert that as man is the captive of Satan, if price for his deliverance is paid at all, it must be to the Evil One. Man is certainly the slave of Satan, but this is only a secondary view of his bondage. Who is it that delivers him over to Satan, on account of his

* Matt. xx. 28. † Rom. iii. 24. ‡ Eph. i. 7. Col. i. 14.
§ 1 Tim. ii. 6. || Tit. ii. 14. ¶ 1 Peter i. 18, 19.

sins? Is it not by divine justice that he is bound over to punishment? The prince of darkness is only the *executioner* of God's righteous sentence. It is to God the debt of obedience or suffering is due. It is God who has the right to detain him in prison. The detaining power is the equity of the divine law and government, but for which, Satan could not hold him in thraldom a single moment. The passages, thus, without controversy, prove the fact that salvation is effected by the blood or death of the Lord Jesus Christ, which is offered to and accepted of by God, as a perfect satisfaction, a proper equivalent for the sins of such as are made partakers of redemption. They are not their own, but BOUGHT WITH A PRICE. Can anything more distinctly express the idea of substitutionary satisfaction, which is just the idea of atonement?

There are two texts in the writings of Paul, strikingly analogous, and which set forth the doctrine of atonement in the strongest possible manner. The one is:—"He hath made him to be sin (ἁμαρτιαν) for us who knew no sin."* The other:—"Christ hath redeemed us from the curse of the law, being made a curse (καταρα) for us."† In the one, Christ is said to be made *sin*; in the other, to be made a *curse*. The former text is often explained to mean only that he was made a sin-offering; and the latter, that he was subjected to the cursed death of the cross. Even in this view, the passages are strong proofs of our doctrine. But we are inclined to take them literally as they stand, and to view them as meaning that *sin* and *guilt* were actually laid upon Christ, or imputed to him; he was, in law reckoning, regarded as if he had sinned, treated as if he had been accursed. This, as before remarked, was necessary to the penal character of his sufferings; and without it they could have been regarded only in the light of afflictions or calamities, which may, and often do, befall those who are innocent. But if Christ was made sin and a curse, it must have been in the room of others; he had no sin

* 2 Cor. v. 21.   † Gal. iii. 13.

of his own; "he knew no sin;" in himself, he ever "continued in all things written in the book of the law to do them." Here then again, have we the doctrine of Christ's substitution in the place of others, affirmed in the most forcible manner.

The passages in which Christ is said to have been made a *sacrifice* are not to be overlooked. In some of these the death of Christ is spoken of, in the plainest terms, as being a sacrifice:—"Christ hath loved us, and hath given himself for us an offering and a sacrifice (θυσίαν) to God."* "Now once in the end of the world hath he appeared to put away sin by the sacrifice (θυσίας) of himself."† "This man, after he had offered one sacrifice (θυσίαν) for sins, for ever sat down on the right hand of God."‡ In many more passages than we can quote, is the death of Christ spoken of in the same sacrificial terms, which are elsewhere applied to the offerings of the law. We have already exposed the untenableness of the theory which would account for this, on the principle of its being merely in figurative allusion to the rites of the Mosaic dispensation; and assigned our reasons for believing that the only real sacrifice, properly speaking, which was ever presented, was the sacrifice of Christ. It will not do to take refuge from the proof for atonement, deduced from the circumstance of which we are now speaking, by referring to the cases in which the moral and religious services of God's people are represented as sacrifices, or things devoted to God, as if the work of Christ was a sacrifice in no other or higher sense than this.§ For let it be remarked, that under the law there were other than atoning sacrifices, sacrifices that were eucharistical not expiatory, thank-offerings as well as sin-offerings, in which sense the services of the people of God may receive the same designation. But there were also burnt-offerings, sacrifices for sin, of a distinctly penal, expiatory, substitutionary character; and when what Christ did is spoken of as a sacrifice, it is in language of the same kind that we find used with

* Eph. v. 2.   † Heb. ix. 26.   ‡ Heb. x. 12.
§ Rom. xii. 1. Heb. xiii. 15. 1 Peter ii. 5.

regard to these. The services of believers are never spoken of as sacrifices *for sin*, sacrifices offered *to put away sin;* yet such is uniformly the style in which the death of Christ is alluded to in the New Testament. The inference, to every candid mind, must therefore be, that Christ's death is a sacrifice, in no figurative or inferior sense, but as a penal, substitutionary, expiatory satisfaction for the sins of those whom he came to redeem, that is to say, an atoning sacrifice."*

We come now to speak of the language of *substitution*, which is plainly and directly employed, by the writers of the New Testament, in relation to the sufferings and death of Christ. We allude to the frequent use of the preposition FOR, as in the following passages:—" The Son of Man came not to be ministered unto, but to minister, and to give his life a ransom FOR (ἀντί) many.—In due time Christ died FOR (ὑπέρ) the ungodly. He spared not his own Son, but delivered him up FOR (ὑπέρ) us all.—Christ our passover is sacrificed FOR (ὑπέρ) us.—He hath made him to be sin FOR (ὑπέρ) us, who knew no sin.—Christ hath redeemed us from the curse of the law, being made a curse FOR (ὑπέρ) us.—Christ also hath loved us and given himself FOR (ὑπέρ) us, an offering and a sacrifice to God. Our Lord Jesus Christ who died FOR (ὑπέρ) us.—Who gave himself a ransom FOR (ὑπέρ) all.—Who gave himself FOR (ὑπέρ, us.—Christ also suffered FOR (ὑπέρ) us.—He laid down his life FOR (ὑπέρ) us."†—The prepositions employed in these texts naturally denote the idea of substitution. The Greek language has no terms by which such an idea can be more significantly expressed; and it is not to be questioned that both sacred and profane writers use them in this acceptation. The first of them,—ἀντί,—literally involves the idea of apposition, of one thing set over against another; whence naturally spring those of commutation, recompense, and substitution. Xenophon, speaking of Artax-

---

* Smith on Sac., p. 286.

† Matt. xx. 28. Rom. v. 6; viii. 32. 1 Cor. v. 7. 2 Cor. v. 21. Gal. iii. 13. Eph. v. 2. 1 Thess. v. 10. 1 Tim. ii. 6. Titus ii. 14. 1 Peter ii. 21. 1 John iii. 16.

erxes being made a subject instead of a king, expresses it thus:—ὡς δοῦλον ἀντὶ βασιλέως.—Our Lord says, "Or if he ask a fish, will he FOR a fish give him a serpent?"*—ἀντὶ ἰχθύος ὄφιν ἐπιδώσει αὐτῷ; In these cases the idea of substitution is sufficiently apparent. Nor is it less so surely when Christ is said to give his life a ransom for many—λύτρον ἀντὶ πολλῶν; to give himself a ransom for all—ἀντίλυτρον ὑπὲρ πάντων.—The other preposition, —ὑπὲρ,—which most commonly occurs, literally signifies *over*, and thus denotes the idea of covering, protection, substitution—that which is placed over another to save that other by receiving what must otherwise have wrought his destruction. The phrase ὑπὲρ τούτου ἀποθανεῖν occurs in Xenophon, in the sense of to die in the stead of one. The same is the sense in which the word occurs in John xv. 13: "Greater love hath no man than this, that a man lay down his life *for* his friends," τὴν ψυχὴν αὐτοῦ ὑπὲρ τῶν φίλων αὐτοῦ. Such being the case, we are naturally led to conclude that the same is the import of the preposition in the numerous passages quoted above with reference to the death of Christ, namely, that he died in our stead, that his death was substituted for ours.

It forms no valid objection to this conclusion, that the same phraseology occurs in circumstances which do not admit of precisely the same terms being employed in explanation. The same preposition, or one of similar import, is used with reference to *sin*, as is employed in the above texts with reference to the *sinner*. Thus it is said, speaking of Christ:—"Who was delivered FOR (διὰ) our offences.—Christ died FOR (ὑπὲρ) our sins.—Who gave himself FOR (ὑπὲρ) our sins. —Christ also hath once suffered FOR (περὶ) sins.—He is the propitiation FOR (περὶ) our sins; and not FOR (περὶ) ours only, but also FOR (περὶ) the sins of the whole world.—He loved us, and sent his Son to be the propitiation FOR (περὶ) our sins."† Now, it is admitted that in these and similar passages the preposition FOR

---
* Luke xi. 11.
† Rom. iv. 25; 1 Cor. xv. 3; Gal. i. 4; 1 Pet. iii. 18; 1 John ii. 2 John iv. 10.

cannot have exactly the same meaning as when used with respect to persons. We can say with propriety that Christ died *in our stead*, but not that he died *in stead of our offences*. In the latter case, *for* must be viewed as synonymous with *on account of*—he gave himself *on account of* our sins; he was delived *on account of* our offences. But this does not prove that the sense of the preposition, in the other case, is not correctly expressed by the phrase in question. It only shows that the same preposition has different meanings, or admits of being taken in different senses, according to the subject to which it happens to be applied. It is not necessary, neither is it possible even on the theory of our opponents, to give one uniform meaning to the word in every case where it occurs. Of course its being used in one set of passages in one specific sense agreeable to the nature of the subject spoken of, is no proof that it is not employed in another set of passages in another specific sense agreeable to the nature of the subject treated of in those passages. And this conclusion will appear the more tenable, when it is observed, that, although different shades of meaning attach to the same word in the respective phrases, the phrases themselves, taken as a whole, express but one doctrinal truth. In the propositions *Christ died for us*, and *Christ died for our sins* the word *for* bears different significations, but the propositions themselves are equivalent; both statements contain the same idea; the meaning of each is consistent with that of the other. Christ's dying *on account of* our sins, and dying *in the stead of* us sinners, amount to the same thing. To reason from the sense of the preposition in the one phrase, against that in which it is used in the other, when the phrases themselves are notwithstanding identical, is utterly futile and nugatory.

But the enemies of atonement will insist that the proper meaning of the term in question, in all the cases in which it occurs, is *on account of*, or, *for our advantage*—that it denotes the *final cause*, and not *substitution*. It is perfectly true that Christ died for our benefit, that he suffered on our account, and this is doubtless implied in the phraseology in question; but that it is *all* that is implied, that it does not imply also that the way in which our advantage was promoted was by the substitution of another in our stead, we are not prepared to admit.—First of all, it is worthy of remark that the above explanation does not preserve a uniformity of meaning in the passages in question. That the phrase *Christ died for us* should mean that he died *for our benefit* is intelligible enough; but does the phrase *Christ died for our sins* mean that he died *for the benefit of our sins?*—Besides, if those passages which teach that Christ died for our sins, offences, &c., mean nothing more than that we reap important advantages from his death with respect to the pardon of sin, inasmuch as that death was a means of confirming or making known to us the doctrine of forgiveness which he taught, it seems impossible to account for such a beneficial result being connected exclusively with his death, and not with his ministry, his miracles, his example, or his resurrection. It is manifest that one and all of *these* contributed to our advantage in respect of our being made acquainted with the doctrine of pardon, at least as much as—not to say, more than—his death. In his ministry he taught the doctrine; by his miracles he confirmed it; in his life he exemplified it; while his resurrection added strength to the evidence by which all that he taught was supported. Yet is it never said that *Christ preached for our sins;* that *he healed the sick,* or *raised the dead,* or *gave sight to the blind for our sins;* or that he *lived for our sins;* or that he *rose the third day for our offences.* On the supposition we are combating, however, such phraseology should have occurred as frequently as that of which we are endeavoring to ascertain the meaning. And from its non-occurrence, from its manifest uncouthness and unintelligibility, we conclude that, when the inspired writers speak of Christ dying for our offences, there must be some other connection between the death of Christ and man's deliverance from sin, than that which is supposed in the former being a confirmation of the doctrine of pardon; in short, that the death of Christ not merely confirmed the doctrine, but *procured* the benefit, of remission.

But the untenableness of this method of explaining the phraseology in question may be placed in a still stronger light. If the sufferings and death of Christ are *for us* in no higher sense than that of being *for our benefit,* then might the same language have been used with respect to the apostles and disciples of our Lord. It cannot be doubted, that numerous and important advantages result to believers, from the sufferings of the apostles and primitive Christians. Their constancy in suffering, and their heroism in submitting to martyrdom, not only taught the most valuable moral lessons, but tended to strengthen the evidence by which the divine origin of the religion they professed is supported. Of this circumstance they were distinctly aware, and they recognized the fact with disinterested satisfaction. "Yea and if I be offered," says Paul, "upon the sacrifice and service of your faith, I joy and rejoice with you all."* "Who now rejoice," says he on another occasion, "in my sufferings for you, and fill up that which is behind of the afflictions of Christ in my flesh for his body's sake, which is the church,"†—"and whether we be afflicted, it is for your consolation and salvation."‡ But are we at liberty to infer, from this language, that the sufferings of Christ bear no other relation to the advantages of his people than do those of the apostles? Was Christ delivered for our offences in no higher sense than Paul the apostle may be said to have been? On the theory of interpretation we are combating, we must regard them as exactly parallel. But this is a conclusion from which, at least, Paul himself would have shrunk back with abhorrence. What else can we make of his appeal to the Corinthians:—"Was Paul crucified for you?"§ Surely he could never have employed such language, had he believed that the crucifixion of Christ had no other relation to the

* Phil. ii. 17.   † Col. i. 24.   ‡ 2 Cor. i. 6.   § 1 Cor. i. 13.

salvation of Christians than that merely of being for their benefit.

Such is the proof of the atonement of Christ, derived from the writings of the New Testament. The doctrine of the remission of sins through the atoning blood of Jesus, indeed, pervades these writings, and like the sun, invests their pages with a sacred light. "That the sufferings of the Redeemer," says the eloquent Robert Hall, " were vicarious and piacular, that he appeared in the character of a substitute for sinners, in distinction from a mere example, teacher, or martyr, is so unquestionably the doctrine of the inspired writers, that to deny it, is not so properly to mistake, as to contradict their testimony; it must be ascribed, not to any obscurity in revelation itself, but to a want of submission to its authority. The doctrine in question is so often asserted in the clearest terms, and tacitly assumed as a fundamental principle in so many more; it is intermingled so closely with all the statements of truth, and inculcations of duty throughout the holy Scriptures, that to endeavor to exclude it from revelation is as hopeless an attempt as to separate color from the rainbow, or extension from matter."* To the same purpose is the testimony of another eminent writer, with whose words we conclude our adduction of proof:—" That Christ suffered and died as an atonement for the sins of mankind, is a doctrine so constantly and so strongly enforced through every part of the New Testament, that whoever will seriously peruse those writings, and deny that it is there, may with as much reason and truth, after reading the works of Thucydides and Livy, assert, that in them no mention is made of any facts relative to the histories of Greece and Rome."†

We have, thus, given a view of the evidence by which the fact of Christ's atonement is supported. In the antiquity and universal prevalence of vicarious

---

* Hall's Works, i. 489.
† Soame Jenyn's View of the Internal Evidence, &c., ninth edition, . 22, note.

sacrifices, for whose existence we have found it impossible to account excepting on the principle of being instituted by God to prefigure the sacrifices of Christ, we have one argument. In the sacrifices of the Levitical economy, purposely designed, and eminently calculated, to lead to Christ, we have another argument. The prophecies of the Old Testament supply us with a third. The facts of Christ's sufferings, of which it is otherwise impossible to give a satisfactory explanation, furnish us with a fourth. While the passages in the New Testament scriptures which speak of Christ making reconciliation; of his being a propitiation; of his giving a ransom and making redemption; of his being made sin, a curse, a sacrifice; and of his dying for us and our sins, add a fifth proof to this body of evidence. The whole of these arguments are taken from the word of God. Some of them are deduced by way of inference from established premises; others are derived from a careful exegesis of scripture language; but each rests on a basis of infallible truth, and all together constitute a mass of evidence so clear, cogent, and convincing, as nothing but the most wilful enmity to the truth can resist. If the sacred scriptures, and not our own preconceived opinions and prejudices, are the standard to which we are to appeal, it seems impossible, but by the most obstinate moral perversity, to refuse the testimony they bear on this momentous subject. In short, unless the doctrine of substitution is admitted, the sacred volume seems reduced to a mass of unintelligible, meaningless, contradictory assertions; the feelings of the writers seem to be out of all harmonious proportion with the nature of their subject; their elevation is fanaticism, their enthusiasm idolatry, and their transports of passion indicate only zeal without knowledge: we may safely join issue with those who represent them as "babblers," for, in this case, their reasonings are inconclusive, their inferences unsupported by their premises, and their premises themselves at variance with fact. Let us beware of adopting opinions, or acting a part which leads to such frightful consequences; and let us yield our minds up, with all becoming submission, to the divinely authoritative testimony by which it is affirmed that CHRIST HATH LOVED US AND HATH GIVEN HIMSELF FOR US, AN OFFERING AND A SACRIFICE TO GOD, FOR A SWEET-SMELLING SAVOR.

SECTION IX.

MATTER OR SUBSTANCE OF CHRIST'S ATONEMENT.

HERE we are to inquire what it was by which Christ made atonement for sin. That he did make an atonement, we consider as established in some preceding sections; it is natural next to ask how this was effected. Christ did many things while on earth; he taught, he obeyed, he suffered, he died. Now, the thing to be ascertained, is, by which of these he gave that satisfaction to the law and justice of God in which we conceive the essence of atonement to consist. The truth, on this topic, we are inclined to think, lies in the following statement:—That Christ made atonement by sufferings alone; that all his sufferings were comprehended in the matter of his atonement; and that a peculiar importance attaches, in this connection, to the sufferings of his soul and of the concluding period of his life. Let us attend to the several branches of this position.

I. Christ made atonement by his *sufferings alone.*

This statement has been questioned by some of the older writers on the subject, and the opinion it involves has been deemed heretical. To this conclusion, they have been led, by taking a more extensive view of the nature of atonement than respect to strict accuracy of definition seems to warrant. Indeed the whole controversy, on this point, depends on the extent of meaning which is attached to the word atonement. If understood to embrace the whole of the Saviour's work for the redemption of man, then more than his sufferings ought to be included in its substance. On the other hand, if by the atonement of Christ is meant only a particular department of the work performed by him for our salvation, correct thinking will require us to restrict our view of its matter to his sufferings alone.

To obviate all difficulty on this subject, it seems necessary only to advert to our definition of atonement. It is this—That satisfaction given to the law and justice of God, by the sufferings and death of Jesus Christ, on behalf of elect sinners of mankind, on account of which they are delivered from condemnation. From the terms of this definition, the atonement of Christ is understood to consist in giving satisfaction to the law of God, so as to procure escape from its curse; and, taking this as a correct view of the *nature* of atonement, it follows, as a thing of course, that its *matter* should be restricted to suffering.

This will appear in a clearer light if the following observations are attended to. The law of God is to be viewed in a twofold light,—in its precept and in its penalty; the one prescribing duty and demanding obedience, the other denouncing punishment on the guilty violator. Corresponding to these, there is a twofold view to be taken of man's relation to the law,—consisting in an obligation to obey the precept, and an obnoxiousness to suffer the penalty in case of transgression. Man's subjection to the law, again, may be viewed in three lights,—natural, federal, and penal. Natural subjection to the law arises necessarily out of man's circumstances as a moral creature, and cannot be increased, or diminished, or nullified, by anything which is done either by himself or by another in his stead: it remains unalterably the same at all times, and abides through eternity: it belongs to man as a moral being, and continues during the period of his existence: it could not be obliterated, but by an entire change of nature, which is tantamount to an annihilation of his existence. Federal subjection springs from the covenant form of the law, in which the fulfilment of duties is enforced, not merely by a threatening of punishment, which seems to be essential to the very nature of a law, but by a promise of reward which the abstract view of law does not necessarily require. This belongs not to man as a creature, but as a party in a voluntary transaction or economical arrangement, the obligation of which is supposed to cease when the object for which it has been entered into has been accomplished; that is to say, when the condition of the covenant is fulfilled. Penal subjection consists in an obligation to suffer the punishment due to the breach of the law, and is incurred by a violation of its requirements. These different kinds of subjection are founded on different views of the divine character, and are alike indispensable, excepting on the principle that the claims of Deity are answered. The first is founded on the nature of God, and is necessarily immutable. The second is founded on the will of God, and can only be dispensed with by a fulfilment of the whole condition of the covenant. The third is founded on the retributive justice of God, and can cease only when the penalty has been fully borne.

Fallen man is to be regarded as under subjection to the law of God in these three lights:—naturally, federally, penally. He is under natural subjection, as a creature. He is under federal subjection, as included in the covenant which God made with Adam in his character of legal representative of his posterity. He is under penal subjection, as involved in the guilt resulting from the violation of the original covenant engagement, and from his own actual transgression.

Now, man's *need* of salvation arises out of his inability to meet this threefold obligation of God's holy and righteous law. He is under subjection, but he cannot fulfil what that subjection supposes to be required of him. He is under natural subjection; but he cannot meet the requirements of the law, because morally depraved. He is under federal subjection; but he cannot yield the perfect obedience which is the condition of the covenant, because he is without strength. He is under penal subjection; but he can never fully endure what the sanction of the law prescribes, because the punishment it denounces is everlasting.

The salvation of man must, therefore, include two things:—deliverance from the federal and penal obligation of the law, and qualification for the fulfilment of that natural obligation from which there can be no deliverance. To qualify man for complying with what his natural obligation to the law imposes, is the work of the Holy Spirit, in regeneration and sanctification. To deliver man from the federal and penal obligation of the law, is the work of Jesus Christ. But the work of Christ, it will thus be seen, must consist of two parts, or rather is to be viewed in two lights—as a satisfaction to the federal demands of the law, and as a compliance with its penal sanction. The former is necessary to give man a title to the life promised in the covenant, and is effected by positive obedience to the whole precepts of the law. The latter is necessary to free man from the death or curse denounced in the covenant on human disobedience, and is effected by suffering the whole amount of the penalty. Now, it is the last of these objects which is contemplated by the atonement, and hence the necessity of restricting its matter to suffering.

It is not to be understood, that, in making this distinction between the positive obedience and penal suffering of Christ, it is meant to be insinuated that these were ever actually separated from one another. *Is Christ divided?* No, by no means. The work of Christ is one, although it may be advantageously viewed in different lights, or as including different parts. It is not supposed, that in some acts he obeyed, and that in other acts he suffered only. Obedience and suffering are different views, or, if you will, different parts of his mediatorial work; but they are inseparable from one another—inseparable in covenant, in act, and in consequence. They are inseparably connected in the covenant, both being included in the stipulated condition which he engaged to fulfil, namely that he should make reconciliation for iniquity and bring in an everlasting righteousness. They were inseparably united in what he did;—while he suffered he obeyed, and while he obeyed he suffered; he became *obedient unto death*. They are inseparable in the consequences of his work; that is to say, no one ever reaps the fruits of the one, without reaping also those of the other; whoever is delivered from death, is made a partaker also of life; whoever is freed from condemnation, is put in possession of a valid title to glory; whoever *receives forgiveness of sins*, obtains, at the same time, *inheritance among them who are sanctified*. Yet, though thus indissolubly united, they are nevertheless distinguishable from one another; and the work of the Redeemer admits of a corresponding distinction, in the aspects in which it may be viewed. The formal matter or substance of Christ's atonement is, thus, his sufferings, by which he fulfilled the penal obligation of the law, and procured the pardon of sin or deliverance from guilt; as distinguished from his formal obedience, by which he complied with the preceptive demands of the law, and in virtue of which his people are regarded as righteous and entitled to glory.

II. The *whole* of Christ's sufferings are comprehended in the matter of his atonement.

It was not by those of his soul to the exclusion of those of his body, or by those of the latter period of his life on earth to the exclusion of those of an earlier date, that he effected the purchase of our salvation. All were necessary, from his birth to his death, from the feeble cry of infancy to the piercing complaint of desertion. From the benevolence of God we conclude, that not a single pang was inflicted more than was requisite. Every pain he endured, every grief which he felt, constituted an indispensable part of that sacrifice by which he made reconciliation for the iniquities of his people. All his sufferings were of a vicarious, none of them of a personal nature. In every case he suffered *for us*, never for *himself;* he suffered, the just for the unjust, that he might bring us to God.

Some have held the opinion, that as a creature, Christ was under natural obligation to the law for himself. This we reckon an objectional statement, as it overlooks the circumstance that he had no personal existence as man, and it is a person alone that can be the subject of a law; as well as that his being under the law naturally for himself as a creature, must have disqualified him for coming under it federally for others as a surety. But even were it admitted that he was under *natural* subjection to the law on his own account, it is never supposed by any that he was under *penal* subjection to the law for himself; he had no sin, consequently was entitled to no degree of suffering on his own account; he had no iniquity of his own for which he required to atone by his sufferings; nor was there any moral discipline of a personal nature to be subserved by what he endured. It pleased God, indeed, to make the captain of our salvation perfect through suffering; but it was a relative perfection as the surety of sinners, not a personal perfection as the Son of God, that was, in this way, promoted. What is said of his death, may be affirmed of every suffering by which it was preceded—it was NOT FOR HIMSELF. Not one throb of pain did he feel, not one pang of sorrow did he experience, not one sigh of anguish did he heave, not one tear of grief did he shed, for himself. All were for men; all were for us. If not one of his sufferings was personal, it follows that they were all substitutionary, that they were all, of course, included in the matter or substance of his atoning sacrifice. During the whole period of his mortal life the victim was a-slaying. At the moment of his birth, the sword of justice was unsheathed against the man who is Jehovah's fellow, and returned not to its scabbard till it had been bathed in the blood of Calvary.

It may be deemed at variance with this view of the subject, that the redemption of man is sometimes in scripture ascribed simply to the blood of Christ, or to his death alone. But such language is not to be understood as limiting the atonement of Christ to the simple act of dying, or to those sufferings in which there was an effusion of literal blood. The bloody agony of the garden, and the accursed death of the cross, were prominent and concluding parts of his sufferings, and, by a common figure, were fit representatives of the whole. They were the last portions, so to speak, the completion of his humiliation, without which all that went before must have been vain; and may be regarded as having procured salvation, in the same way as the last instalment of a sum which is paid by degrees, may be supposed to cancel the debt and procure a discharge. But, as when Christ is said to have been "obedient unto death," we are to understand the phrase, not of a *single act,* but of the *duration* of his obedience throughout the whole period of his life, so may it be said that he *suffered unto death,* as expressive of the duration of his suffering throughout the whole of his earthly course.

III. Yet it is not intended by these remarks to deny that *a special importance attaches to the sufferings of Christ's soul, and of the concluding period of his life.*

It is impossible to peruse the Scriptures attentively and not perceive that a special emphasis is put upon these. We are not to confine the matter of atonement to any one kind or degree of suffering; but as little are we at liberty to overlook the speciality that attaches to those sufferings to which we now refer. His bodily pains were of consequence, but the agonies of his holy soul were of more consequence. The suffering of infancy and childhood and youth are not to be lost sight of, but those of the final conflict call for particular notice.

The soul is often spoken of with peculiar emphasis. " Thou shalt make his SOUL an offering for sin—The waters are come in unto my SOUL—My SOUL is full of troubles, and my life draweth nigh to the grave—My SOUL is exceeding sorrowful even unto death—Now is my SOUL troubled, and what shall I say ?"* What our divine surety suffered in his soul must ever surpass all

Isa. iii. 11. Ps. lxix. 1; lxxxviii. 3. Matt. xxvi. 38. John xii. 27.

our powers of description or conception. The language used by the inspired writers denotes the highes pitch of intensity, while we have the best reason to suppose that every variety of inward agony which a sinless spirit can possibly feel was experienced by him. *His soul was exceeding sorrowful;*—the most pungent sorrow filled his bosom; his heart was pierced through with many sorrows; he was a man of sorrows and acquainted with grief. *He began to be very heavy:*— an unutterable load of dejection, an overpowering weight of consternation pressed down his spirits to the lowest depth of depression. *He was sore amazed:*— filled with inexpressible wonder and horrific terror at the evil of sin, and the magnitude of the curse to be endured for its expiation. *His soul was troubled;*— agitated with alarm, filled with apprehension, overwhelmed with anguish, at thought of that awful wrath which he had to endure; at sight of that thick darkness, that midnight gloom of hell which he had to approach and to dissipate; at experience of that condemnation which now weighed him down under its mountain load; at taste of that cup of gall which had to be drunk with all its wormwood bitterness. Well might he take up the complaint, " My soul is full of troubles; the waters are come in unto my soul." And thus was it that " he made his soul an offering for sin."

Nor can it be doubted that the sufferings of the latter period of his life possess a speciality of interest. The period of his mysterious agony, his awful desertion, and his actual death calls for particular notice. This is what is emphatically called "his hour—the hour and the power of darkness—the hour that he should depart out of this world."* It was now that he was subjected to that inexplicable agony which, in the absence of every adequate external cause, covered him over with a copious sweat of blood. It was now that he was cruelly deserted by all his former friends, there not being among the whole multitude of those whom he had cured of their sicknesses, to whom he had preached the Gospel of salvation, and whom he

* John vii. 30. Luke xxii. 53 John xiii. 1.

had chosen as his disciples, one to abide with him in his dire extremity, but being left to utter the heavy complaint, "I looked for some to take pity, but there was none; and for comforters, but I found none."* It was now that he suffered the withdrawment of all sensible tokens of his Father's love; the suspension of every kind of sensible support, of every display of divine complacency; the felt manifestation of God's righteous displeasure at sin; the total eclipse of the hallowed light which had formerly cheered him amid the deepest gloom; the paternal desertion which drew from him the deep groan of bereavement, "My God, my God, why hast thou forsaken me." It was now that he suffered the pains of actual dissolution; he died the death of the cross; he bowed the head and gave up the ghost. It was no faint, no swoon, no temporary suspension of the vital functions. It was death—a complete separation of the soul and body; the heart having been pierced by the soldier's spear, and his enemies themselves bearing witness to the reality of his departure. "Then came the soldiers and brake the legs of the first, and of the other which was crucified with him: but when they came to Jesus and saw that HE WAS DEAD ALREADY, they brake not his legs; but one of the soldiers with a spear pierced his side, and forthwith came thereout blood and water."† This was the period when emphatically the Son of God made atonement for sin; when the tide of suffering rose to its height; when the dregs of the bitter cup of anguish were wrung out; when the sentence of woe reached its climax. A period, into which whatever is painful in torture, ignominious in shame, distressing in privation, terrific in satanic assault, and overwhelming in experienced wrath, was, as it were, compressed!— a period, whether to the sufferer himself or to the guilty world whose cause he undertook, the most awfully momentous that had ever occurred since the commencement of time.

Such, then, is what constitutes the matter or substance of Christ's atonement,—his sufferings, all his

---

* Psalm lxix. 20.   † John xix. 32—34.

sufferings, and the sufferings of his soul, and of the concluding period of his life in particular. It is not necessary to suppose that the sufferings which Christ endured on our behalf were precisely the same in kind and degree which are experienced by the wicked in the place of final woe. There are, on the one hand, ingredients in *their* misery which *he* could not feel, as remorse, despair, and the fury of evil passions. Remorse he could not feel, for his soul was a stranger to personal guilt. Despair he could not feel, for he had full assurance of deliverance from the bondage of death and the prison of the grave. And as for sinful passions, they had at no time a seat in his breast. On the other hand, there were ingredients in the sufferings of Christ, arising from the repugnance of his pure soul at moral defilement, which those who go down to the pit are incapable of feeling. " It is, I humbly conceive," says Dr. Pye Smith, " worse than improper to represent the sufferings of Jesus Christ, in their last and most terrible extremity, as the same with those of condemned sinners in the state of punishment. In the case of such incorrigible and wretched criminals, there is a leading circumstance which could not, by any possibility, exist in the suffering Saviour. *They eat of the fruit of their own way, and are filled with their own devices.* A most material part of their misery consists in the unrestrained power of sinful passions, for ever raging, but for ever ungratified. Their minds are constantly torn with the racking consciousness of personal guilt; with mutual aggravations and insults; with the remorse of despair: with malice, envy, and blasphemy against the Holy and Blessed God himself; and with an indubitable sense of Jehovah's righteous abhorrence and rejection of them. No such passions as these, nor the slightest tincture of them, could have place in the breast of the holy Jesus. That meek and purest Lamb offered himself without spot. His heart, though broken and bleeding with agonies to us unknown, ever felt a perfect resignation to the hand that smote him, and a full acquiescence in all the bitterness of the cup which was appointed him to drink: the resignation and acquiescence of love and conv'ction. He suffered in such a manner as a being perfectly holy could suffer Though animated by the joy that was set before him, he endured the cross and despised the shame; yet there appear to have been seasons in the hour of his deepest extremity, in which he underwent the entire absence of divine joy and every kind of comfort or sensible support. What but a total eclipse of the sun of consolation, could have wrung from him that exceedingly bitter and piercing cry, *My God! My God! why hast thou forsaken me?*—The fire of Heaven consumed the sacrifice. The tremendous manifestations of God's displeasure against sin he endured, though in him was no sin: and he endured them in a manner of which even those unhappy spirits who shall drink the fierceness of the wrath of Almighty God, will never be able to form an adequate idea! They know not the HOLY and EXQUISITE SENSIBILITY which belonged to this immaculate sacrifice. That clear sight of the transgressions of his people in all their heinousness and atrocity, and that acute sense of the infinite vileness of sin, its baseness, ingratitude, and evil in every respect which he possessed,—must have produced, *in him*, a feeling of extreme distress, of a kind, and to a degree which no creature, whose moral sense is impaired by personal sin, can justly conceive. As such a feeling would accrue from the purity and ardor of his love to God and holiness, acting in his perfectly peculiar circumstances; so it would be increased by the pity and tenderness which he ever felt towards the objects of his redeeming love. A wise and good father is more deeply distressed by a crime which his beloved child has perpetrated, than by the same offence if committed by an indifferent person.' *

* Disc. on Sac., pp. 45—47.

SECTION X.

VALUE OF CHRIST'S ATONEMENT.

Whatever may be the philosophical difficulties in which the subject is involved, there is no idea with which we are more familiar than that of causality. The terms *power, cause* and *effect,* are in daily and constant use. It seems capable of satisfactory demonstration that the only correct notion attachable to these words, is that of invariable *antecedence* and *consequence.* There are certain things which never exist without being immediately followed by certain definite events. To the antecedent we give the name of *cause,* to the consequent the name of *effect ;* and the proper notion of *power* is, not that in the antecedent there is anything which produces the consequent, but the simple fact of their combination,—the naked circumstance of immediate invariable antecedence. The *fact of the conjunction* of the objects is all that we know or are capable of perceiving in the matter ; the *bond of connection,* the tie which binds them together, the connecting link, is an incomprehensible mystery, in every case impenetrable to human sagacity. It seems, therefore, reasonable to conclude, that the real immediate cause of every effect is the will of the Supreme Intelligence : and that those invariable antecedences and consequences in events, which we denominate causes and effects, are nothing but the order of that perfect harmonious system which the Almighty has established in the universe. It is not, however to be inferred from this, that the connection of cause and effect has no other foundation than mere arbitrary will, or capricious appointment. Far from us be the unworthy thought. From the known character of God we are bound to believe that, in every case, a wise and righteous ground of connection exists. This inference is no way invalidated by the circumstance that we are unable, in any instance, to tell what that is which constitutes the bond of connection. Such, we are inclined to think, is the uniform procedure of the Almighty in all his works—the true account of the phenomena of the universe, which exhibits a constituted series of antecedents and consequents, under the control and direction of infinite wisdom, infinite holiness, and infinite power.

To this grand law of God's universal government, the economy of human salvation, it is humbly presumed, will be found to present not the shadow of an exception. For the production of the *effect*, which is in this case salvation, there exists a proper and adequate *cause* in the vicarious sufferings of the Son of God. The means bear a true relation to the end. The great object of redeeming mercy is effected in perfect and beautiful consistency with legislative rectitude. These are but parts of the one all-wise system of the universe, and the connection betwixt them rests on a basis of infinite wisdom and justice. This basis is the formation of a moral constitution, according to which, on the one hand, guilt and punishment should be transferred to a divine Substitute, and, on the other hand, the obedience and sufferings of this surety imputed to those who are to be saved. This transference of sin and imputation of merit proceed, let it be distinctly marked, on principles of right reason and perfect equity, on a divinely-constituted union of nature and federal relationship between the spotless victim and those who reap the advantages of his meritorious sufferings. By this constitution, such a reciprocal proprietorship is made to exist betwixt the parties, that, as regards the benevolent issue, the universal law of cause and effect which God has established, is upheld and illustrated rather than infringed. Taking the benevolent intention and holy nature of Deity into the account, that the sufferings and death of the Son of God should procure the salvation of sinners, rests on as firm a basis of philosophical truth as any other case of antecedence and consequence in the universe.*

This brings us directly to the subject of this section, which is to inquire what it was about the sacrifice of Christ which rendered it an adequate *cause* to produce the *effect* of human salvation; that is to say, what it is that constitutes the moral worth or value of Christ's atonement.

The value of Christ's atonement we conceive to arise, not from the nature, or intensity, or continuance of his sufferings. The work of Jesus was not a mere commercial affair of debt and payment. We have no conception that, had the number of those for whom he suffered been greater than it was, or had their sins been more numerous or more aggravated than they were, his sufferings must have been proportionably increased. Neither can we subscribe to the notion that one pang or pain of all that he endured was itself sufficient to effect atonement. We conceive, on the contrary, that he suffered nothing but what was necessary, that if less could have sufficed less would have been required; while, on the other hand, the intrinsic worth of what he actually endured was such as to render it sufficient for the salvation of many more than shall be ultimately saved, had God only seen meet to extend to them his mercy in Christ Jesus. The sufferings of Christ we regard as a moral satisfaction to the law and government of God, which would have been necessary had there been only one to be saved, and which would have been found sufficient had the whole human race, without exception, been to rank among the redeemed. Just as the arrangement which exists for the outward illumination of our globe, would have been required had there been but one inhabitant to reap the benefit presently enjoyed, and would have been sufficient had there been many more millions in existence than actually inhabit the earth. The worth or value of Christ's atoning sacrifice we conceive to have arisen, not from one circumstance alone, but from several circumstances combined, none of which can

* See Smith's Disc. on Sac., pp 38, 282.

be dispensed with in forming a proper estimate on the subject. These circumstances we shall now attempt to unfold.

I. The first is *the dignity of the Saviour's person.*

He who, in making atonement, is at once the priest and the sacrifice, is divine. He is the Son of God, the brightness of his glory, and the express image of his person. He is God himself, co-equal with the Father, Jehovah's fellow. Titles which involve essential dignity are unhesitatingly ascribed to him. He is spoken of as possessing all the necessary attributes of Deity. Works which belong only to God, are said to be performed by him. And the highest forms of divine worship are used by all moral creatures, in doing him homage. The truth of these assertions we must be permitted to take for granted, as to exhibit even an outline of their evidence would lead us into an improper digression. The doctrine of Christ's dignity is prominently set forth in the volume of revealed truth. It is the glory of Christianity. It sparkles, like a radiant gem, in every part of the sacred field. It invests the whole Christian system with heavenly beauty. It imparts a peculiar grandeur and sublimity to the doctrines of the cross.

From the dignity of the party offended by man's sin, it was requisite that he, who should successfully transact for pardon, should possess a corresponding elevation of character. He who is offended is the infinite Jehovah, the great God of heaven and of earth. It is the infinite Majesty whose honor has been violated; it is the throne of the Eternal whose stability and authority have been invaded. To effect reconciliation, in such a case, is a work to which no man, no angel, no superangelic creature is adequate. No priest of less personal consequence than the Lord of glory, is competent to the office of appeasing the wrath of the high and lofty One who inhabiteth eternity. But we have such an High Priest, who is set on the right hand of the throne of the majesty in the heavens.

The sacrifice by which atonement is made for offences of infinite moral turpitude, must be possessed of infinite moral worth. The relative value arising from divine appointment is not enough; else it could never have been said, "It is not possible that the blood of bulls and of goats could take away sin." The blood of inferior animals was as capable as any other of all the worth which mere appointment can impart. But an intrinsic worth was required, which could be possessed by nothing short of "blood divine." Hence the sacrifice of Christ is so often spoken of in scripture as being *himself*. "Christ has loved us and given HIMSELF for us an offering and a sacrifice to God.—Who gave HIMSELF a ransom for all.—When he had by HIMSELF purged our sins.—He offered up HIMSELF.—He appeared to put away sin by the sacrifice of HIMSELF."*

As the substance of Christ's atoning sacrifice consisted in his sufferings or death, it has been alleged that its intrinsic worth could be nothing more than human, as his human nature alone could suffer and die. But the close and inseparable union subsisting between the divine and human natures in the person of the Son of God is here to be remembered. Although the human nature alone could either suffer or die, it was the Son of God, as possessed of this nature, who endured the sufferings and died the death of the cross. The possession of a human nature qualified him for suffering; the divinity of his person gave to his suffering a worth equivalent to its own dignity. Although the human nature was alone capable of suffering, it was nevertheless the person to whom this nature belonged who suffered. It may be thought that at this rate, as the person was divine, such an assertion involves the blasphemy that Deity suffered. By no means. When a person suffers, it does not follow that he suffers in all that pertains to him. He may suffer in his property and not suffer in his honor; he may suffer in his happiness and not in his character; he may suffer in his body and not in his soul; still it is the person who suffers. So, in the case before us, while the Son of God suffers in his human nature it is still the person which

* Eph. v. 2. 1 Tim. ii. 6. Heb. i. 3; vii. 27; ix. 26.

suffers. If, before we are entitled to say that a person suffers, all that pertains to him must suffer, it follows that we can never say a person dies, as the soul, an essential constituent part of the person, never dies.

But, granting that it is the person who suffers, it may still be said that the value of these sufferings is to be estimated only by the nature of that in which he suffers. When a martyr suffers death, as it is the body only that dies, there cannot belong to his death a worth proportioned to his soul. In like manner, when Christ suffers, as Deity cannot suffer, his sufferings, it may be said, can possess only the worth of humanity. But this is to leave out of consideration altogether a circumstance which is allowed by all to have the effect of increasing the value of certain acts and sufferings. The circumstance to which I refer is *dignity of character*. There are some things which are of the same value, by whomsoever performed. Money, for example, paid by a prince, is of no more mercantile value than money paid by any other man. But there are other things in which the case is widely different, their value depending, in some measure, on the dignity of him by whom they are performed. The relative value of certain actions depends on the rank in the scale of intellectual, or moral, or social being of the person who performs them. To the action of an inferior animal we attach less value than to that of a human creature;—to that of a man less, again, than to that of an angel. On the same principle, the action of a peasant and that of a king may differ materially, with regard to relative worth. In one point of view, the life of a slave and the life of a monarch are of equal value; they are both human creatures. But, in another point of view, the life of a king is of far greater value than the life of a slave: and the act of laying down his life involves a higher degree of worth in the one than in the other. This distinction is recognized in the address of the people to king David, when he would go forth with them to battle:—"Thou shalt not go forth: for if we flee away, they will not care for us; neither if half of us die, will they care for us:

but now THOU ART WORTH TEN THOUSAND OF US."* For a king to submit to excruciating tortures and an ignominious death, with a view to save some one of his subjects, will be reckoned by all a more meritorious piece of conduct than if such had been submitted to by one who held the place merely of a fellow subject. Yet here it might be said, it is humanity and not royalty which suffers, and why attach to it a value arising from the latter, rather than confine it to that which springs from the former circumstance? The case is parallel to that of which we are now speaking. The humanity of Christ alone could either suffer or die, but that humanity belonged to a person who is divine, and this gave to his sufferings and death the value of divinity.†

How it comes to pass, that the personal dignity of the sufferer conveys to the sufferings of his humanity a worth proportioned to *him* who suffers rather than to *that* which suffers, we pretend not fully to explain. The above observations, however, serve to show that the principle on which this is affirmed, is one on which we are not altogether unaccustomed to reason. It is not meant to be inferred that any analogies, such as

---

* 2 Sam. xviii. 3.

† " To suppose, because humanity only is capable of suffering, that therefore humanity only is necessary to atonement, is to render *dignity of character* of no account. When Zeleucus, one of the Grecian kings, had made a law against adultery, that whosoever was guilty of this crime should lose both his eyes, his own son is said to have been the first transgressor. To preserve the honor of the law, and at the same time to save his own son from total blindness, the father had recourse to an expedient of losing one of his own eyes, and his son one of his. This expedient, though it did not conform to the letter of the law, yet was well adapted to preserve the spirit of it, as it served to evince to the nation the determination of the king to punish adultery, as much, perhaps more than if the sentence had been put into execution against the offender. But if instead of this he had appointed that one eye of an animal should be put out in order to save that of his son, or if a common subject had offered to lose an eye, would either have answered the purpose? The animal and the subject were each possessed of an eye, as well as the sovereign. It might be added, too, that it was mere bodily pain; and seeing it was in the body only that this penalty could be endured, any being that possessed a body was equally capable of enduring it. True, they might endure it, but would their suffering answer the same end? Would it have satisfied justice? Would it have had the same effect upon the nation, or tended equally to restore the tone of injured authority ?"—Works of Andrew Fuller, vol. v p. 565.

that resorted to above, can give us a complete idea of the nature of a case which is transcendently and awfully peculiar. It is enough if they serve to neutralize the objections of such as are disposed to cavil at the truth. On a subject of this nature, it ill becomes us to speak either with carelessness or precipitation. It is to be approached only with cautious reverence. Here, if anywhere, we should be careful to be "lowly wise." Yet we may be permitted to show the reasonableness of a doctrine, and to expose the temerity and presumption of its adversaries, without laying ourselves open to the charge of being wise above what is written. The following statement may not altogether be without its use, in shedding a ray of light on this acknowledgedly great and profound mystery:—A person only can perform moral acts: The human nature of Christ possessed no personal subsistence: Of course, although the human nature of Christ alone could either suffer or obey, the obedience and sufferings of his humanity, viewed in themselves could have no moral character: To give them a moral character they must be viewed in connection with his person Whence it follows that, the obedience and sufferings of Christ, *physically* considered, possessed only the worth of humanity, but *morally* considered possessed a worth proportioned to the dignity of his divine person. Now, the sufferings and death of Christ for the sins of his people were of a moral character, being endured with a view to meet the claims of the divine moral government, to satisfy the law and justice of God. It follows that there attached to them all the value which divine dignity could impart.*

* On this delicate point, I beg to confirm the view I have given, by referring the reader to the following paragraphs by Dr. Pye Smith.

"I. The assumption of human nature by the eternal word, who is God, was the act of an infinite mind, knowing, intending, and contemplating all the *results* of that act of assumption, through the period of the designed humiliation and for ever. To the divine mind, nearness and remoteness of time or space are equal. Consequently, as the actual assumption of human nature was the first result of the omnipotent will, so the same act, or volition, must equally have carried forwards and communicated its original divine value to all the subsequent moral and mediatorial acts of the incarnate Saviour.

But we are more concerned with the evidence of the *fact*, than with the explanation of the *mode*, of this great and important truth. Those who hold the doctrine of Christ's divinity, can never hesitate to admit that the sufficiency or efficacy of his atonement springs from the supreme dignity of his person as the Son of God. The validity of his sacrifice takes its rise from his true and essential divinity. To this the testimony of Scripture is distinctly borne. The epistle to the Hebrews, which treats professedly of the insufficiency of the legal sacrifices, and the intrinsic validity of that of Christ, commences with an elaborate demonstration of Christ's divinity, as the basis on which the subsequent reasoning is made to rest. The High Priest of the Christian profession is explicitly shown to be the brightness of the Father's glory and the express image of his person; to be much better than the angels; to be God whose throne is forever and ever; to be Jehovah who laid the foundations of the earth, who shall remain when all else has perished, who is the same and his years shall not fail. While, in another part of the

"II. The union of the divine and human natures, in his person, was constant and invariable. The Scriptures afford us no reason to think that the Messiah's human nature, though retaining always its essential properties, had ever a separate subsistence. To the mother of Jesus it was announced, 'The holy Being which is born of thee, shall be called the Son of God:' and according to the prophetic declaration, as soon as men could say, 'Unto us a child is born,' so soon was it the fact that his name was called 'The Wonderful, the Counsellor, the Mighty God.' It was the Mediator, *in his whole person*, that acted for the salvation of man; though it was impossible that the divine nature could be subject to suffering.

"From these two positions I infer a third, which I venture to propose, as an unexceptionable mode of stating this important, though profound and difficult subject:—

"III. All the acts of our Lord Jesus Christ that were physical, or merely intellectual, were acts of his human nature alone, being necessary to the subsistence of a human nature: but all his moral acts, and all the moral qualities of his complex acts; or, in other terms, all that he did in and for the execution of his mediatorial office and work,—were impressed with the essential dignity and moral value of his divine perfection.

"These reasons appear to me sufficient to authorize our attributing to this holy sacrifice, a value *properly* INFINITE, on account of the divine nature of him who offered it. A most important conclusion! Rich in blessing to the contrite sinner: full of joy to the obedient believer."— Disc. on Sac., pp. 69—71.

book, the blood of Christ is represented as deriving its superiority over the ceremonial sacrifices, from its being offered "THROUGH THE ETERNAL SPIRIT"—a phrase understood by some of our most eminent critics and divines to refer to the divine dignity of his person. " How much more shall the blood of Christ, who through the Eternal Spirit offered himself without spot of God, purge your conscience from dead works to serve the living God."* It is because *Jesus Christ* is God's *Son* that his blood possesses intrinsic validity *to cleanse from all sin.* The value of the gift and the sufficiency of the propitiatory sacrifice arise from the same circumstance. " *God sent his* SON *to be the propitiation for our sins.*"†

II. But this is not all. *Relationship of nature to those for whom the atonement was made,* is an essential element in its validity.

Christ required to be real and proper *man*, as much as the true *God*. To qualify him for making atonement he must possess opposite attributes, a frail and mortal nature combined with ineffable dignity of person. We allude not now to the necessity of the incarnation to *fit* the Messiah for suffering, to render him *susceptible* of pain and death, to make the offering of himself as a sacrifice a thing *possible.* We refer rather to the possession of human nature as imparting a character of *worth* or *validity* to what he did. This was requisite, not more to *enable* him to suffer, than to impart to his sufferings an essential *value* in the estimation of the divine law. Had the work of our redemption been a mere mercantile transaction, it mattered not by whom the price might have been paid. But being a moral satisfaction to the law of God for the sins of men, there existed a moral fitness or necessity that the satisfaction should be made by one in the nature of those who had sinned and were to be redeemed. The redeemer behooved, as of old, to be a kinsman, a brother. Without this, neither could the moral government of God be vindicated, nor the glory of the divine Lawgiver maintained, nor the

* Heb. ix. 14. † 1 John iv. 10.

principles of the law upheld. The law in its precept was suited to man, and in its curse it had a claim upon man. Its requirements were such as man only could fulfil; its penalty such as one possessing the nature of man only could bear. The penalty was *suffering even unto death;* and no angel, no one who had not a body as well as a soul, could die. The death only of a man could possess a moral and legal congruity to the curse of a law given to man and broken by man. It was not, then, merely to qualify him for suffering that the Messiah took upon him the nature of man, but to qualify him for *such* suffering as should possess validity in the eye of the divine law. *But he that sanctifieth and they who are sanctified* must be ALL OF ONE.* *Therefore in all things it behooved him to be made* LIKE UNTO HIS BRETHREN, *that he might make reconciliation for the sins of the people. Since by* MAN *came death, by* MAN *came also the resurrection of the dead.* The serpent's head could be cruised, only by the SEED OF THE WOMAN.†

III. *Freedom himself from all personal obligation to suffer*, is another essential ingredient in the value of Christ's atonement.

He who makes atonement for others must himself be entirely free from that which renders the atonement necessary. What renders atonement necessary is sin. But Jesus was altogether holy. It would seem to be a dictate of reason and common sense, that vicarious punishment cannot be borne by one who is himself a sharer in the guilt which calls for it. The law, in this case, has a previous claim upon him. His own state renders an atonement necessary. He cannot remove his own guilt by his sufferings, and how can it be possible that he should remove the guilt of others? A substitutionary victim must itself be perfectly spotless and pure.

This was plainly enough pointed out in the Levitical law. The high priest was required to possess a high degree of ceremonial purity. Perfect moral purity

---

* *i. e.* all of one nature.
† Heb. ii. 11, 17; 1 Cor. xv. 21; Gen. iii. 15.

was impossible; but the necessity of this in the antitype, was sufficiently taught, by this legal functionary being required to be free from all bodily defect or deformity, to be the son of one who was a virgin and not a widow when married to his father, and by his being exempted from certain methods of contracting ceremonial defilement. The sacrificial victim, also, was to be a lamb *without blemish and without spot.* To the same purpose was it enacted that the red heifer should not only be one *without spot wherein was no blemish,* but one *upon which never came yoke.**
All this, doubtless, was designed to shadow forth the immaculate purity of the great High-Priest of our profession, who put away sin by the sacrifice of himself.

In virtue of his spotless innocence, Jesus was completely free from all manner of legal obligation to suffer, arising from himself. Legal obligation to the curse may arise from one or both of two things: either from being born under the curse, that is to say, from original sin; or from becoming exposed to the penalty in consequence of a personal breach of its requirements, that is, by actual transgression. Infants of the human family are under it in the former way; adults in both: but Jesus was neither the one nor the other.

He was free from all actual sin. His obedience to the divine law, under which he voluntarily brought himself, was complete. His thoughts were ever pure; guile was not found in his mouth; and he did always those things that pleased his Father. As regarded God, he fully exemplified the duties of religion;—cherishing every pious emotion of love, faith, gratitude, patience, and submission; and scrupulously performing, with punctuality and exactness, every act of devotion, meditation, prayer, praise, and attendance on the services of public worship. As respected men, every social duty, whether of affection and obedience and respect to relatives, or of kindness and fidelity to friends, or of justice and equity and benevolence and

* Num. xix. 2. Deut. xxi. 3.

integrity in general society, was fully exhibited. Nor were the personal duties of temperance, sobriety, circumspection, and self-command, less strictly observed by him.

These are not unsupported assertions. The testimony borne to the innocence of the Saviour's life is most complete and decisive. Prophets spake of him as the "Holy One," who "had done no violence, neither was any deceit in his mouth." The angel announced him as "that holy thing" which should be born of Mary. Himself said, "I do always those things that please the Father—Which of you convinceth me of sin?—The prince of this world cometh and hath nothing in me." His apostles spoke of him as one "who knew no sin"—who was "without sin"—"who was holy, harmless, undefiled, and separate from sinners"—"who did no sin, neither was guilt found in his mouth"—one, of whom it could be said, "in him is no sin." But the most decisive testimony of all is that which was borne by his inveterate enemies. The Jews, who were brim-full of prejudice against his person and claims, were unwillingly compelled to affirm, "He hath done all things well."—The traitor who gave him up to his enemies, exclaimed, under the agonies of conviction, "I have sinned in that I have betrayed *innocent* blood." The judge, who unjustly doomed him to the cross, acknowledged, "I find no fault in this man." Nay, even the fallen spirits were forced to confess, saying, "Let us alone: what have we to do with thee, thou Jesus of Nazareth? Art thou come to destroy us? I know thee who thou art, THE HOLY ONE of God."* Such is the evidence that Christ did not bring himself under the curse.

Some of these passages are quite as decisive in favor of the innocence of the Saviour's *nature*, as of that of his life. That he was not *born* under the curse is as unequivocally taught as that he did not *bring himself* under it. Indeed, an innocent life

---

* Psalm xvi. 10. Isa. liii. 9. Luke i. 35. John viii. 29, 46; xiv. 30. 2 Cor. v. 21. Heb. iv. 15; vii. 26. 1 Pet. ii. 22. 1 John iii. 5. Mark vii. 37. Matt. xxiii. 4. Luke xxiii. 4. Mark i. 24.

would seem to afford very satisfactory proof of an innocent nature. We can conceive of a holy nature lapsing into sin, as has been exemplified both in angels and men; but how a holy life, a life free from the slightest taint of corruption, could spring from a nature in every degree corrupt, is, we must say, to us utterly inconceivable. It seems a natural impossibility. An impure fountain cannot but send forth impure streams: a corrupt tree cannot but bear corrupt fruit. To contend therefore, as some have done, for the sinlessness of the Saviour's life, and yet to maintain the sinfulness of his nature, appears to us to be grossly contradictory and paradoxical. But of the strict innocence of the Saviour's *nature*, of its perfect freedom from whatever should entitle it to the character of "fallen," we should reckon his own words as decisive:—"The prince of this world hath nothing IN ME." To the same effect is the testimony of the writer of the epistle to the Hebrews:—" Who is *holy*," (ὅσιος,) signifying purity of nature, as distinguished from "harmless," (ἄκακος,) meaning freedom from evil in respect of external conduct, and also from "undefiled," (ἀμίαντος,) which seems to denote purity of official qualification and administration. Nor can there be anything more unequivocal than the language of the angel, when, making known his miraculous birth, he calls him " that Holy thing,"(τὸ ἅγιον.) This refers to what was conceived and born of Mary; not "fallen and sinful flesh," but a "holy thing," essentially and naturally holy from the first moment of its existence.

The miraculous nature of the conception of our Lord's humanity affords additional proof of this point. By being born of a virgin, being in a peculiar sense the seed of the woman, the human nature of Christ escaped all connection with the Adamic covenant. It was at once connected with the race of man, and yet free from the contamination springing from Adam's federal representation of his natural descendants. This is what constitutes the incarnation the great mystery of godliness, and but for this it is not only not easy to assign any good reason for the miraculous nature of his conception at all, but even difficult to vindicate it from consequences that are necessarily and positively injurious. If, even notwithstanding its miraculous production, his human nature was fallen and sinful, one can scarce help asking for what purpose a miracle was wrought at all in the matter, seeing that fallen and sinful humanity could have been produced without any miracle whatever. But the miracle was not only in this respect useless: it was, at the same time, calculated to convey the impression that the human nature of Christ differed essentially, in this particular, from man's nature in general,—an impression which, on the supposition against which we are contending, was false and delusive.

We wait not to argue the holiness of Christ's human nature from the oneness of his person; from the necessity of such holiness to his being a proper example to his people; from the impossibility otherwise of his death being voluntary; and from his having survived the conflict with the powers of darkness and the enemy death, which is not else to be accounted for. The discussion of these points would carry us too far away from our general design. But we deem it necessary to mention them. How full, and varied, and unequivocal the testimony of Scripture may be, there are many who will not hesitate unceremoniously to set aside the evidence of particular texts, by having recourse to some vague or loose mode of interpretation. For the sake of such, it must be made known, that the view taken of these particular texts is fully borne out and supported by certain general principles, which, while they harmonize with the meaning attached to individual passages of Scripture, themselves peremptorily and independently require us to admit the immaculate holiness of Christ's atoning sacrifice.

The perfect innocence of the Saviour's nature and life—thus, we hope, satisfactorily established—enters essentially into that which constitutes the moral worth or intrinsic value of his vicarious sufferings. It shows him to have been free from all legal obligation to suffering in himself. The law of God had in this way no claim upon him for subjection to its curse; and he was thus far at liberty to suffer the penalty due to sin on behalf of others. It is on this principle that the apostle speaks of his personal innocence as essential to his sacerdotal character and work. "Such an high priest," says he, "became us, who is *holy, harmless, undefiled, separate from sinners*, and made higher than the heavens, *who needeth not daily to offer up sacrifice first for his own sins*, and then for the people's."

IV. It was further necessary to the validity of Christ's atonement that he should be *entirely at his own disposal.*

It is not enough that the substitute, being innocent, is free from the claims of the law to which he gives satisfaction for others. He may be under obligations to another law, the fulfilment of whose demands may render it impossible for him to occupy the place of a surety. His whole time and energies may be thus, as it were, previously engaged, so as to put it out of his power to make a transfer of any part of them for the behoof of others. This is, indeed, the case with all creatures. Whatever service they are capable of performing, they owe originally and necessarily to God. They are, from their very nature, incapable of meriting anything for *themselves*, much more for *others*. The right of self-disposal belongs not to creatures. Themselves and all that pertains to them, are the property of Him who made and preserves them. They are under law to God, and at liberty to dispose of themselves only as that law directs. It thus appears that an angel of light, though perfectly innocent, and free from all the claims of the particular legal constitution under which man is bound over to punishment, could not have furnished a sacrifice, of value to atone for human guilt. Angels are creatures, and as such, are necessarily under law to God. They are not under the covenant which God made with man, to be sure; but the law under which they exist demands all their energies, it has a claim upon them for the full amount of the service they are capable of performing, and thus denies them all right of giving satisfaction to another law, in behalf of a different order of creatures.

But the Son of God, not being a creature, was originally under no law. He was perfectly at his own disposal. Whatever he might choose, of his own free will, to do or to suffer, was what no existing law had a previous right to. He was not only not under the law which man had broken, but he was under no other law; he was not only innocent, but free to dispose of himself as might seem to him to be fit. He was Lord of all, and subject to none. He, and he only, was entitled to assume such language as this:—" Therefore doth my Father love me, because I lay down my life that I might take it again. No man taketh it from me. but I lay it down of myself: I HAVE POWER TO LAY IT DOWN, and I HAVE POWER TO TAKE IT AGAIN." He here not merely claims to have acted voluntarily, but to have had a right, a legal right, (ἐξουσία) so to do. This is what no creature could ever say. In giving his life a ransom for many, Christ gave what was strictly his own, and entirely at his own disposal. Without this, it does not appear that what he did could have been possessed of value; subjection to one law could not have been yielded without the violation of another, and this was sufficient to deprive it of all moral worth.

V. Christ, in making atonement, was perfectly *voluntary;* and here we have another ingredient in its value.

Without this, it is clear, all the other ingredients were of no avail. Let his person be ever so dignified; let him be ever so closely related to man; let him be as free as possible from all moral contamination; nay, let him be entirely at his own disposal, it is manifest that, unless he chose actually to dispose of himself in the manner in question, no validity could attach to what he did. Vicarious satisfaction can never be compulsory: voluntariness enters into its very essence. Every well-ordered mind revolts at the idea of one person being *compelled* to suffer for another. Such an act involves the highest injustice and the supposition of attempting to satisfy the claims of infinite rectitude by what amounts to a direct violation of the principle of equity, is too monstrous and shocking ever to be entertained. The sacrifice must not be dragged to the altar. So much is this a dictate of reason, that even the heathen reckoned it an unpropitious omen, if the animal showed any reluctance.

In all that he did to make atonement for sin, Jesus manifested no degree of reluctance. At every step we meet with evidence of the most perfect willingness. To the proposal in the eternal covenant he gave his cheerful consent,—" Sacrifice and offering thou didst not desire, burnt-offering and sin-offering hast thou not required. Then said I, Lo, I come: in the volume of the book it is written of me, I delight to do thy will, O my God; yea, thy law is within my heart."* It was the same spirit that dictated the well-known reply to his mother, when yet young,—"How is it that ye sought me? Wist ye not that I must be about my Father's business."† At a later period he said, "I lay down my life: no man ($οὐδείς$, no one) taketh it from me, but I lay it down of myself.‡ In no instance did he manifest the slightest symptom of backwardness. The inspired writers speak of him as submitting to every suffering with a fixed determination of purpose which nothing could shake. "He *gave* his back to the smiters and his cheeks to them that plucked off the hair—He *gave* himself a ransom for all—He *gave* himself for us—He bowed his head and *gave* up the ghost."§

His death was as voluntary as any part of his sufferings. The Roman soldiers, indeed, were employed in crucifying him; and this instrumentality was necessary to prevent his being involved in the guilt of suicide. But we err egregiously if we suppose that, notwithstanding of this, he died otherwise than voluntarily. "I lay down my life; no one taketh it from me," is his own unequivocal and emphatic language. He died, neither from disease nor exhaustion. Just be-

* Psalm xl. 6—8.   † Luke ii. 49.   ‡ John x 17 18.
§ Isa. l. 6, 1 Tim. ii. 6, Eph. v. 25. John xix. 30

fore he expired, ne had strength enough to cry with a loud voice, "It is finished." He could then, or at any other moment, had it so pleased him, have stepped down from the cross, to the confusion of those who assailed him with the bitter taunt, "If thou be the Christ, come down from the cross and save thyself." But then, the Scriptures should not have been fulfilled nor the redemption of man have been effected. Nevertheless, his own decisive words, as well as the fact of his divinity, leave us without a doubt that, had he not cheerfully given it up of his own accord, earth or hell could not have wrung from him his life. Neither could cruel men, nor hellish hosts have borne off his body in triumph to the grave, had he not freely resolved to descend into the tomb. The very time of his death was that of his own choice; for neither could the barbarities of his persecutors precipitate, nor the lingering punishment of crucifixion protract it beyond the period in which he determined himself to yield up the ghost; and, accordingly, when the soldiers came to break his legs, they found that he was dead already.

The voluntary nature of the Saviour's death, it may here be remarked by the way, affords a strong argument in proof of the divinity of his person, and also of the spotless innocence of his humanity. Had he been a creature, even a super-angelic creature, brought into being for the purpose of dying for us, his death could not have been said to be voluntary. Much less could this be said if his human nature had been in any sense sinful, for then he must have died of necessity not of free-will; he must have died, as has been said "by the common property of flesh to die because it was accursed in the loins of our first parents," and then the doctrine of atonement, with all its comforting influences, must have been given up.

This willingness of Christ to suffer and to die, was not the result of ignorance. A person may thoughtlessly engage to submit to treatment, of the amoun of which he may not, at the moment of engagement be aware; and, when the reality comes to be known he may, from the force of honor or some such principle, persevere in his determination to suffer. But such suffering could scarcely be called voluntary. Such, at all events, was not that of Christ. He knew, from the first, the full amount of what he was to endure. It was, with the perfect knowledge of all that should befall him in the Jewish capital, that "he steadfastly set his face to go to Jerusalem."* It was, knowing every bitter ingredient that was infused into the mingled chalice of woe, that he said, "The cup which my Father hath given me, shall I not drink it?"† It was, with a full understanding of all the terrors with which that cloud of Jehovah's wrath was charged, which was soon to burst in awful vengeance on his head, that he magnanimously exclaimed, "I have a baptism to be baptized with, and how am I straitened till it be accomplished."‡ It was no sudden impulse of transient enthusiasm which moved the Son of God to undertake the work of our redemption. It was no momentary movement of generous pity, which the experience of difficulties and dangers might cool or extirpate. No. It was a settled and immovable purpose, which time and obstacles only served to strengthen and confirm. Instead of shrinking from dangers, and seeking excuses for desisting from his expressed determination, his fortitude seemed to gather power in proportion as he approached the final scene of complete woe; and, it is remarkable, that the only occasion on which he ever used language that might be said to indicate a degree of intemperate feeling, was when an attempt was made to dissuade him from suffering. On representing to his disciples that he must go up to Jerusalem and suffer many things, Peter presumed to expostulate with him, saying, "Be it far from thee, Lord: this shall not be unto thee;" but he turned and said unto Peter, "Get thee behind me, Satan; thou art an offence unto me: for thou savorest not the things that be of God, but those that be of men."§

* Luke ix. 51.   † John xviii. 11.   ‡ Luke xii. 50.
§ Matt. xvi. 22, 23.

From all this it appears, that the work of Christ, in giving himself up to suffer and die for us, was strictly voluntary. In no step of that glorious undertaking, was he constrained by anything but his own free will and matchless love. It was a high act of sovereign grace; not a boon forcibly wrung from a reluctant benefactor. To deny this, is to destroy altogether its efficacy. "It is of the utmost importance for us to know," as has been beautifully observed, " that through every step of the painful process through which he passed, the benefits derived to us by his sufferings, were not by constraint wrung from him, but willingly purchased for us; that he was not bound to endurance by the iron chain of his own fallen and sinful personal constitution, but by the golden chain of that love to God, whose glorious perfections he was manifesting to the universe, and of that love to men through whose salvation he was making the manifestation, which no waters could quench, and no floods could drown."*

VI. There is one ingredient still necessary. It is of such essential importance as to have been supposed by many to be all that is requisite. In a compensatory arrangement, such as the atonement is, both parties must be voluntary. Not only must the one party be willing to make the compensation; the other must be willing to accept of it when made. *The appointment of the Father* is no less important than the voluntary engagement of the Son; and this, we have now to state, is a prerequisite to validity which the work of Christ distinctly possessed.

The necessity of divine appointment will appear, if it is considered, that God, being the party offended by man's sin, had a right to determine whether sin should be pardoned at all, and if, to be pardoned, on what ground. It was not enough, that a person heroic and benevolent enough should be found, to offer to substitute himself in the place of the guilty. To the offended sovereign does it belong to determine whether the proposed substitution shall serve all the ends of justice Of this He is the only judge. And, suppos-

* Dods, p. 126.

ing him satisfied on this point, it is still a part of his sovereign prerogative to determine whether he shall be pleased to accept of this, or shall insist that the penalty be inflicted on the person offending. To say otherwise, is to hold the monstrous opinion, that the Almighty could be compelled to adopt a line of procedure pointed out by another. In short, the acceptance of commutative satisfaction is such a deviation from the ordinary course of legislative wisdom, that none but the sovereign legislator himself is qualified to say when it may be wise and proper to put forth so high an exertion of the dispensing power. The power of dispensing, in any particular, with the laws, can reside only in him who has the power of making the laws. Now, in the case before us, there is a dispensing with the letter of the law as far as it requires the personal punishment of the offender. It is thus clear as noon-day that, had not God voluntarily consented to accept of the sufferings of Christ, these sufferings, however otherwise precious, could have been of no avail. They might have been rejected, as an unauthorized interference with the regular flow of legislative procedure. No security could have existed for their ever being accepted. Intrinsically valuable though they were, they might have been relatively worthless; and, as regards the grand design of appeasing the wrath of God, the precious blood of Christ might have been as water spilt upon the ground.

The evidence that the sacrifice of Christ was appointed by God is happily as satisfactory as the necessity for the appointment is indispensable. In giving himself for our sins that he might redeem us from the present evil world, he acted " according to the will of God, even our Father." * It was in consequence of no fortuitous concurrence of circumstances, or private overture of benevolence, that Jesus died, but from " being delivered by the determinate counsel and foreknowledge of God."† The character in which he suffered was stamped with the authority of a divine delegation,—" I was set up from everlasting, from the

* Gal. i. 4. † Acts ii. 23.

beginning, or ever the earth was."* At the very time that he claims for himself the character of entire self-devotement, he fails not to point distinctly to his commission from above,—"I have power to lay it down, and I have power to take it again. *This commandment have I received of my Father.*"† Just before entering on the final scene of woe to which so much importance is attached, did he say, "As the Father gave me *commandment* so I do; arise, let us go hence."‡ Not less decisive is the testimony of the apostles. "Whom," says Paul, "God hath *set forth* (foreordained, προέθετο) to be a propitiation through faith in his blood."§ "For of a truth," says Peter, "against thy holy child Jesus, whom thou hast anointed, both Herod and Pontius Pilate, with the Gentiles, and the people of Israel, were gathered together, for to do whatsoever thy hand and thy counsel *determined before* to be done." And again, "Ye were not redeemed with corruptible things as silver and gold—but with the precious blood of Christ, as of a lamb without blemish and without spot, who verily was *foreordained* before the foundation of the world."‖ In beautiful harmony with these testimonies is the descriptive language of the beloved disciple. "The Lamb slain *from the foundation of the world.*"¶ Thus does it fully appear that, in making atonement for our sins, Jesus acted, not only with the full consent, but under the high commission of God. He it was who awaked, by his vindictive call, the fiery sword of vengeance against the Shepherd, the man that was his fellow, which continued to smite with relentless severity till justice was satisfied, and could not be quiet because *the Lord had given it a charge.* So true is it that "the Father sent the Son to be the Saviour of the world."

These are circumstances, then, which constitute the validity of Christ's atonement. They are all of them necessary; not one can be dispensed with. Exclude

* Prov. viii. 23. † John x. 18. ‡ John xiv. 31.
§ Rom. iii. 25. ‖ Acts iv. 27, 28. Pet. i. 19. 20. ¶ Rev. xiii 8.

any one of them, and it will be instantly seen to nullity all the rest. They resolve themselves into supreme divinity, perfect humanity, and divine appointment. These, not singly but together, are what conferred on the sufferings and death of our Mediator that high character of intrinsic and relative worth, which rendered them a complete atonement to the law and justice of God for the sins of men. Without these, they had had no efficacy. In this case, the dying conqueror had never given utterance to the expiring shout of exultation, " It is finished :" Never had he arisen from the grave, and ascended to glory, and sat down at the right hand of God, amid the welcoming shouts of enraptured seraphim : The mediatorial glory which eclipses the splendors of the shekinah, had never thrown around him its celestial radiance : Nor had the sceptre of universal empire ever been put into his hand. From the perfection of his atonement, arising out of the circumstances specified above, does it proceed, that he makes intercession for us within the vail of the upper sanctuary; that he dispenses with a munificent hand the gifts of his purchase, and causes the prey of a great spoil to be divided. And peace, and pardon, and redemption, and holiness, and eternal glory, are among the rich fruits of the royal and triumphant conquest he achieved, when, by his infinitely meritorious death, he spoiled principalities and powers, and made a show of them openly. With the most entire confidence, then, may the needy sinner, smitten with the deepest sense of conscious unworthiness, rely for salvation on this all-sufficient atonement.

SECTION XI.

EXTENT OF CHRIST'S ATONEMENT

The point of which we are now to treat has been extensively agitated, as well in ancient as in modern times. At a very remote period, Faustus, the leader of the Pelagians, and Sirmandus, an acknowledged Semipelagian, advocated the sentiment that Christ died for all men; and were opposed by Augustine, Prosper, Fulgentius, Remigius, and other fearless defenders of the truth. In the Romish church, this controversy was carried on with no small degree of warmth, the Jesuits espousing the one side, and the Jansenists the other. From the Papists it passed to the Protestants, Lutherans and Arminians advocating the cause of universality, while the Calvinists contended for a definite or restricted extent. The opinion of the remonstrants on this topic was pointedly condemned by the synod of Dort.* It still constitutes a prominent feature in the controversy between Arminians and Calvinists; and even some, who are otherwise free from the Arminian taint, have adopted notions on this point that are at variance with the Calvinistic creed. Thd Hopkinsian controversy, which has of late distracted the American churches, involves, amongst its peculiarities, the point in question. And in our own country, as cannot but be known to many of our readers, the question respecting the extent of Christ's atonement has been agitated of late with considerable keenness; nor has the side of what we conceive to be truth, been always espoused by those who are otherwise evangelical in their doctrinal opinions.

I. Before going into anything like argument, it will be proper to attend to some preliminary EXPLANATIONS.
On the extent of Christ's atonement, the two opin-

---
* Turretini Institutio, vol. ii. pp. 495, 496.

ions that have long divided the church are expressed by the terms *definite* and *indefinite*. The former means that Christ died, satisfied divine justice, and made atonement, *only for such as are saved*. The latter means that Christ died, satisfied divine justice, or made atonement, for *all mankind without exception*, as well those who are not saved as those who are. The one regards the death of Christ as a *legal satisfaction* to the law and justice of God on behalf of elect sinners: the other regards it as a *general moral vindication* of the divine government, without respect to those to whom it may be rendered effectual, and of course equally applicable to all. The former opinion, or what is called *definite* atonement, is that which we adopt, and which we shall endeavor to explain, prove, and defend, in our subsequent observations. It may be thus stated:—THAT THE LORD JESUS CHRIST MADE ATONEMENT TO GOD BY HIS DEATH, ONLY FOR THE SINS OF THOSE, TO WHOM, IN THE SOVEREIGN GOOD PLEASURE OF THE ALMIGHTY, THE BENEFITS OF HIS DEATH SHALL BE FINALLY APPLIED. By this definition, the extent of Christ's atonement is limited to those who ultimately enjoy its fruits; it is restricted to the elect of God, for whom *alone* we conceive him to have laid down his life. However, to prevent mistakes, and to give us a clear understanding of the point in dispute, it may be necessary to offer a few explanatory remarks.

1. The point in dispute, let it be carefully observed, does not respect *the intrinsic worth* of Christ's death. This is admitted, on both hands, to be *infinite*. There is no room for controversy here. As has been shown in the preceding section, the inherent worth of Christ's atonement arises not from the nature, intensity, or continuance of his sufferings, but from his personal dignity and other concurrent circumstances, which stamp a character of infinite value on all that he endured. On this ground we hold that the sacrifice of the Lord Jesus Christ possessed an intrinsic value *sufficient* for the salvation of the whole world. In this sense it was adequate to the redemption of every human being— able to procure the expiation of every man's sins that

ever existed or ever shall exist to the end of time Here we feel no hesitation; nor can we qualify these assertions in the slightest degree. We shall yield to none in our estimate of the intrinsic worth of Christ's atonement. That worth we hold to be, in the strictest sense of the term, INFINITE—ABSOLUTE—ALL-SUFFICIENT. If sufficiency were the point on which the controversy turned, it might soon be ended; and we are strongly inclined to believe, that nothing more than this is meant by many of those who contend for Christ's having died for all men: it is with such persons a mistake of words more than of opinion. In the fullest sense of the terms, then, we regard the atonement of Christ as SUFFICIENT FOR ALL. This all-sufficiency is what lays foundation for the unrestricted universality of the Gospel call. And from every such view of the atonement as would imply that it was not sufficient for all, or that there was not an ample warrant in the invitations of the Gospel for all to look to it for salvation, we utterly dissent. Against every such limitation or restriction we enter our solemn and deliberate protest, as alike dishonoring to Christ, and unwarranted by the testimony of Scripture. Nor would we hesitate for a moment to adopt the following strong protestation of an eminent writer, as expressive of our own settled conviction on the subject: —"Such is my impression of its sufficiency, that were all the guilt of all the millions of mankind that have ever lived concentrated in my own person, I should see no reason, relying on that blood which *cleanseth from all sin*, to indulge despair."*

2. Neither does the present controversy turn on the *application* of Christ's atonement. The extent of application is also allowed, on both hands, to be limited. Our opponents must admit that the atonement is *made effectual only to some*. Only such as believe, ultimately come to share in the benefits of the Redeemer's purchase; and it is admitted that all men have not faith. There have been persons—as Puccius and Huberas among the ancients—who have maintained

* Dr. Wardlaw.

that all men actually reap the saving benefits of Christ's blood; and there are those even in our own day, who contend for the ultimate eternal welfare of the whole race of mankind: but as these sentiments are held in connection with the most vague and erroneous views of the nature of the Redeemer's work, in connection in short with a denial of the doctrine of atonement, with those who maintain them we cannot consider ourselves as having at present any dispute. Those with whom we contend restrict the application of atonement to believers, while they allow that many shall perish finally and eternally in a state of unbelief.

3. The present question, then, hinges solely on the *divine intention* regarding the subjects of atonement, or what is called the *destination* of Christ's death. This, some maintain, extends to all mankind, without exception, and not to those merely who are saved by it in the end. This is the turning point of the controversy. The question is not, whether Christ's atonement is sufficient for all, or whether all finally enjoy the benefit of his atonement: but whether it was the secret design, intention, or determination of God that his Son should make atonement for all, or only for the select specified number who are finally saved. Now, confining ourselves to the divine intention or design regarding the objects of the atonement, there are only these supposable cases, one of which must constitute the truth on this important and much litigated point:— The design or intention of God must have been, that his Son should make atonement by his death;—either for SOME of the sins of ALL men—or for ALL the sins of ALL men—or for ALL the sins of SOME men—or for t..e sins of NO man in particular, but for SIN IN GENERAL. The first of these suppositions we do not know to be held by any, nor is this wonderful, when it is considered, that to die for only some of the sins of men would avail nothing for salvation, as what remained unatoned for would be sufficient to insure condemnation. The second and the fourth are involved in one another, as the advocates of universal or indefinite atonement seem to mean, by Christ's dying for the sins

of all men, that his death was a moral satisfaction to the divine law for sin in general, which, without a designed reference to any one in particular, was capable of being applied to all. Now this is the sentiment which we mean to oppose, by proving and vindicating the third supposition, namely, that it was the design or intention of God that his Son should make atonement for ALL the sins of SOME men only.

II. These explanations prepare the way for the PROOF that the atonement is definite or limited as to its extent, that is to say, that Christ made atonement for the sins of only some men.

1. And here we appeal, first of all, to *the speciality and immutability of the divine purpose respecting the subjects of salvation.*

We enter not on the wide field of controversy connected with the doctrine of divine decrees. A sovereign act of election from all everlasting is admitted, we believe, by those with whom we at present contend. Indeed, it is difficult to see how this can be denied by any who believe in the wisdom and foreknowledge of God, or who pay respect to the direct testimony of Scripture. It is admitted that there is such a thing as salvation, and that this salvation is the privilege, not of all, but only of some of the human race. It must also be admitted, that, in effecting salvation, the Divine Being acts agreeably to a preconceived plan or designed arrangement. To deny this is to impute to the infinitely wise God conduct such as we ascribe only to the most foolish and thoughtless among men; conduct such as is exemplified in no other department of the Almighty's works, for in all of them we meet with such order and regularity as evince the existence of an original purpose or design. Well, then, if God, in the matter of salvation, acts according to design, and it so happens that salvation is limited in its application to some, does it not follow that it was the design of God that it should be so limited? And, if it was the eternal purpose of God that only some should be saved by the death of Christ, with what propriety can it be held that it was his design that Christ should die for all? Does not this amount to the supposition, that God designed his Son should die for some to whom it was not his design that his death should be effectual? That is to say, that it was God's design that the death of Christ should be ineffectual with regard to some of those for whom it was designed—that God designed the existence of a cause which should not be attended with its designed effect. This appears to us to be unworthy a Being of infinite wisdom, and at variance with the direct Scripture testimony, that *whom he did predestinate to be conformed to the image of his Son, them he also called, and whom he called them he also justified, and whom he justified them he also glorified.*

Besides, the purposes of God must be allowed to be immutable. Scripture asserts, and reason approves the assertion, that his *counsel stands and he will do all his pleasure.* All the designs of a Being of infinite wisdom and almighty power must be fulfilled. It is impossible to see how they can ever be frustrated. To assert that they can, savors of blasphemy. If, therefore, it was the design of God that Christ should make atonement for all, this design must be accomplished in the salvation of all. But, if the fact is that only some are saved, it must have been the design of God that atonement should be made only for some, else the designs of God may be frustrated—the intentions of the divine will may be disappointed. If it was the purpose of God that atonement should be made for all, and yet the fact turns out to be that only some are benefited by the atonement, how comes it about that it fails with regard to the others? It cannot be from any deficiency of knowledge, for God is omniscient. It cannot be from any deficiency of wisdom, for his understanding is infinite. It cannot be from any alteration of affection, for he rests in his love. It cannot be from any defect of power, for his arm is omnipotent, and who hath resisted his will? We are reduced to the conclusion that the design of God, whatever it is, is infallibly accomplished, and of course, are compelled to adopt the opinion, that, as the atonement actually extends but to some, it was the original purpose of the divine will that it should not extend further. The fact is the best interpreter of the divine intention.

2. *The rectitude of the divine character* conducts to the same inference.

Shall not the Judge of all the earth do right? A God of truth, and without iniquity, just and right is he. Reason, conscience, revelation, and providence all concur in attesting this perfection of his nature. The Supreme Being gives to every one his due. This principle cannot be violated in a single instance. He cannot, according to this, either remit sin without satisfaction, or punish sin where satisfaction for it has been received. The one is as inconsistent with perfect equity as the other. If the punishment for sin has been borne, the remission of the offence follows of course. The principles of rectitude suppose this, nay peremptorily demand it; justice could not be satisfied without it. Agreeably to this reasoning it follows, that the death of Christ being a legal satisfaction for sin, all for whom he died must enjoy the remission of their offences. It is as much at variance with strict justice or equity that any for whom Christ has given satisfaction should continue under condemnation, as that they should have been delivered from guilt without a satisfaction being given for them at all. But it is admitted that all are not delivered from the punishment of sin, that there are many who perish in final condemnation. We are therefore compelled to infer, that for such no satisfaction has been given to the claims of infinite justice—no atonement has been made. If this is denied, the monstrous impossibility must be maintained, that the infallible Judge refuses to remit the punishment of some for whose offences he has received a full com pensation; that he finally condemns some, the price of whose deliverance from condemnation has been paid to him; that, with regard to the sins of some of mankind, he seeks satisfaction in their personal punishment after having obtained satisfaction for them in the sufferings of Christ; that is to say, that an infinitely righteous God takes double payment for the same debt, double satisfaction for the same offence, first from the surety, and then from those for whom the surety stood bound. It is needless to add that these conclusions are revolting to every right feeling of equity, and must be totally inapplicable to the procedure of Him who "*loveth righteousness and hateth wickedness*"

3. Let *the connection of the atonement with the covenant of grace* be considered, and farther confirmation will be given to our argument.

The Scriptures represent the divine persons as entering into a federal agreement for the salvation of men. In this covenant of peace, the Father is the representative of the Godhead, and the Son representative of those who are to be redeemed. He is on this account called the Mediator and the Surety of the covenant. Whatever he did as Mediator or Surety, must, therefore, have been done in connection with the covenant. His death was the condition of the covenant. It was stipulated, as the condition of his having a seed to serve him, that he should make his soul an offering for sin; that he should bear their iniquities; that he should pour out his soul unto death. In reference to this, the blood of the ancient sacrifices was called *the blood of the covenant*, while, of his own, the Saviour testifies, *this cup is the new testament in my blood.* The blood of Christ was not shed by accident, it was not poured out at random or on a venture. No: he laid down his life by covenant. The terms of the covenant must, therefore, define the designed extent of the objects of his death. If all mankind are included in the covenant,—if the Surety of the covenant represented, in this eternal transaction, the whole human race, then the atonement of Christ must have been indefinite. But, if the children of the covenant, as is admitted, are only a given specified number of the human family, then must the atonement of the Mediator be restricted to *them*. There seems no evading this inference. To give the designed objects of the Saviour's atonement a greater extension than the covenant of grace, is to nullify its character as the stipulated condition of the covenant, and to render nugatory and unavailing the consolatory address by which the heart of many an awakened sinner has been soothed, "Behold the blood of the covenant."

4. We may refer, also, to *the very nature of atonement.*

What is the atonement of Christ? It has been already defined and explained as that perfect satisfaction to the law and justice of God, on account of which sinners are delivered from condemnation. Or, in other words, it is that which removes the offence subsisting between God and men, and procures a reconciliation. It supposes a compensation to be made to the lawgiver, in consideration of which certain specific blessings flow out to men. From its very nature, then, all for whom the atonement is made must reap its fruits. It is no atonement without this. That any of those for whom Christ died should fail to enjoy the benefits of his death, is, in this way, utterly inconceivable. It is not more at variance with the purpose of God, or the equity of the divine character, or the tenor of the covenant of grace, than with the very nature of the Saviour's work. His work is an atonement, that is, a reconciliation; and to talk of his making atonement for such as are never reconciled, is a contradiction in terms; it is to say he makes atonement and yet no atonement, in the case of the same individuals. The same conclusion follows from other descriptions of the work of Christ. He is said to give satisfaction for sin; but how can he have given satisfaction for the sins of those on whom the law is to take satisfaction eternally? He is said to appease divine justice; but can the justice of God be appeased, in the case of those against whom its flaming sword shall awake forever and ever? He is said to expiate our offences; but how can those sins for which the guilty perpetrators are to suffer everlastingly have been expiated? He is said to redeem from the curse of the law; but how can those who are to be kept in eternal thraldom have redemption through his blood? He is spoken of as propitiating the wrath of God; but how can those be interested in his propitiation who are to be the objects of Jehovah's unceasing displeasure? He is described, in fine, as procuring by his death, grace and glory; but how can this apply to the case of those who continue under the power of corruption here, and sink hereafter into never-ending perdition? We appeal, then, to the very nature of atonement: we revert to the terms of our definition, in proof of the definite object of Christ's death. Any other view is directly at variance with these terms, and this we should conceive as sufficient in itself to determine the controversy. All views of an indefinite extent are at once put to flight by this question, What is the atonement?

What renders the present argument more emphatic is, that, previous to the atonement being actually made, multitudes had been placed beyond the reach of ever being benefited by it. Before Christ died many of the human race had gone to the place of woe, where God has forgotten to be gracious, and where his mercy is clean gone. But, according to the opinion we are combating, the eternal salvation of these was included in the designed extent of the atonement. And what have we here? Why, the supposition, not merely that Christ made atonement on Calvary for many who should afterwards, through unbelief, come short of an actual participation in the benefits of his death, but that he made atonement for thousands who, long before he did so, had gone down to irretrievable perdition, and were on this account, at the very time, placed beyond the possibility of ever receiving from his death a single benefit. Such are the palpable inconsistencies, nay, the monstrous absurdities, which the error in question compels men to adopt.

5. *The connection of the death of Christ with his resurrection and his intercession, and with the gift of the Spirit,* is here deserving of attention.

The death and resurrection of the Saviour bear a close relation to each other. In whatever character he died, in the same character he rose from the dead. If he laid down his life as Head of the church, and Surety of his people, and Mediator of the covenant, in the same capacities did he take it up again. The persons interested in the one event and in the other, are the same. "Christ died for *our* sins, and rose again for *our* justification."* He died for none, for whose sake he did not rise. And for whom did he rise? Who are they who are benefited by his resurrection? Those, surely, who "shall come forth unto the resurrection of life." "Now Christ is risen from the dead and become the *first-fruits of them that slept.*"† The sleep here is not the sleep of death merely, which all undergo, but that *refreshing rest* to which the death of the righteous is compared. and which is called, by the same apostle, in another of his writings, *sleeping in Jesus ;*—" Them also which sleep in Jesus will God bring with him."‡ Then he adds, in language fully corroborative of the restricted extent of those who profit by his resurrection, " Every man in his own order ; Christ the first-fruits ; afterwards *they that are Christ's* at his coming."§ Those, then, to whom Christ in his resurrection stood in the relation of the first-fruits, are they *who sleep in Christ*, they *who are Christ's*, and not the whole race of mankind. And, from the connection subsisting between his resurrection and his death, for these only can he be held to have died.

A similar relation subsists betwixt the death and the intercession of Christ. Such is the economy of our salvation, that his intercession is necessary to a participation of the fruits of his death. No one can ever partake of the latter without the former. Of course, he cannot be supposed to have died for any for whom he does not intercede, as he cannot be supposed to intercede for any for whom he has not died. And for whom does he make intercession? For all, or only some of the human race? Let us see. " I PRAY NOT FOR THE WORLD, BUT FOR THEM WHICH THOU HAST GIVEN ME."—" Father, I will that THEY WHOM THOU HAST GIVEN ME, be with me where I am."‖ If he died for all, how comes it that he prays only for some ? Are there any for whom he died, for whom he neglects or refuses to pray ? The thing is incredible, impossible

---

* Rom. iv. 25.   † 1 Cor. xv. 20.   ‡ 1 Thess. iv. 14.
§ 1 Cor. xv. 23.   ‖ John xvii. 9, 24.

on every view that can be taken of the Redeemer's character and work. If he died for all, he must pray for all; and, if he prays for all, all must be saved, for *him the Father heareth always.* But the intercession is manifestly special and restricted, as respects the persons who are the subjects of it. Whence, we feel warranted to conclude, that an analogous restriction attends his death.

The work of Christ and that of the Holy Spirit are also closely connected, and bear an exact correspondence the one to the other. It is not our object to trace this correspondence extensively. The fact, however, is abundantly evident. " This is he that came by *water and blood,* even Jesus Christ; not by water only, but by water and blood: and it is the Spirit that beareth witness, because the Spirit is truth."* The ancient ceremony of the two birds, one of which was to be killed in an earthen vessel over running water, and the other to be dipt alive in the blood of the slain bird, significantly prefigured this connection. Nor do the writers of the New Testament fail to call our attention to the circumstance. " The blessing of Abraham comes on the Gentiles through Jesus Christ, that we might receive the promise of the Spirit through faith."† God's having " sent forth his Son, made of a woman, made under the law, to redeem them that were under the law," bears a distinct relation to His " sending forth the Spirit of his Son into our hearts, crying, Abba, Father."‡ How appropriate and expressive, in this view, was the act of the divine Saviour, when, just after his resurrection from the dead, " he breathed on the disciples, and said unto them, Receive ye the Holy Ghost."§ In the economy of redemption, they bear so close a relation to one another, as to induce the belief that they must necessarily be co-extensive as regards those who are their objects. The connection is, indeed, inseparable. If the atonement removes the legal obstructions to man's salvation, the Spirit removes such as are moral; but it were alike preposterous and nugatory to conceive that there are

* 1 John v. 6.   † Gal. iii. 14.   ‡ Gal. iv. 4—6.   § John xx. 22.

any who enjoy the one without the other,—any who are delivered by Christ from the condemnation, without being rescued by the Spirit from the power, of sin. If the atonement opens the door of the heavenly sanctuary, the Spirit's work is necessary to fit for inhabiting the holy place ; and it were of no avail that the one of these were secured for any without the other. If the atonement of Christ lays the foundation, the Spirit by his work rears the superstructure of grace ; but it were a reflection alike on the wisdom and goodness of our covenant God, to suppose that there are any who possess the former of these blessings without the latter, which is necessary to its perfection and utility. The question, then, comes to be, do all receive the gift of the Spirit ? Are all actually regenerated, sanctified, and put in possession of eternal life ? If not, we have no ground for supposing that all are interested in the atoning virtue of Christ's precious blood ; for, as we have seen, the work of Christ and the fruits of the Spirit have a corresponding extent. "He who spared not his own Son, but delivered him up for us all, how shall he not with him also freely give us all things ?" This is good reasoning, but it is fatal to the opinion we are combating, as it infallibly establishes that all for whom God delivered up his own Son shall certainly come to the enjoyment of every fruit of his purchase.

6. Some weight is deserving of being attached to *the limited application and even revelation of the atonement.*

The argument from the limited application, is substantially involved in what we have already said respecting the nature of atonement, and its inseparable connection with the work of the Spirit. Of the designed extent of Christ's atonement, we may judge from that of its influence. Is the effect or application of the atonement universal or restricted ? Restricted, as we have already seen is acknowledged on all hands. But as the omnipotent and omniscient God cannot fail in any of his designs, the *actual* effect lets us know the extent of the *designed* effect. Betwixt these there can never exist any proper disagreement. And as the effects of atonement, namely, redemption, reconciliation, sanctification, and glory, extend but to some, we are bound to apply to the atonement itself a similar restriction in the designed extent of its subjects.

Even the limited extent to which the atonement has been revealed, would seem to point to the same conclusion. A knowledge of the fact, is, according to the plan of our salvation, necessary, in the case of adults, to a participation in its fruits. " Believe in the Lord Jesus Christ and thou shalt be saved :" but " faith cometh by hearing, and hearing by the word of God ;" and " how shall they believe in him of whom they have not heard, and how shall they hear without a preacher ?" It seems to follow from this, that all for whom the remedy revealed in the Gospel is designed, must be put in possession of the Gospel. They must believe that they may be saved ;—they must know that they may believe ;—and they must hear that they may know. Many, for whose ultimate benefit the remedy itself is not secretly designed, *may* possess the revelation of it ; but all, for whom it is so designed, *must*. Now, in connection with this, consider the limited diffusion of the Gospel. In every age of the world, the revelation of mercy has been, in fact, restricted to a few. In ancient times, the Almighty showed his word to Jacob, and his judgments to Israel, while the nations at large sat in darkness. In later times, although the diffusion has been more wide, and the command has been that the Gospel should be preached to every creature, it has actually been greatly limited compared with the population of the world. To this hour there are hundreds of millions of our race who remain unvisited by the day-spring from on high. And if we suppose that for these the atonement which the Gospel reveals was as much designed as for the others, we shall be led to the most unworthy views of the divine character. God could have made it known to all, and yet it seems he has not. It is vain to plead the remissness of those whose duty it was to diffuse the benefit of Gospel light among their benighted fellow men; for as they were completely under his sovereign control, this, although it leaves them inexcusable, leaves the fact wholly unexplained as regards the purpose and design of God. The thing has happened under his superintending providence, and must, therefore, be in harmony with the secret councils of his will. It is, of course, utterly irreconcilable with the notion that the atonement of Jesus Christ was designed for all. What would men think of the prince, who, designing to emancipate all the inhabitants of a rebellious province of his empire, should provide a sufficient ground of escape for all, but should communicate the knowledge of this merciful provision only to a few, while the greater number were allowed to continue in perpetual durance in consequence of their unhappy ignorance? Or what would men think of the physician, who should benevolently devise and prepare a medicine designed to cure a disease of universal prevalence, and yet suffer multitudes for whom it was so designed to remain ignorant of its existence, thus rendering it impossible for them to avail themselves of its healing virtues? Such things might occur among men, with whom generosity, and humanity, and consistency, and wisdom, are but rare qualities, but that anything analogous should ever occur in the arrangements of Him whose understanding is infinite, whose nature is love, and in whom compassion flows, is utterly inconceivable. We hold, then, the limited diffusion of the Gospel to be demonstrative of the definite nature of Christ's atonement.

7. We take the liberty of adverting to *the absurdity that attends every other supposition* but that of a definite atonement.

There are, as we have seen, only four suppositions on the subject:—that Christ died, either for some of the sins of all men; or for all the sins of all men; or for all the sins of some men; or for the sins of no one in particular, but for sin in general. The first is held by none: the third is that which it is our object to prove: the second and fourth are what are held by the opponents of our doctrine: and these, we are now to show, involve such as maintain them in absurdity. That Christ made atonement for all the sins of all men, is a supposition fraught with absurdity. As we have already seen, it supposes him to be the Saviour of those who are never saved, the Redeemer of those who are never redeemed, the Deliverer of thousands who are never delivered, but remain under eternal condemnation. But this is not the absurdity we have at present in view. When those who hold the sentiment that Christ made atonement for the sins of all men, are asked, why, in this case, it happens that any are condemned? they readily reply, that salvation was procured for men on the condition that they should believe, and, not believing, they of course cannot be saved. The reason, in short, why many of those for whom Christ died fail to reap the benefits of his death, is their unbelief. Now here is a series of absurdities. It is supposed, for one thing, that many are condemned for unbelief, although, as we have seen, they had not an opportunity of believing, never having been put in possession of the Gospel. Then, again, it is supposed that men are able of themselves to believe— that faith is a spontaneous act of the natural man, irrespective of the death of Christ, and that without which the death of Christ can have no efficacy; whereas, according to the Scriptures, faith is the gift of God, an act of the new man only, and an effect, not the cause of the efficacy of Christ's death. This being the case, it is absurd to talk of its being the condition of man's salvation, on the fulfilment of which the effect of the atonement hinges. For, if man cannot believe of himself, if the power to do so is God's gift, conferred out of respect to and in consequence of the virtue of Christ's atonement, it is as absurd to speak of Christ's making atonement for men on condition that they believe, as it would be to offer a blind man a sum of money on condition that he will open his eyes. Besides, on this supposition, the death of Christ might have been utterly and forever unavailing, with respect to the whole human race. The efficacy of the atonement is thus suspended on the condition of man's belief; the reason why it proves inefficacious, in the case of any, is the unbelief of the persons in question; but had all chosen not to believe—and what some do, all might have done—the atonement had been rendered altogether useless. Every view of salvation, then, is absurd, which does not provide security for the existence of faith in all for whom it is designed. Christ died, not to render salvation *possible* merely, but *certain*.

Nor are these the only absurdities with which this supposition is burdened. The benefit of Christ's atonement, it is said, extends not to all men, because of the unbelief of some. But unbelief is either a sin or not a sin. If it is not a sin, it is unaccountable that any should be condemned, or come short of salvation, on account of it. If a sin, Christ either made atonement for it, or did not make atonement for it. If Christ made atonement for the sin of unbelief in all men, it is inconceivable that any should perish on account of that sin. If Christ did not make atonement for it, then he made not atonement for all the sins of all men. To say then that Christ made atonement for all the sins of all men, and yet that many perish because of unbelief, is absurd. From this dilemma we see no way of escape; and the abettors of the point in dispute must lay their account with being tossed on one or other of its horns, till they are pleased to abandon the untenable position they have assumed.

That Christ made atonement for no man's sins in particular, but for sin in general, is a supposition as absurd as that we have now exposed. We are afraid the idea is not uncommonly entertained, that the death of Christ was only a public exhibition of God's displeasure at sin, introduced simply with a view to maintain the honor of the divine moral government. Not to mention other objections to this view of the subject, we remark at present that it leads to absurdity Christ, according to this, did not die for *sinners*, but for *sin*. But sin, apart from sinners, has no counterpart in nature: it is a metaphysical abstraction, a nonentity. Sin is a moral quality, which, like all other qualities, supposes necessarily a subject to which it belongs; and it were every whit as rational to talk of redness existing apart from an object that is red, or roundness apart from an object that is round, as of sin apart from a sinner. Separate sin from sinners and you have a mere abstraction, for which it is dishonoring to the character of the blessed Saviour to suppose him to make atonement.

Add to all, that sin in general,—sin in the abstract, includes the sin of angels as well as that of men. And, if Christ died only to make a public display of the divine abhorrence at sin in general, we see not why the extent of the atonement should be limited even to the human family; we see not why, besides comprehending the whole race of man, it should not also embrace all the fallen angels without exception. So absurd in itself, and so subversive in its tendency of the whole Gospel economy, is the supposition we have thus endeavored to overthrow.

8. But let us close our proof with a direct appeal to *the testimony of the divine word*.

What say the Scriptures? The arguments already adduced, it is not doubted, are Scriptural arguments. They are founded on views of the divine character, the covenant of grace, and the Saviour's work, which are taken from the word of God. But, in advancing them, we may be said rather to be " reasoning out of the Scriptures," than to be appealing directly to the Scriptures themselves. The former line of procedure serves to show the harmony of our doctrine with the system of revealed truth at large: the latter calls the attention to individual texts which have a direct bearing on the subject, and which, by confining ourselves to the other, would be in danger of being overlooked. We shall give a specimen of the texts which might easily be marshalled in overpowering numbers, and this we shall do in the order of the books of Scripture in which they occur.

We pass over the Old Testament writings, with one remark of a general kind, namely, that they everywhere suppose and recognize a distinction between the people of God or the Israelites, and the Gentiles or the nations of the world: and that the benefits of the sacrificial rite, which prefigured the atonement of Christ, were exclusively limited to those who are included under the former description. This distinction is incorporated in the very first intimation given to man of the divine Victim, an intimation in which the seed of the serpent and the Seed of the woman are placed in striking and instructive antithesis; nor is it ever afterwards suffered to drop out of sight. We wait not to advert, in particular, to such expressions as these, " For the transgression of *my people* was he stricken," " He bare the sins of *many;*" but proceed to the writings of the New Testament, to which we principally make appeal in this department of our argument.

Let the reader candidly peruse these words—" Not every one that saith unto me, Lord, Lord, shall enter into the kingdom of heaven; but he that doeth the will of my Father which is in heaven. Many will say to me in that day, Lord, Lord, have we not prophesied in thy name? and in thy name have cast out devils? and in thy name done many wonderful works? And then will I profess unto them, I NEVER KNEW YOU: depart from me ye that work iniquity."* Here a broad line of distinction is drawn between two classes of the human family, with respect to one of which the Saviour makes the appalling affirmation, " I never knew you." The import of the words, according to Scripture usage, it is by no means difficult to ascertain. The doctrine of the Saviour's omniscience precludes the idea that simple knowledge is all that is designed. The antagonist assertions, " You only have I known of all the families of the earth," and " The Lord knoweth them that are his,"† leave us no room to hesitate. The reference can only be to *a special saving cognizance*, of which some are the objects, and others not. But with what shadow of plausibility can such knowledge be denied, with regard to any for whom Jesus suffered, whose sins he actually bore in his own body on the tree? Are there any such whom he *never knew?*

---

* Matt. vii. 21—23.   † Amos iii. 2. 2 Tim. ii. 19.

Take another testimony from the same evangelist: —" At that time Jesus answered and said, I thank thee, O Father, Lord of heaven and earth, because thou hast hid these things from the wise and prudent, and hast revealed them unto babes."* It is here affirmed, as plainly as language can do it, that there are some of mankind from whom the saving benefits of Christ's kingdom are " hid." Now, we are not concerned what interpretation is put upon this phrase. That it imports some awful privation in the matter of the soul's eternal interests, cannot be denied. What we have to do with is this, *whether Christ's being said to have hid these things from the wise and prudent, can be made to comport or agree with his having procured these very things for the same individuals by his death.* Can it be honoring to " the only wise God, our Saviour," to suppose in his conduct so glaring a contradiction, as that of first purchasing, at the expense of his own precious blood, saving benefits for men, and then deliberately hiding these purchased benefits from those for whom they were thus expensively provided? Take what view you will of the hiding from the wise and prudent, it will be found to be incompatible with the persons in question ever having been interested in the atonement of Christ.

In the following passages, the distinction made between *the sheep* and the goats or the wolves, for the former of whom only Christ is said to lay down his life, ought to be carefully marked and duly weighed: —" I am the good shepherd : the good shepherd *giveth his life for* THE SHEEP. *I lay down my life for* THE SHEEP. But ye believe not, because ye are not of MY SHEEP, as I said unto you. MY SHEEP hear my voice, and I know them, and they follow me: and I give unto them eternal life, and they shall never perish neither shall any pluck them out of my hand."† Besides the restriction of Christ's laying down his life,— that is, his atonement,—to the sheep, the identity of those for whom he laid down his life and those to whom

* Matt. xi. 25.   † John x. 11, 15, 26, 27, 28

is given eternal life so that they shall never perish, is deserving of particular notice.

The singularly decided passage in our Lord's intercessory prayer has already been commented on, and here requires only to be noted:—"*I pray not for the world but for them which thou hast given me. For their sakes* I sanctify myself, that they also might be sanctified through the truth. Father, I will that *they also whom thou hast given me* be with me where I am."*

Paul says, " But God commended his love towards us, in that, while we were yet sinners, Christ died for us. Much more then, being now justified by his blood, we shall be saved from wrath through him."† We know not how it could be more clearly taught that those for whom Christ died are justified by his blood and delivered from the wrath to come: but this cannot be affirmed of all. To the same purpose this apostle gives utterance to the challenge, " Who shall lay anything to the charge of God's elect? It is God that justifieth. Who is he that condemneth? It is Christ that died." The death of Christ is thus supposed to be the best possible security against condemnation: none for whom Christ died can ever be exposed to the curse; but there are some on whom the curse will press forever: of course it cannot be said that for such Christ died.

The next text we adduce is this:—" For he hath made him to be sin for us who knew no sin, that we might be made the righteousness of God in him."‡ It will be allowed, that by Christ being *made sin*, is meant his suffering for our atonement. But the object of his being made sin is, that those for whom he is so made, might be made the righteousness of God in him. These are of the same extent, as regards the persons interested in them. They are, in fact, the very same persons for whom he was made sin, and who are, in consequence, made the righteousness of God in him. Now, that all are not made the righteousness of God in Christ need not to be proved; and we have only to

* John xvii. 9, 19, 24.   † Rom. v. 8, 9.   ‡ 2 Cor. v. 21.

draw the inference, that for all he has not been made sin.

Two other kindred passages may close this department of proof:—" Husbands, love your wives, even as Christ loved the church, and gave himself for it."* Two points, in favor of our position, are furnished by this text:—in the first place, it is *the church*, and not the world, for which Christ gave himself: and, in the second place, the love of Christ, by which he was actuated in so doing, is *peculiar* and *exclusive* towards the church, as that of husbands is required to be towards their wives. The latter consideration completely sets aside the discreditable shift by which some have endeavored to get rid of this passage, namely, by alleging that Christ's giving himself for the church does not imply that he gave himself for no others. On this principle, we should be obliged to admit that Christ's loving the church does not imply that he loved none else; and, then, what becomes of the passage as setting forth an example or pattern for the imitation of husbands? Analogous to this text is that of the same apostle, in his epistle to Titus:—" Who gave himself *for us*, that he might redeem us from all iniquity, and purify unto himself a *peculiar people*, zealous of good works."† This requires no comment. Those for whom Christ gave himself are a *peculiar people*, and not the whole race of mankind indiscriminately.

III. Opposed to these arguments are certain OBJECTIONS to the doctrine of a definite atonement, which, it is proper, we should weigh with candor, and against which it becomes us to vindicate the position we have taken up.

1. It is objected that the restriction for which we contend is *derogatory to the honor and the merits of Christ*.

To this we reply, that it belongs not to man to determine the share of honor due to the Saviour. This is the prerogative of God. And, supposing it admitted —which it is not—that less honor would redound to Christ from his atonement being definite, if the honor

* Eph. v. 25. † Tit. ii. 14.

of making a definite atonement is all that God designed he should have, or all which he himself claims or expects, what right have men to interfere and say it is not sufficient? On the principle on which this objection rests, might it be contended that Christ made atonement for fallen angels as well as for men, because, forsooth, it may be supposed to be more honoring to Christ to hold such a sentiment than the other. The thing with which we have to do is, not which of two suppositions reflects the greatest degree of honor on the Redeemer, but which is the fact. Jesus claims the honor only of what he performs. He makes not atonement for angels, and claims not the honor of so doing: and if he makes atonement only for some of the human family, the honor of so doing is all he requires, and more he will not receive.

But all this proceeds on the assumption, that what is alleged is the fact, namely, that the theory of our opponents is, abstractly speaking, more honoring to Christ than the doctrine for which we contend. This, however, is more than we are disposed to concede. The objection overlooks whence it is that the merit or honor of Christ's atonement proceeds; it proceeds not from its *efficiency*, but from its *sufficiency*. Its worth is to be estimated, not by what it *effects*, but by what it is *capable* of effecting. The latter arises from its intrinsic merit, and is, as we have seen, infinite: the former depends on the sovereign will of God, and may be held to be limited, as in fact it is, without detracting the slightest degree from the honor and merit of the Saviour. The restriction of the atonement is attributable solely to the divine purpose, and leaves altogether unaffected the intrinsic merits of the Redeemer's work. Sufficiency and efficiency are not always co-extensive, even in the works of God. The evidences of revealed religion supply an apt confirmation of this remark. Every believer in the Bible must admit that these evidences are *sufficient* to convince all, but we know that they are *efficient* to convince only some. But the restricted extent of their *actual efficiency* is no valid objection against their *perfect suffi-*

ciency. Our readers can easily apply this illustration to the point in hand.

Nor is this all. The objection may be fairly retorted on those who make it. It is, in our humble opinion, the doctrine of an indefinite atonement which reflects dishonor on Christ. We think it might safely be left to the candid decision of any unprejudiced judge to determine, whether it be more dishonoring to Christ to suppose, as our doctrine does, that all for whom he died shall be saved and finally secured in the possession of every gracious benefit; or to suppose, as the doctrine of our opponents does, that the greater number of those for whom he died shall be eternally lost, without deriving from his death a single saving blessing. No rational mind can hesitate to conclude, that it is more glorifying to the High Priest of our profession, to regard his atoning sacrifice as one which infallibly secures the eternal well-being of all for whom it was offered, than to regard it of such a nature as to admit of many for whom it was offered being doomed in justice to everlasting woe. Whether, we ask, is it more creditable to an intelligent agent to maintain that what he performs effects its design, or that it comes short, to a great extent, of accomplishing the object for which it is wrought?

2. It is alleged against our view of the extent of the atonement that it supposes an *unnecessary redundancy in the merits of Christ's death.*

If Christ's death be, intrinsically considered, of value sufficient for all, and yet designed only for some, does not this suppose a superabundance of merit, which is available for no end whatever, and with regard to which the question may be asked, " To what purpose is this *waste?*"

To this we reply, in the first place, that, even admitting the divine intention with respect to the atonement to be unlimited, the same difficulty meets us with regard to a restricted application. Whatever is the extent of destination, it is admitted that the actual efficiency is limited. Now, as in this case the degree of available merit exceeds the extent of actual good done every one must perceive that there is as much room as in the other case for the question, "To what purpose is this waste?" The difficulty presses with as great force on the opinion of our opponents as on ours.

Again, it may be remarked, that it accords with the general procedure of God in other departments of his works, to confer his favors with a profusion which to many may seem redundant and unnecessary. For example, he causes his rain to fall on barren deserts, sterile rocks, and the watery deep, as well as on fertile hills and valleys. There are many fertile tracts of land which have never been cultivated; much spontaneous fruit grows in regions where there is not an inhabitant. And how many flowers expand their blossoms and diffuse their fragrance, in wilds where there is not a human being to admire their beauty or inhale their sweets. Are we at liberty to say that, in such cases, there is a wasteful exuberance of divine goodness or of providential care? No more can it be said that, in the case before us, there is an unnecessary redundance of merit. We must not, in the one case any more than in the other, presume to limit the Almighty, or to sit in judgment on the works of his hands; but firmly believe it will be seen in the end that he has done nothing in vain.

Moreover; let it be observed, that the objection proceeds on the mistaken supposition, that the atonement of Christ is an exact equivalent for the sins of men, and that, had the number to be saved been either more or less than they are, or had their sins been of greater or less amount, the sufferings of the Redeemer must have varied in proportion. Now, to this view of the subject there are insuperable objections. It is at variance with what we have before established, namely, the infinite intrinsic value of Christ's atonement. It overlooks the grand design of the atonement, which was, not simply to secure a mere commutative satisfaction to the justice of God, but to glorify all the divine perfections, and to make an illustrious manifestation of the principles of his government before the whole universe of moral creatures. It leaves no room for such an unlimited offer of Christ in the Gospel, as to render those who reject him without excuse; for if the atonement of Christ bore an exact proportion, in point of worth, to the sins of those who are actually saved by it, then the salvation of any others was a *natural impossibility*, and no blame could attach to such for neglecting to embrace the proffered boon; indeed there would be no ground on which such an offer could be made. Nay, it would require us to believe, that a far greater display of the righteousness of God and his abhorrence at sin could have been made by the sufferings of men than by those of Christ; for, as, on the supposition in question, the number actually saved is limited, and the sufferings of Christ were an exact counterpart of the sufferings due to the sins of that limited number, it was only necessary that the whole human race should have suffered for their own sins, to secure an amount of suffering greatly superior to that of the Saviour of sinners. For these reasons, we reject the theory of atonement against which the objection is pointed, and hold by the view already explained, namely, that the sufferings of Christ are to be regarded in the light of a moral satisfaction to the law and justice of God, which would have been requisite had there been but one sinner to be saved, and had that sinner had but one sin, and which would have been adequate had the number to be saved been to any conceivable extent greater than it is. But to this view of the subject the objection does not apply, as the merit of the atonement is not greater than, according to this, is absolutely indispensable.

3. *The universal offer made of Christ in the Gospel*, has been urged as another objection.

The fact on which this objection is founded we admit without reservation. We contend for the unlimited extent of the Gospel call, and regard every attempt to restrict it as hostile alike to the letter and the spirit of the Gospel. Here we take the phrases "every creature"—"all the world"—"every one"— "whosoever will," &c., in the fullest extent of acceptation of which they admit. The ministers of religion ought to esteem it a privilege and a pleasure, not less than a duty, to be permitted, as ambassadors for Christ, beseechingly to say to all who come within the reach of their voice, " We pray you, in Christ's stead, be ye reconciled to God." Nor is it denied that the general invitations of the Gospel rest, as their basis, on the atonement of Jesus Christ. " We pray you, in Christ's stead, be ye reconciled to God, for he hath made him to be sin for us who knew no sin." " All things are ready—come unto the marriage."* We do not pretend to be able to remove every difficulty, connected with the reconcilableness of the unrestricted offer of salvation and particular redemption. The subject involves all the difficulties connected with the profound abyss of the divine decrees, which it is not for shortsighted man to pretend ability to fathom. If we can only say what may be sufficient to nullify the objection, to show the unreasonableness of cavillers, or to remove the perplexity of humble inquirers, we shall not come short of our aim. With these views, we beg to submit, with all deference, the following considerations.

It would not be a sufficient reason for rejecting, either the doctrine of a definite atonement, or that of an unlimited Gospel call, that we found it impossible to reconcile them with one another. That *we* are incapable of reconciling them does not prove them to be irreconcilable. God may be capable of reconciling them ; creatures of a higher intellectual and moral rank may see their reconcilableness ; or we ourselves, when elevated to a brighter sphere of being, may yet be fully equal to the difficult problem. Their perfect consistency with one another, is not the ground on which we are required to believe either the one or the other. This ground is, with regard to both, the testimony of God in his word. To this testimony we must yield implicit submission, and we must beware of the daring presumption of refusing to receive what God has made known, because of its appearing to our

* 2 Cor. v. 20, 21.   Matt. xxii. 4.

reason either unintelligible in itself, or inconsistent with some other acknowledged dictate of inspiration.

The principles of human obligation are not affected by the secret will of God. What *man ought to do*, is one thing; what *God will do*, is another thing. Now, the Gospel call may be regarded as expressive of man's duty, rather than of the divine intention. God may, and does command many things, which he knows the persons commanded will never fulfil. These things it is the duty of man to do, but it is not the secret will of God to accomplish. By the warnings, and remonstrances, and solemn admonitions of Noah, he called the antidiluvians to repent, and be saved from the waters of the deluge; and that it was their duty to do so, is not surely disproved by what we now know, from the fact, that it was not the secret design of God to save them. By means of his servant Moses, God commanded Pharaoh to let Israel go, as a means of saving his own life and those of his people; it was his duty certainly to obey this command; but it was not the secret intention of God that the Egyptians and their king should escape the destruction of the Red Sea. The Jews and Roman soldiers were under obligation, from the command "Thou shalt not kill," not to put Jesus of Nazareth to death; yet it was in consequence of being delivered by the determinate counsel and foreknowledge of God, that he was taken, and by wicked hands crucified and slain. In like manner, may we not say, that the unlimited offer of the Gospel proves only that it is the duty of all men to believe in Christ for salvation, and not that it is the design or intention of God that all should be saved by him, or that he should obtain salvation for all.

The unlimited nature of the Gospel call necessarily results from God's plan of salvation. It is God's method to save men by faith. With his reasons for so doing we are not at present concerned. It is enough for us to know, that "it hath pleased God by the foolishness of preaching to save them which believe." Now, to this the unrestricted offer of Christ is essential, as otherwise men could have no warrant for faith. The warrant of faith is the testimony of God in the Gospel. And, it may be asked, could not this testimony have been made only to those to whom it was his design to give grace to receive it? We answer,—not, without doing away with that mixed state of human existence, which God has appointed for important purposes;—not, without making a premature disclosure of who are the objects of his special favor, and who are not, to the entire subversion of that moral economy, under which it is the good pleasure of his will that men should subsist in this world; —not, without even subverting the very design of salvation by faith. For, on this supposition, the very communicating of the divine testimony to any one would amount to a virtual intimation of his own personal salvation; it would make that salvation as sure as it could possibly be made; and where, in this case, would there be room for that faith which is the substance of things *hoped for*, the evidence of things *not seen?* Thus does it appear, that, if God should choose to save some of the human family by faith in the Gospel message, it is necessary to this design that the publication of this message, be universal. We must either deny that God has a right to save any by means of faith in the Gospel—and who are they that will take upon them thus to limit the Holy One of Israel?—or admit that an unrestricted Gospel offer is perfectly consistent and indispensable.

The objection we are considering militates as directly against the limited application, as against the restricted intention, of Christ's atonement. It is asked, how can God offer to all salvation by Christ, if this salvation has not been purchased for all? We ask, on the same principle, how can God offer to all salvation by Christ, when, even supposing it purchased, it is his intention not to confer it on all? And when our opponents have given a satisfactory reply to the latter question, we shall have no difficulty whatever in replying to the former. A designed limited application, which our opponents admit, affords no broader a basis for the universal offer, than a designed limited purchase. The difficulty is only, by this means, shifted a step forward, where it presses, not only with all its original weight, but with that of other encumbrances which it has gathered in its progress.

The ground on which the universality of the Gospel offer proceeds, is the *all-sufficiency* of Christ's atonement. This the universal Gospel message supposes and affirms. It is not said in the Gospel, that Christ died with the intention that all should be saved, but that his atonement is a sufficient ground of salvation to all, and that all who rest on this ground by faith shall be saved. This is all that the Gospel asserts; and there is nothing here but what is true, and fit to be made known to all. Nor is anything more requisite to vindicate the universality of the Gospel offer from the charge of inconsistency or insincerity. The atonement of Christ being sufficient for all, possessing a glorious, infinite, all-sufficiency, it is with propriety made known and offered to the acceptance of all. There is, in this case, no natural impossibility in the salvation of any man. The secret design of God, by which the application is restricted, has no causal influence in producing unbelief. The obstacles to salvation are all moral, that is to say, are such only as arise from the native rebellion and hardness of man's own heart. A sufficient ground of salvation exists; the appropriate means of salvation are provided; and, of course, a proper foundation is laid for man's accountability, so that, in rejecting salvation by Christ, he is absolutely without excuse. " He that believeth not shall be condemned."

Add to these considerations, that the universality of the Gospel offer is necessary to glorify God. We are too apt to limit our views, in this matter, to the interests of man. But the gracious character of Deity, and the beauty of the scheme of mercy, are also concerned in it. By the universal offer, means of salvation are provided for all, and God's willingness to save all that come unto him is widely proclaimed. It is thus made known, that he is " long-suffering to us-ward, not willing that any should perish, but that all should come to repentance." He is revealed as "God our Saviour, who will have all men to be saved, and to come unto the knowledge of the truth." And the sincerity of his own remarkable declaration is seen and vindicated,—" As I live, saith the Lord God, I have no pleasure in the death of the wicked, but that the wicked turn from his way and live: turn ye, turn ye, from your evil ways; for why will ye die, O house of Israel." It is, further, made to appear, that the reason, the sole reason, why men perish in their sins, is not, in any sense, because Christ did not die for them, but because they would not avail themselves of the merits of his death, by believing the record which God hath given of his Son. The character of God is vindicated from every aspersion, and the blame of eternal misery is seen to rest with the unbelieving themselves. " This is the condemnation, that light is come into the world, and men loved darkness rather than light, because their deeds were evil."

4. The *universal terms* used in scripture, in speaking of the subjects of Christ's atonement, constitute the most plausible objection to the view we have adopted.

Before proceeding to consider the particular terms and phrases in question, we crave attention to some general remarks, applicable to the whole, and which, in our opinion, ought of themselves to go far, in the way of removing any difficulty that may be felt on that head.

First then, the difference betwixt the Old and New Testament dispensations, with regard to extent, is deserving of marked attention. The former was greatly restricted; it was almost exclusively confined to one people; and to this limitation the members of the church had been long accustomed. The new dispensation, again, was possessed of an opposite character; it was distinguished by a universal extension of its privileges; it threw down the middle wall of partition by which the Jews were kept separate from the other nations of the earth, broadly maintained that there was no difference between the Jew and the Gentile, and opened its arms to Greek and Jew, Barbarian and Scythian, bond and free. But the previous state of things had given rise to deep-seated prejudices in favor of exclusive privilege, which it was no easy matter to uproot. Although the Saviour had manifested a regard for a Roman centurion, and for a woman of Canaan, and had even plainly declared " other sheep I have which are not of this fold," still the exclusive sentiment appears to have retained a firm hold on the minds even of his own disciples. They were Jews, and were manifestly reluctant to descend to a common level with others, in regard to the enjoyment of religious privilege; a miracle was even required to be wrought to convince an apostle that God is no respector of persons, and to carry home to him the lesson, " What God hath cleansed, that call not thou common."* If such narrow views were entertained by those who had the best opportunities of correct information, we need not wonder at the bigoted prejudices of others. The preaching of the Gospel to the Gentiles awakened the jealousy of the Jews, and to such a length did they carry their opposition, that they even persecuted the preachers, " forbidding them to speak to the Gentiles, that they might be saved."† Take one specimen:—" And the next Sabbath-day came almost the whole city together to hear the word of God. But when the Jews saw the multitudes, they were filled with envy, and spake against those things which were spoken by Paul, contradicting and blaspheming. Then Paul and Barnabas waxed bold, and said it was necessary that the word of God should first have been spoken to you: but seeing ye put it from you, and judge yourselves unworthy of everlasting life, lo, we turn to the Gentiles: for so hath the Lord commanded us, saying, I have set thee to be a light of the Gentiles, that thou shouldest be for salvation unto the ends of the earth."‡ Considering such a state of things, it is surely not difficult to account for the use of terms of extensive import, in speaking of the blessings of the

* Acts xi. 9. † 1 Thess ii. 15, 16. ‡ Acts xiii. 41—47.

new economy. To mark the contrast, the strongest language that could be employed became necessary. In these circumstances, we can conceive of nothing more natural than to use the phrases *all men, all the world*, &c., to denote men in general, without regard to national distinction. Nor let it be surmised that, in giving this explanation, we are supposing language to be employed which is not strictly true or correct. We make no such supposition; we reason on the commonly received principle of verbal interpretation: it is an ordinary occurrence to use a general designation, when it is intended to express a general principle, and not to include each individual comprehended in the general designation employed. Take, as an explanation of what we mean, these words uttered in reference to the conversion of Cornelius:—"Then hath God also to the Gentiles granted repentance unto life." What do they express? Not that to every individual of the Gentile world God had granted repentance unto life; but that the conversion of Cornelius, a Roman soldier, evolved and established the principle that Gentiles as well as Jews were eligible to the enjoyment of saving blessings. In precisely the same way, are we warranted to explain the phrases in question as meaning, not that Christ died for *all men* without exception, or for every individual in the world, but for all without distinction of national character. Bearing this in mind, and remembering that it is the language of a Jew addressed to Jews, the words of John can not be misunderstood.—"If any man sin we have an advocate with the Father, Jesus Christ the righteous: and he is the propitiation for OUR sins, and not for OURS only, but also for the sins of THE WHOLE WORLD."[*] The same principle will apply to many similar passages. The difference between *all without exception* and *all without distinction* is deserving of particular attention in this controversy. If we do not greatly mistake, it supplies the true solution of the apparent difficulty on which the objection before us is founded. That Christ made atonement for *all without distinction*

[*] 1 John ii. 1, 2.

is freely conceded; that he made atonement for *all without exception* cannot be maintained, as we have seen, without involving ourselves in the most palpable contradiction; nor is there anything, it appears, in the language of scripture, which requires us to adopt such a supposition.

But further, it may even be admitted that there are certain advantages or privileges, not of a saving nature, resulting from the death of Christ, the participation of which, by those who live under the Gospel, may be held to be strictly universal. The preservation of the human race itself may be traced up to this source; and certainly we are indebted to it for the means of moral and religious improvement, for much valuable and useful knowledge, for a more full and clear exhibition of duty, for greater restraints on wickedness, and stronger incentives to righteousness, and benevolence, and purity; with many other things, contributing to the prosperity of society and the welfare of individuals; which unassisted reason or civil legislation could never have secured.* The system of grace, established on earth and resting as its basis on the atonement of Christ, surrounds, so to speak, "our guilty world with an atmosphere of natural and moral good, and scatters an endless variety of personal and social enjoyments." These advantages are strictly universal; and if the sentiment that Christ died for all men, were understood to have no higher reference than these, we might not feel ourselves called upon to dispute it. Still, at the same time, we should be disposed to question the propriety of the language employed to express the sentiment in question. Because certain benefits, not of a saving nature, spring to all men from the death of Christ, we do not conceive it proper to say that Christ died for all men. It is plain that, in this sense, the phrase expresses a meaning different altogether from that which it bears when used with reference to the subjects of saving grace, or the objects of God's purpose of mercy. And, with nearly the same propriety, might it be affirmed that Christ

---

* Hill's Lectures, vol. iii. p. 9.

died for angels, for it is not to be disputed, as we shall afterwards see, that they also derive important advantages from the death of Christ, more especially an enlargement of knowledge and an accession of companions, which, but for this, they could never have enjoyed.

Besides; it ought to be observed, that universal terms are not to be stretched beyond that with reference to which they are used. They denote all comprehended within a specified *whole*, but the whole itself may be limited. In this sense, the term *all* may express an endless variety of extension: it may be all the members of a family, or all the citizens of a town, or all the population of a country, or all the inhabitants of the globe. Its meaning must be defined by that which is spoken of. That Christ died for all, is certainly affirmed; but for all whom? This is the question. Whether for all the human family? or only for all that were given him by his Father,—for all his own, for all his church? Because, in speaking of privileges secured for the people of Great Britain, a writer should happen to say that these privileges were secured for *all*, it would surely be unfair to infer that he meant they were secured for all the inhabitants of the earth. Not less unwarrantable is it, because Christ is said to have died for all, when the whole context is treating of the privileges of the people of God, to draw the conclusion, that he died for all the human family without exception. And it is here not a little noticeable, that, in the whole compass of revelation, so far as we are aware, it is never once said, in so many terms, that Christ died for *all men*, or for *every man*. In the received version, it is true, the words *men* and *man* occur, but there are no corresponding terms in the original; *all* and *every one* are the words employed, leaving the sense to be filled up by the connection. It may here also be remarked, that the Greek language possesses terms more strictly expressive of absolute universality than those which are used in treating of the extent of Christ's death;* so that we may infer, it was

---

* Πᾶς is the word most commonly employed; but it is allowed not to

not the design of the inspired writers to express the greatest degree of universality, else these more extensive terms would have been employed.

Having made these general observations, we are now prepared for entering on a more close review of the particular passages of scripture, on which the objection we are considering is founded. These passages may be arranged into two classes:—Such as connect the death of Christ with *the world* or *the whole world*—and such as speak of his having died for *all men* or for *every man*.

The passages which connect the death of Christ with *the world* or the *whole world*, are six in number. It may be premised, that the term *world* is used in scripture *subjectively* for the material world, or the world *containing;* as in the expressions, " the world was made by him," and " the field is the world."* It is also used *adjunctively* for the world *contained*, that is, the men in the world; as when God is said to "judge the world."† It is scarcely necessary to remark, that it is in the latter sense the term occurs in the present controversy. But even in this sense, its meaning is not always uniform; it sometimes means all men collectively, and at other times all distributively, that is, some of all classes. Nothing is clearer than that the phrases *the world, all the world,* and *the whole world,* often occur in circumstances where absolute collective universality is perfectly inadmissible. Such is the case in the following passages:—" There went out a decree from Cæsar Augustus that all the world should be taxed;"‡ where *all the world* can mean only the inhabitants of the Roman Empire:— " The world knew him not;"§ where all the inhabitants of the earth cannot be meant, as there certainly existed, even then, some who knew Christ:—" Perceive ye how ye prevail nothing; behold the world is gone after him;"|| where, as denoting those who

have the same intensity as ἅπας, σύμπας, or ἕκαστος, which we believe are not used in this connection.

* John i. 10. Matt. xiii. 39. † Rom. iii. 6. ‡ Luke ii. 1.
§ John i. 10. || John xii. 29.

waited on the ministry of Jesus, a very restricted sense only of the term can be applicable:—" The whole world lieth in wickedness;"* where, though more extensive than in the last quotation, universality is totally inadmissible, as, at the time this language was used, there were, at least, several thousand godly persons in the world:—" All the world wondered after the beast;"† at the time to which this language applies there were with the Lamb on Mount Zion a hundred and forty and four thousand, who had not the mark of the beast in their forehead. Thus it is distinctly proved that the phrases in question do not *necessarily* denote universality. If absolute universality is to be understood, when they occur in reference to the death of Christ, it must be on some other ground than the scripture usage of the language. And if the extent of import attachable to the words is to be determined by circumstances connected with the thing spoken of, we candidly submit whether the principles formerly advanced, from the purposes of God, the covenant of grace, the resurrection and intercession of Christ, and the work of the Holy Spirit, are not sufficient to warrant a restricted import, while the general observations, lately made, determine the nature and extent of this limitation. But let us look at the passages themselves in which these phrases occur.

" Behold the Lamb of God which taketh away the sin of the world."‡ Here, the fact that the Lamb of God does not take away the sin of every individual in the world, peremptorily demands that the term shall be taken in a restricted acceptation; while the circumstance of the address having been made originally to Jews, sufficiently accounts, on a principle formerly explained, for the use of an extensive term. John was sent to announce a new order of things, widely different, in point of extent, from the levitical economy, which had now waxed old, and was ready to vanish away.

" For God so loved the world that he gave his only

* 1 John v. 19.   † Rev. xiii. 3.   ‡ John i. 29.

begotten Son, that whosoever believeth in him should not perish, but have everlasting life. For God sent not his Son into the world to condemn the world, but that the world through him might be saved."* The same remarks apply to this passage as to the last. The latter expression in t explains what is meant by the world. We have only to ask, whether every individual in the world is actually saved by God's only begotten Son, to ascertain the extent of that world which is the object of God's redeeming love; for it must be blasphemy to suppose that the design for which God sent his Son into the world, could, even in the slightest degree, be thwarted.

" We have heard him ourselves, and know that this is indeed the Christ, the Saviour of the world."† This expresses the opinion of certain Samaritans, and, as they were believers, it may be supposed to be according to truth. It represents Jesus as *the Saviour of the world.* If the appellation be understood to denote only fulness of merit or sufficiency of means for salvation, there can be no difficulty in explaining it. But if it be supposed to denote the actual procurement of salvation, then the ultimate fact comes in to determine that the term " world" shall be taken in a restricted sense, for it is not more a solecism in language than revolting to every right and honorable conception regarding Christ, to speak of him as the *Saviour* of those who are *lost.*

The same remarks apply, in all their force, to the Saviour's own words :—" The bread that I will give is my flesh, which I will give for the life of the world."‡ An express contrast is designed between the privileges of ancient Israel and those of which Jesus was to be the immediate author, which sufficiently accounts for the universal term in this place; while, as in all the other instances, the fact obliges us to adopt a limited interpretation.

The same principles must guide us in explaining the apostle's words :—" God was in Christ reconciling the world unto himself, not imputing their trespasses unto them."§ It is enough here to ask whether *all* without

---
* John iii. 16, 17.   † John iv. 42.   ‡ John vi. 51.   § 2 Cor. v. 19.

exception are reconciled to God?—whether *all* participate in the blessedness of the man to whom the Lord imputeth not his sin?

"If any man sin, we have an advocate with the Father, Jesus Christ the righteous; and he is the propitiation for our sins; and not for ours only, but also for the sins of the whole world."* This seems, at first sight, the strongest passage of all in support of the objection, yet there is not one, which, when viewed in its connection, is more easily explained in consistency with the view we have adopted. The chief explanation has already been brought forward, in speaking of the comparative extent of the New and Old Testament privileges. The contrast is here plainly marked —"*our* sins; the sins of *the whole world*." The aim of the passage, too, is clearly to afford consolation to believers when they fall into sin, not to hold out encouragement to the wicked to commit iniquity. "Propitiation" itself supposes an actual deliverance from the wrath of the Almighty, in which we are certain all do not share, for we read of some on whom the wrath of God abideth forever. Moreover, the propitiation for sin is connected with advocacy, by which, as before explained, the reference of the former term is necessarily limited. Not to mention the passages before adduced, in which the very same phrase occurs in a connection which necessarily precludes absolute universality: to which we here beg leave to add other two:—" I also will keep thee from the hour of temptation which shall come upon *all the world.*—The great dragon, called the devil and Satan, which deceiveth *the whole world.*"†

The second class of texts, on which the objection in question is founded, consists of those in which Christ is said to die for *all men* or for *every man*. We must here remind the reader of the established canon of criticism before laid down, namely, that the extent of import attaching to universal terms depends on the subject in reference to which they are used. Now, the term *all* is often employed in scripture in a restricted, or distributive sense. For example, when Paul says,

* 2 Cor v. 10.   † 1 John ii. 1, 2.   ‡ Rev. iii. 10; xii. 9.

"For *all* seek their own, not the things that are Jesus Christ's,"* the term must be restricted to those selfish persons of whom he complains in the context, yet the term itself is as naked and general as in any case in which it is used in connection with the death of Christ. Again, when the same writer says, "marriage is honorable in *all*,"† the term must likewise be restricted, as there are not only many who enter into marriage dishonorably, but many who never marry at all. Further, when he says, "I exhort, that supplications, prayers, intercessions, and giving of thanks, be made for *all* men,"‡ that the term is to be understood not collectively but distributively, is plain from what follows, "for kings and for all that are in authority." Keeping these things in mind, the passages in which similar language is used, in connection with the death of Christ, can give us no difficulty. But it may be proper to look a little more closely into these passages themselves.

"And I, if I be lifted up from the earth, will draw all men unto me."§ The word "men" is a supplement; the original is "all" ($\pi\acute{a}\nu\tau\alpha\varsigma$,) leaving the sense to be filled up agreeably to the nature of that which is spoken of. What is spoken of is, the attractive power of the Saviour's cross in drawing men to him. The power is exemplified in justification, regeneration, communion, and perfect salvation; and is rather moral than legal in its nature. It is the *actual efficacy* of the crucifixion of Christ that is the subject of this assertion, and this, by the acknowledgment of all, is limited with respect to the number of its subjects. Besides, the words were spoken in consequence of certain *Greeks*, who had come up to worship at the feast, having expressed a desire, through Andrew and Philip, to be introduced to Jesus, from which it is fair to infer that the "all" here means all *without distinction*, not all *without exception*.

"The free gift came upon all men unto justification."‖ Here also, the actual result, justification, is

---

* Phil. ii. 21.   † Heb. xiii. 4.   ‡ 1 Tim. ii. 1, 2.
§ John xii. 32.   ‖ Rom. v. 18.

spoken of. Are all men, without exception, actually justified, that is, delivered from condemnation and accepted of God?

"For as in Adam all die, so in Christ shall all be made alive."* It would be out of place here, to enter into the controversy, whether the death in this passage means anything more than temporal death, and the life anything more than the bodily resurrection which is common to the righteous and the wicked. There seems to us to be very satisfactory grounds for rejecting this view.† But we submit the following remarks, as, in our humble opinion, sufficient to neutralize the objection founded on this and similar texts in the writings of Paul.—There is good reason to believe that the comparison or parallelism instituted between Adam and Christ refers to the public representative capacities of both; which brings the matter to the question, whether Christ stood in a federal relation to the whole human race, and, if he did not, because the *all* represented by Adam are all without exception, to conclude that the *all* represented by Christ must be so too, is an unfounded inference. The comparison is, also, obviously meant to be understood with reference to the actual efficacy of what is performed by each: and as the offence of Adam has not merely procured condemnation for all, which may or may not come into operation, according to circumstances, but has actually brought all in him under the curse of death, so we are bound to admit that the *all* who are made alive in Christ, are not merely—according to the supposition of our opponents—those for whom Christ has procured life, but those on whom this blessing is actually bestowed‡.

"For the love of Christ constraineth us, because we thus judge, that if one died for all, then were all dead, and that he died for all that they which live should not henceforth live unto themselves, but unto him who died

---

* 1 Cor. xv. 22. † Wardlaw's Essays, pp. 247—270.
‡ Such as wish to pursue this subject will find an able and satisfactory disquisition on the passages in which a parallelism is instituted betwixt Christ and Adam, in Dr. Wardlaw's Essays, pp. 297—310

for them, and rose again."* What does this passage affirm? Not that Christ died for *all who were dead*, but that *all for whom he died were previously dead.* There is a vast difference betwixt these two things; the latter, however, is all that is either affirmed or supposed, and leaves room for the supposition, that there might be many more who were dead than those for whom Christ died. Besides, the very words themselves limit the *all* to those who feel the obligation arising from the death of Christ to promote his glory: —" he died for all, that they who live—or rather, that these all living, ἵνα οἱ ζῶντες—should not live to themselves," &c. Moreover, the passage establishes the inseparable connection between the death and resurrection of Christ—" him who died for them and rose again"—which, as before shown, necessarily requires a limitation in the number of those for whom he died.

" Who gave himself a ransom for all, to be testified in due time."† The context leaves no room to doubt that the universal term is employed, in this instance, distributively, as meaning all without distinction. The reference, in what goes before, is to kings and persons in authority, (v. 2 ;) and, in what follows, to the " Gentiles," (v. 7.) And this explains the apparent difficulty, (v. 4,) " who will have all men to be saved," as if there were a contrariety between the " secret and revealed will of God," or between the purpose of Deity and the real state of things. We are exhorted to pray for men of all ranks and descriptions; for it is God's will that men of all ranks and descriptions should be saved; and of this we have sufficient evidence in Christ's having given himself a ransom for all ranks and descriptions of men. Such is plainly the connection of the various clauses in this chapter, and how far is it, in this view, from giving any support to the doctrine of indefinite atonement!

" We trust in the living God, who is the Saviour of all men, especially of those that believe."‡ A Saviour is one, not merely who designs to save, but who actually effects salvation; and as all men without ex

---

* 2 Cor. v. 14, 15.   † 1 Tim. ii. 5.   ‡ 1 Tim. iv. 10.

ception are not actually saved from sin, the term "Saviour," in this passage, must have some other meaning. It means *Preserver;* and in this sense the living God is the Saviour of all men without exception; he upholds them in being, he sustains them in temporal life, in him they live, and move, and have their being; while he extends a peculiar care to believers who are partakers of his special grace.

"We see Jesus, who was made a little lower than the angels for the suffering of death, crowned with glory and honor; that he, by the grace of God, should taste death for every man."* The word *man* here is not in the original; the phrase runs *for every one*—ὑπὲρ παντός. Now, the rule with regard to universal terms is, not to extend them beyond the subject of which the writer happens to be treating; and, in the case before us, the persons spoken of are the "sons" whom the Captain of salvation brings to glory,— "they who are sanctified,"—" his brethren,"—" the children which God had given him;" from all which we are surely warranted to presume the meaning of the disputed expression to be, that Jesus tasted death for every one of *these,* and not for every one of the human race. Nor is this interpretation different from what we are required to adopt in similar instances, in which even stronger language is employed in the original. "But the manifestation of the Spirit is given to every man (ἑκάστῳ) to profit withal."† This cannot possibly be understood universally. Neither can the following, where even the term *man* occurs in the Greek—" Whom we preach, warning every man (πάντα ἄνθρωπον,) and teaching every man," (πάντα ἄνθρωπον.)‡

These, we believe, are all the passages in which the phrases in question occur, in connection with the death of Christ. Or, if there are any others, they are to be explained on the same principles. The sources of explanation are chiefly two: *that universal terms are not to be extended beyond the subject in reference to which they are used—and, that " all," with special*

* Heb. ii. 9.   † Cor xi 7.   ‡ Col. i. 28.

reference to the greater extension of New Testament blessings, means all WITHOUT DISTINCTION, *and not all* WITHOUT EXCEPTION. These canons kept in view and applied, will serve to explain every difficulty which may be supposed to arise from the use of universal terms, in speaking of the subjects of Christ's death.

5. There remains but one other objection, that, namely, which rests on those passages of Scripture which seem to imply a *possibility of some perishing for whom Christ died.*

If such a thing could be shown to be fact, or even proved to be possible, then would the doctrine of a definite atonement be overthrown, and the theory of universality would possess a high degree of probability. But the passages referred to, when closely examined, give support to no such idea. Let us give our attention for a little to these passages.

"Those that thou gavest me I have kept, and none of them is lost, but the son of perdition: that the scripture might be fulfilled."* Here, it is supposed that one of those who were given to Christ to be redeemed by his blood is said to be lost. The explanation of this passage depends on the view taken of the phrase, "those that thou gavest me." If this refers officially to the giving to Christ of certain persons to be his apostles, then there is nothing which impugns our doctrine in what is expressed, namely, that Judas, one of the apostles, had apostatized and fallen from his apostleship. But we apprehend that by those given to Christ, we are to understand the elect of God, the redeemed from among men, who in the context are said to have "kept his word," and to have "believed in him." To this number, Judas, who was always a hypocrite, never belonged. The particle *but* ($\epsilon\iota$ $\mu\eta$) is thus not *exceptive* but *adversative;* it does not suppose the son of perdition to be *included* in the number of those given to Christ, but to be *contrasted* with such; the language is elliptical, and the ellipsis requires but to be supplied, to render the passage one of the strongest in the Bible in our favor: "those that thou hast

* John xvii. 12.

given me I have kept, and none of them is lost. But the son of perdition *is lost*, that the scripture might be fulfilled." Such is the force of the particle in in many other passages, which may serve to illustrate and confirm this explanation :—" No man knoweth the Son, but the Father—(εἰ μὴ ὁ Πατὴρ, i. e. but the Father knoweth the Son); neither knoweth any man the Father, but the Son,"* (εἰ μὴ ὁ Υἱὸς, i. e. but the Son knoweth the Father.) "Many widows were in Israel in the days of Elias—but unto none of them was Elias sent, save unto Sarepta (εἰ μὴ εἰς Σάρεπτα,) a city of Sidon, unto a woman that was a widow."† That the particle is here adversative, not exceptive, is plain from the circumstance that *Serepta* was not in *Judea*, and of course the widow who abode there was not a widow in *Israel;* the manner in which God treated this widow, by sending to her his prophet, is *contrasted* with his treatment of the many widows in Israel, to whom he sent him not. Thus, also, in the passage which immediately follows :—" Many lepers were in Israel in the time of Eliseus the prophet; and none of them was cleansed, saving (εἰ μὴ) Naaman the Syrian."‡ Naaman the *Syrian* was not a leper in *Israel;* the force of the passage lies in the implied contrast ;—" none of THEM was cleansed. But NAAMAN THE SYRIAN *was cleansed*." Take two other examples of the adversative force of the particle :—" And it was commanded them that they should not hurt the grass of the earth, neither any green thing, neither any tree; but only (εἰ μὴ) those men which have not the seal of God in their foreheads," i. e. only those men shall they hurt. "And there shall in no wise enter into it anything that defileth, neither whatsoever worketh abomination, or maketh a lie ; but (εἰ μὴ) they which are written in the Lamb's book of life :" i. e. they shall enter into it.§ Surely, after these passages are considered, no candid person will insist that Judas, the son of perdition, was included among those who were given to Christ to be redeemed by his blood ; for

---

* Matt. xi. 27. † Luke iv. 25, 26.
‡ Luke iv. 37. § Rev. ix. 4; xvi. 27

on the same principle might it be maintained, that the Father was a man, that Sarepta was a city of Judea, that Naaman the *Syrian* was a leper in *Israel*, that the men who had not the seal of God in their foreheads were grass and trees, and that those who are written in the Lamb's book of life were persons who are defiled, and work abomination, and make a lie. That a mere English reader might be led, by the passage under consideration, to adopt the idea, that those for whom Christ died may possibly perish, would not be wonderful, although the texts in which a parallel phraseology occurs might have prevented even such from error; but that persons conversant with the original language should take such a view of it, is utterly inexcusable, inasmuch as the very opposite is what the original terms import.

" But if thy brother be grieved with thy meat, now walkest thou not charitably. Destroy not him with thy meat for whom Christ died."* Similar to this is a passage in another epistle of the same writer, which must be explained on the same principles:—" And through thy knowledge shall the weak brother perish, for whom Christ died?"† These texts seem at first sight to be formidable; but they are capable of being satisfactorily explained. It occurs to remark, at the outset, that, if they actually imply that those who are redeemed by the blood of Christ may finally fall away and perish, then do they directly contradict other passages of scripture, which as expressly teach us the contrary of all this; such as the following:—" All that the Father hath given me shall come to me; and him that cometh to me I will in no wise cast out. This is the Father's will which hath sent me, that of all which he hath given me I should lose nothing.—I give unto them eternal life, and they shall NEVER PERISH, neither shall any pluck them out of my hand.—Who shall also CONFIRM you unto the end, that ye may be blameless unto the day of our Lord Jesus Christ.—The Lord is faithful who shall STABLISH you and keep you from evil.—Who are kept by the power of God, through

* Rom. xiv. 15.   † 1 Cor. viii. 11.

faith unto salvation."* Such as maintain the possibility of any for whom Christ died perishing, will find it difficult to explain these passages in consistency with this opinion; but they are as much bound to reconcile the passages on which they found the sentiment in question with those we have now adduced, as are the advocates of a definite atonement to reconcile the same passages with the sentiment they have espoused. Nay, we greatly mistake if the latter be not a much more easy task than the former.

There are several ways in which these passages may be fully explained. "The brother for whom Christ died," may be taken in its popular sense to denote one who professes or seems to be such, although he may not be so in reality. It is in this way that the persons to whom the apostolical espistles are addressed are designated, "saints," "elect," &c., because as members of the church they profess to be such, and, while they do nothing to belie their profession, we are bound in charity to suppose them what they profess to be; and that some who thus profess to be brethren may perish, is perfectly possible.—Besides, the peace or comfort of a person's mind may be destroyed, without supposing the destruction of the soul; and it is not improbable that, in the former of the passages on which we are commenting, this may be the thing that is meant, as a contrast is manifestly designed between the untender conduct of the uncharitable brother, and the grace of Christ in giving himself unto the death for us.—Or rather, the true explanation of these passages seem to be, that the *tendency* of the wicked conduct denounced is what is pointed out. The tendency is to destroy, or make to perish, the brother for whom Christ died. All sin tends to the destruction of the soul; and such, in every case, would be its effect, were there nothing to prevent it. This is the case with the sins of the people of God as well as those of others; and nothing but the justifying righteousness of the Redeemer in which they are interested by faith, prevents this end from supervening. Such, of course, is

* John vi. 37, 39; x. 28. 1 Cor. i. 8. 2 Thess. iii. 3. 1 Pet. i. 5.

the case with the temptations to sin to which they are exposed from others: the tendency of these temptations is to bring about their destruction, to cause them to perish. Because such a consummation shall not be permitted to take place, it is not less true that it is the tendency of the conduct in question to lead to it. And, in speaking of a line of evil conduct, and setting forth its enormity with a view to deter from pursuing it, what more natural or fitting than to describe it by its evil and pernicious tendency! It is thus that he who believeth not God is said to make God a liar. The tendency of the conduct is to such an end; but the end itself can never be in reality. So in the case before us; the tendency of the conduct described is to cause the brother to perish for whom Christ died, although such is the grace of God that this consummation shall never be permitted to take place.

"Of how much sorer punishment, suppose ye, shall he be thought worthy, who hath trodden under foot the Son of God, and hath counted the blood of the covenant wherewith he was sanctified, an unholy thing, and hath done despite unto the Spirit of grace."* The apostle is showing the aggravated criminality of apostasy from the Gospel. One aggravating circumstance is, that the apostate treats with contempt the blood of the covenant; which blood is said to be, as magnifying still more the crime, that "wherewith he was sanctified." The question here is, who is it that is referred to by the pronoun "he?" Who is it that was sanctified? Is it the apostate himself? or is it the Son of God? The former is, of course, understood by those who adduce the passage as an objection to the doctrine of a definite atonement. But this we are disposed to question; the immediate antecedent is the Son of God; thus understood, the passage is rendered more strongly expressive of the writer's object; and this is the view which is taken of it by some of our best writers. That the blood, which apostates from the Gospel profane, is that by which the Son of God was himself consecrated or set apart to his mediatorial offices, is surely a con-

* Heb. x. 29.

sideration fitted to deepen their crime. But admitting that the apostate himself is meant, the passage presents no opposition to our doctrine. In the first place, the word "sanctified," often means nothing more than consecration to the service of God, which may apply to hypocrites as well as true saints in respect of their profession of the Gospel; making that profession, they avowedly set themselves apart to the service of the Most High. And in the second place, supposing the word *sanctified* to be used in its more frequent acceptation to mean inward purification of the soul, may we not understand the apostle here to reason regarding the guilt of apostasy, on supposition of the truth of what the apostate professes? The hypocrite professes to be sanctified by the blood of the covenant, claims the character of one who has felt the cleansing virtue of the blood of the Son of God, and, supposing it for a moment to be true, how does it aggravate his guilt, that he by his apostasy counts this very blood, wherewith he professses to be sanctified, a common thing? Nothing can be more natural than such a train of reasoning; and, in this light, the passage presents no opposition to the view of Christ's death for which we contend.

"But there were false prophets also among the people, even as there shall be false teachers among you, who privily shall bring in damnable heresies, even denying the Lord that bought them, and bring upon themselves swift destruction."* Some are of opinion that "the Lord" here does not refer to Christ; and certainly the original term (δεσπότην) is not that by which the Saviour is commonly designated. Others, again, think that the *buying* here does not refer to the meritorious purchase which Christ made of the church with his blood, but to the redemption from Egypt or some other thing of inferior importance. But we are willing to admit that Christ is "the Lord" spoken of, and that the purchase of redemption by his blood is what is meant by the word "bought:" and yet we see nothing in the text that opposes our doctrine. It is not

* 2 Peter ii. 1.

necessary to suppose that the false teachers who were to bring on themselves swift destruction were *actually* bought with the blood of Christ. It is enough for the apostle's purpose that they were *professedly* so. He argues against them *on their own principles*, and shows thus that their conduct was heinous and dangerous in the extreme. And in doing so, he only follows the example of the Saviour himself, who confuted the Pharisees who professed to be righteous and were not, on their own acknowledged principles:—" I say unto you, that likewise joy shall be in heaven over one sinner that repenteth, more than over ninety and nine just persons which need no repentance."* Are we to conclude, from this, that there were any such *just persons who needed no repentance?* Surely not; but there were persons who made pretensions to this character; and against these was the reproof contained in the passage directed. Neither are we, from the expression under consideration, to conclude that the persons spoken of were actually "*bought*" with the price of Christ's blood; but there were persons who pretended to be so, and yet acted inconsistently with the supposition; and such pretension certainly tended to enhance the enormity of their guilt.

Thus have we brought to a conclusion the argument respecting the extent of Christ's atonement. We have endeavored clearly to exhibit the state of the question; have stated, it is hoped, with fairness, the difficulties with which the subject is beset; and have brought forward what has seemed to us sufficient to refute what we conceive to be error, and to support what we conceive to be the truth on this important point. It is to be feared that, in the case of many, the opposition shown to a definite atonement, springs from the objections to the doctrine of divine sovereignty, and we have reason to be on our guard against this fruitful source of error. Let us beware, too, of being carried away with the mere sound of scripture language, to the overthrow of the analogy of faith. Let saints rejoice that not one of those for whom Christ died shall

* Luke xv.

come snort of eternal life, for whom God did predestinate to be conformed to the image of his Son, them he shall certainly glorify. But let it not be thought, from anything we have said, that we have a wish to limit unduly the saving virtue of the Redeemer's blood. We repeat, that, in intrinsic worth, we regard it as infinite; nor would we be understood to mean that its actual efficacy is not greatly extensive. We deny that it is universal, but we rejoice to think, notwithstanding, that it extends to a multitude which no man can number—that "number without number" of redeemed men, who, gathered from every nation, and people, and kindred, and tongue, shall, with harmonious voices and grateful hearts, sing praises to the Lamb that sitteth on the throne forever and ever.

SECTION XII.

RESULTS OF CHRIST'S ATONEMENT.

The results of the great doctrine we have thus endeavored to explain, establish, and defend, are so numerous and diversified that an attempt fully to discuss, or even to enumerate them all cannot be presumed. But the present work might be deemed to be essentially defective were these altogether passed over without notice. We beg the reader's attention to the following.

I. *The atonement serves to illustrate, in the most interesting manner, the* CHARACTER OF GOD.

Even the *natural* perfections of Deity are thus illustriously manifested. What *wisdom* is shown in devising a way by which the grand object of redeeming mercy might be gained, in consistency with legislative rectitude, and the seemingly inharmonious conjunction of characters might be effected—" a just God and a Saviour." No mortal mind, no angelic intellect could ever have conceived this plan, could ever have solved this problem. Well may it be characterized as a display of "the manifold *wisdom* of God;" nor can we express ourselves regarding it in more appropriate terms than by saying, "He hath abounded toward us in all *wisdom*."

In it we see the *power*, not less than the wisdom, of God. Powerful love, love stronger than death, must it have been, which moved the appointment of such a plan of salvation. Such a load of guilt as pressed on him who "bare our iniquities," such a weight of wrath as was endured by him whom "it pleased the Father to bruise," could have been borne by no power less than almighty. The curse which he sustained was sufficient to sink the whole guilty world of sinful men to the depths of perdition. What even when inflicted on angels who "excel in strength," requires to be broken up into portions and dealt out through the successive ages of eternity, was poured forth on the head of Emmanuel at once and in one unbroken torrent of accumulated vengeance. Nor do the effects resulting from the atonement of Christ, in his taking the prey from the mighty, calling into being a new creation, and performing all those acts of almighty grace which evince the Gospel to be "the power of God unto salvation to every one that believeth," give a less striking display of omnipotence.

Here also the *moral* attributes of God shine forth. Nowhere else do we meet with such a display of divine *holiness*. He is manifested, indeed, to be the Holy One, of purer eyes than to behold iniquity, who cannot look upon sin; for such is the immaculate purity of his nature that moral guilt must not be cancelled by a sovereign act of will, nor moral pollution wiped away by a mere effort of power, but sin signally stamped with the brand of Jehovah's deepest abhorrence by the substitutionary sufferings of his own Son. By God's sparing not his own Son, but delivering him up for us all, we are more impressively taught the inviolability of divine *justice* than we could be by laying open the caverns of endless despair, and disclosing to view the horrid and appalling scenes of suffering and woe which they present. In the cross of Heaven's spotless Victim we read most plainly that God will by no means clear the guilty. The wrath of God is here revealed as it is nowhere else, against all ungodliness and unrighteousness of men. The immovable determination of the divine nature, to visit every deviation from rectitude with its merited and appropriate award of judgment, is unanswerably demonstrated. Nor can anything be conceived, better fitted to fill with terror such as perseveringly outrage the authority of the divine law; for, if the sword of justice was made to awake against the Shepherd, and smite the man who is Jehovah's fellow, who, continuing in a course of sin and unbelief, can expect to escape the vengeance of eternal fire! If such things were done in the green tree, what shall be done in the dry?

But it is the *gracious* character of God that is principally exhibited in the atonement of Christ. Compassion, mercy, love, grace, beam with refulgent splendor from the cross, and from the cross only. Wisdom and power, holiness and justice, though here transcendently magnified, are elsewhere displayed to a certain extent: but the atoning sacrifice of Christ is what alone gives any intimation, even the slightest, of forgiving mercy and redeeming love. If left to creation and providence, our anticipations might well be of a different character, seeing the pains, and privations, and sorrows, and death, which everywhere prevail, would seem to announce God's fixed determination to avenge the quarrel of his covenant. But, in the face of the suffering Saviour, we read distinct intimations of mercy and love. Gethsemane and Calvary thus disclose what the fairest scenes in nature can never exhibit. The "human face divine," even when marred with grief, and lacerated with thorns, and foul with weeping, and pale with death, reflects more of the divine glory than the sun when shining in his strength. The hour of midnight gloom, and darkness, and desertion which came upon the holy soul of the Redeemer, was, so to speak, the noon-tide of God's eternal love, the meridian splendor of mercy to perishing men, the reign and triumph of superabounding grace,—" God commendeth his love toward us in that, when we were yet sinners, Christ died for us." " Herein is love, not that we loved God, but that he loved us and gave his Son to be a propitiation for our sins." " Grace reigns through righteousness unto eternal life by Jesus Christ our Lord."

II. *It vindicates the honor, and establishes the principles of the Divine moral Government in general, and of the moral Law in particular.*

The homage to his excellence which the Lord of the universe demands of all his rational creatures, of whatever class, together with a duly apportioned expression of his approbation or disapprobation, according as their conduct meets, or falls short of, his demands, constitutes what we understand by the divine moral government in general. The moral Law again, is that special moral constitution given to the human race in particular, comprehending the divine requirements obligatory on man. The one is just a branch of the other, and, as far as their claims, sanctions, and obligations are concerned, they may be regarded as identical.

The original claims of God's moral government and law are high,—entire affection, and perpetual and devoted obedience. These claims are founded on the undoubted supremacy, intrinsic excellence, and inherent proprietorship of God. No testimony to their equity could be more unequivocal than that which the death of Christ supplies. Had they not been at first perfectly equitable, had they been essentially unjust, or even in the slightest degree over-rigorous, their tone would certainly have been relaxed, rather than that the Son of God should be subjected to suffer the accursed death of the cross. His being so subjected thus proclaims in the most determinate accents that the law is holy, just, and good.

The sanctions of the Divine moral government are necessary as well as its claims. Without these, neither could the displeasure of the Supreme moral Governor at the breach of his law be adequately expressed, nor could the subjects of this law ever be deterred from sin. While it is obvious, that to effect these ends they require to be awful, it is equally plain, that the moral Governor himself is alone entitled to determine what shall be thought adequate. This he did by giving forth the appalling declarations, " In the day thou eatest thereof thou shalt surely die"—" cursed is every one that continueth not in all things that are written in the book of the law to do them." But the doctrine of atonement which supposes this curse of the law to be borne by the Son of God himself, surely strikingly demonstrates, that these sanctions, however awful, were nothing more than just, nothing more than necessary; that they were dictated by no little feeling of revenge, founded on no pitiful calculation of expediency, and were utterly incapable of being departed from in any one instance.

Thus, the permanent obligation of the requirements and sanctions of the supreme moral government was satisfactorily and forever established. It appears that these obligations are not to be violated with impunity, nor altered, nor abated in the slightest degree. No abrogation, or abridgment, or modification of them can take place out of respect to man's disinclination, or to what is called *human frailty*. Though palpably irrational, the heart of man has been wicked enough to conceive this monstrous supposition; and, but for the direct confutation it receives from the vicarious sufferings of the Redeemer, there is reason to fear that the base and pernicious principle would have been extensively adopted. But for these sufferings, on the supposition that man had been saved, it must have gone forth to the moral universe, that the law, though requiring perfect obedience, would be satisfied with less, and though denouncing condemnation on every guilty violator, would permit the perpetrator to escape with impunity. And the consequence of this announcement must have been, to give such a view of the Lawgiver and his law, as could not fail to encourage moral subjects, of every order, to revolt, and embark in the most hardened and extensive rebellion. The atonement, on the other hand, proclaims the stability of the law, and the unflinching rectitude of the Lawgiver. It assures us that the one is not to be insulted, nor the other to be trifled with; that either God must be obeyed, or the consequences of disobedience must be borne; that the throne of the divine moral government is strictly inviolable, and that his rectoral powers are not to be let down to the most presumptuous mortal on earth, or to the most ambitious archfiend in hell. The law is magnified and made honorable. Christ appears to be the end of the law for righteousness. He came not to destroy the law but to fulfil it. And God hath set forth a propitiation through faith in his blood, to declare his righteousness.

III. *It affords a demonstration of the exceeding evil of sin.*

That sin could not be pardoned without a satisfaction, and that no satisfaction could suffice but the death of God's own well-beloved Son, are surely demonstrative of the dreadful and malignant nature of moral evil. No proof equal to this was ever given. Abstract reasonings from the infinite excellence and holiness of God, and practical comments on the overthrow of angels, the drowning of the Antediluvians, the burning of Sodom, and the extermination of the Canaanites, must all yield to the affecting scene of Calvary. Even the most profound study of the law itself, to which sin is opposed, could convey no such impression of its deep demerit. The cross is "the mirror which reflects the true features and lineaments of moral evil." It is when looking upon Him whom we have pierced, that we see sin in such light as to induce us to mourn as one mourneth for a first-born, and to be in bitterness as one that is in bitterness for an only son. Men, in their ignorance and partiality, may conceive of it as a small matter, and speak of it as "a little thing;" they may palliate their offences and plead excuses for them, as if they were too light to be noticed, or too trivial to be severely punished. But let them seriously weigh the momentous truth, that Christ died for our sins, that the Son of God had to pour out his soul unto death before a single transgression could be forgiven; let them recall the contradiction of sinners and the fury of devils, the agonies of the garden and the tortures of the cross, the desertion of his friends and the hidings of his Father's face, to which he had to submit before one iniquity could be pardoned, and then say whether sin does not now assume a new character; whether it does not appear to be an evil and a bitter thing; whether they are not better prepared to appreciate the language in which it is spoken of as "exceeding sinful"—"the abominable thing which God hates." It is thus that we learn to entertain right views, and to cherish right feelings, with regard to moral evil. Grief, and shame, and abhorrence can only be inspired by a believing view of this doctrine; and thus only can those pungent convictions for the past, and those vigorous determinations to resist it in future, be felt, which are the essential characteristics and ingredients of genuine repentance. Nowhere do the tears of godly sorrow flow with such profusion as at the foot of the cross; nor is there another station so well calculated to nerve the penitent with the resolution to say, "I have done iniquity, I will do so no more." Oh, who is there that, living under the habitual influence of the cross of Christ, is not induced to hate sin with a perfect hatred? Who is there, with the sufferings of a crucified Saviour full in his view, that can bring himself to love sin, or roll it as a sweet morsel under his tongue; that is not rather impelled to purify himself from all filthiness of the flesh and of the spirit, and to perfect holiness in the fear of the Lord?

IV. *It infallibly secures the perfect and everlasting salvation of the chosen of God.*

This is the grand benevolent purpose of the divine will, whose nature, preparations, and consequences bespeak its transcendent magnitude and importance; and every barrier to which, whether arising from the perfections of Deity, or the principles of the divine government, or the moral corruption of man's nature, has been removed by the blood of atonement.

Every legal obstruction to the salvation of man is thus taken away. Guilt is atoned; redemption from condemnation is procured; and every demand which the law can prefer against the sinner, whether of requirement or of sanction, is completely answered. "He hath redeemed us from the curse of the law, being made a curse for us." "We have redemption through his blood, even the forgiveness of sins." No impediment to the most ample pardon now exists. "There is now no condemnation to them that are in Christ Jesus." Through faith in the atoning death of Emmanuel, those who before could only give vent to the shriek of horror, may now sing in full anthem, "Thou art worthy, for thou wast slain, and hast redeemed us to God by thy blood." And the sinner, who formerly crouched, and trembled in every nerve at the sanctions of the law, may now lift his head in humble confidence, and, bidding defiance to a whole universe of accusation, say, "Who shall lay anything to the charge of God's elect? Who is he that condemneth? It is Christ that died."

The moral obstructions to man's salvation are thus also removed. God's benevolent design embraces sanctification as well as pardon. There must be emancipation from corruption as well as from the curse; an active, vital, and prevailing holiness, as well as forgiveness. Now, Christ "gave himself for us, that he might redeem us from ALL iniquity, and *purify* to himself a peculiar people, zealous of *good works*." "The blood of Jesus Christ *cleanseth* from all sin." "For what the law could not do, in that it was weak through the flesh, God, sending his own Son in the likeness of sinful flesh, and for sin, *condemned sin in the flesh*." "We are *sanctified* through the offering of the body of Jesus Christ, once for all." "Wherefore Jesus, that he might *sanctify* the people with his own blood, suffered without the gate." With such passages as these before them, it is wonderful that the doctrine of atonement should ever have been represented by its enemies as hostile to the interests of morality, or that any who profess to believe it, should ever have taken occasion from it to indulge in sloth or wallow in licentiousness. The moral influence of the cross is great and direct, through the accompanying power of the Spirit. It restores to the favor of God; lays restraints on the springs of moral corruption; weakens the power of temptation; dissuades from the practice of sin; and furnishes the most powerful motives to sincere, constant, and universal obedience. Its tendency to inspire a hatred of sin has already been remarked. Nor does it supply a less energetic stimulus to the cultivation of personal holiness. The view which it gives of the divine purity, and justice, and love, the demonstration it furnishes of the rectitude and inviolability of the divine law, and the obligations of gratitude and love under which it brings us, are all directly favorable to the interests of moral obedience. It is even the grand instrument in bringing about a moral regeneration of nature; it being by the influence of this doctrine, that the divine Sprit melts and subdues the adamantine heart of the sinner, and transforms it into the image of Christ.

It no less infallibly secures the happiness of man, here and hereafter. The sovereign purpose of God extends to man's deliverance from misery, as well as from guilt and pollution. And, by the sufferings of the Son of God in our stead, was foundation laid for whatever can contribute to his present or eternal felicity. That communion with God, which is the source of all true enjoyment, is to be had only through this medium "Through him we have access by one Spirit unto the Father." "Seeing that we have a great high priest, let us *come boldly* unto the throne of grace." "Having an high priest over the house of God, let us *draw near* with a true heart, in the full assurance of faith." Those prayers and praises, by means of which the intercourse with heaven is kept up, are accepted only for the sake of the Angel with the golden *censer*, who ministers at the golden *altar* which is before the throne, and out of whose hand the smoke of the *incense* ascends up before God. It also opens up a well-spring of consola tion to the believer, amid the innumerable ills to which he is exposed in this evil world. When burdened with guilt, it "purges the conscience from dead works." When beset with Satan's wiles, it affords him comfort to reflect that, " in that the merciful and faithful high priest himself hath suffered, being tempted, he is able to succor them that are tempted." When visited with afflictions and trials, he is comforted and upheld with the thought that "we have not an high priest who cannot be touched with the feeling of our infirmities." When in the arms of death, and the soul about to be dismissed from the body, a believing view of the Son of man standing on the right hand of God, "a lamb as if he had been slain," can enable him calmly to resign himself, in the spirit and language of the proto-martyr, " Lord Jesus, receive my spirit." Nay, when anticipating the day of final account, and conceiving himself to stand before the bar of a righteous God, he can possess himself in patience, seeing he knows that there " shall be no condemnation to them that are in Christ Jesus," and that the blood of the covenant shall secure for him an honorable acquittal, and infallibly protect him from the wrath to come: the tribunal of eternal justice appears to be encircled with the rainbow of mercy, and, instead of the shriek of shuddering horror, he is enabled to give expression to the language of confiding hope and exulting anticipation, " Thou wilt show me the path of life: in thy presence is fulness of joy: at thy right hand there are pleasures for evermore."

It is, besides, the procuring cause and sole security of eternal glory. Through faith in this blessed truth alone can any of our outcast family " rejoice in hope of the glory of God." Heaven is procured, prepared, taken possession of, and retained, by means of the atonement. The blood of the covenant constitutes the title to its possession. The heavenly things themselves are purified with better sacrifices, than those by which the patterns of things in the heavens were purified. We have boldness to enter into the holiest of all only by the blood of Christ, and to the

Lamb in the midst of the throne are the redeemed in debted for the permanency of their glory and bliss. Those immortal honors, those glorious hopes, those perennial enjoyments, which are imaged by crowns of glory, palms of victory, harps of gold, and rivers of life, have all their meritorious source in the cross. Heaven has everything about it to deepen the recollections of Calvary; and, could we conceive a soul suddenly snatched from the foot of the cross to the sanctuary above, it would undergo no violent change of feeling, for it would still breathe the atmosphere and be surrounded with the symbols and memorials of atonement. Yes: the central object of attraction to men and angels is " the *Lamb* in the midst of the throne." The robes of the redeemed are " made white in the blood of the *Lamb*." " Worthy is the *Lamb* that was slain," is the burden of the celestial song. And those enlivening, gladdening streams which send forth into the heart an ever-welling tide of unmingled bliss, " proceed out of the throne of God and of the *Lamb*." " Not one thought in the crowd of eternal ideas, not one note in the compass of eternal anthems, not one moment in the round of eternal ages, can there be, but refers to Christ crucified. Heaven is no place for flight from the recollections of Calvary! It is filled with the apparatus and monuments of atonement! Its atmosphere is brightened by it—redolent of it—vocal with it."

V. *By the atonement, a way is opened up for the honorable egress of divine mercy in the bestowment of salvation; sinners have ample encouragement to rely on this mercy; and foundation is laid for every pious emotion in the breasts of saints.*

The exercise of mercy in consistency with the claims of justice, is the perplexing problem which only the doctrine of atonement solves. To the flow of the former the demands of the latter seem to present insuperable barriers. These demands must be satisfied, and, if satisfied in those on whom they primarily take hold, the way of mercy is necessarily shut up.

> "Die man, or justice must, unless for him
> Some other, able, or as willing, pay
> The rigid satisfaction, death for death."

It was the revelation of the all-momentous fact of Christ's atoning death, that enabled the gifted poet to hint even at this method of extrication from the above dilemma. Nought else could supply a reconciling principle. No tears of penitence however copious, no prayers however fervent, no good works however sincere, could warrant "a just God" to "justify the ungodly." The sufferings of Christ solve the difficulty; by these every obstruction to the consistent exercise of mercy is removed; the stream of the Lord's blood has opened up a channel in which full, free, and abundant grace might flow unobstructedly and forever to the very chief of sinners. "God is *in Christ* reconciling the world to himself, not imputing unto men their trespasses." Not only *is* this the way by which God has seen meet to make an harmonious display of the perfections of his nature, but it may even, without presumption, be affirmed to be the *only* method by which he *could* do so. It is not, indeed, for us to limit the Mighty One, whose understanding is infinite. Yet, considering the constitution of things, and the peculiarity of the case, we may safely affirm, that the method which he *has* adopted is the best that *could* have been adopted; and, as it is impossible that a Being infinitely wise can do other than what is best, it follows that it was the *only* plan which even divine wisdom could employ. The necessity, be it observed, which is here supposed, is a *moral* necessity; and, in asserting that God could not save men otherwise than by the atonement of his Son, we no more impeach the perfection of his nature, than when we say that he cannot lie, cannot love sin, cannot contradict himself: we just affirm that *he cannot but do what is best.*

By the atonement every encouragement is held out to sinners to rely on the divine mercy in Christ for salvation. If the view which it exhibits of the rigors of justice and the inviolability of the law are fit to cause the sinner " meditate terror,' the view which it at the same time, gives of the greatness of God's mercy and of his willingness to save to the uttermost cannot but awaken hope. If God spared not his own Son, but delivered him up for us all, will he refuse such as come to him humbly soliciting pardon? The gift of his own Son is such a demonstration of his merciful design that no sinner need despair; and the merits of Jesus Christ, the intrinsic worth and sufficiency of his sacrifice, are sufficient to inspire the hope of forgiveness, even should our sins be in number as the sand of the sea, and in aggravation as crimson and scarlet. "It is a faithful saying and worthy of all acceptation, that Christ Jesus came into the world to save sinners, even the chief." "He came not to call the righteous but *sinners* to repentance." No degree of guilt can exceed the worth, no depth of pollution surpass the cleansing virtue of the Saviour's blood. To the timid, the conscience-stricken, the heavy-laden, the bowed down, he says, "Come unto me, and I will give you rest." And even should "the whole head be sick and the whole heart faint, and from the sole of the foot even unto the crown of the head there be no soundness," his call is still, "Come now and let us reason together; though your sins be as scarlet they shall be white as snow; though they be red like crimson they shall be as wool." Unbelief and despair are thus totally without excuse.

As the atonement is the hope of sinners, so is it also the source of every pious emotion in the breasts of saints. It is the very object of faith; "Christ is the end of the law for righteousness to every one that believeth." It is the spring of repentance; "they shall look on me whom they have pierced and they shall *mourn*." The wisdom it displays, the amazing love it discloses, and the mighty power which it exhibits, are all fitted to fill the bosom with adoring wonder. Gratitude, the strongest gratitude, is awakened by a view of the magnitude of the blessings with which it is fraught, and the sacrifices which required to be made in order to secure them. Who that thinks of the Son of God, who, being in the form of God, and think-ng it no robbery to be equal with God, yet made himself of no reputation, took upon him the form of a servant, and was made in the likeness of men, and being found in fashion as a man, humbled himself, and became obedient unto death, even the death of the cross;—who, that remembers that, though rich, for our sakes he became poor, that we through his poverty might be made rich, but must feel impelled to " offer the sacrifice of praise to God continually, that is the fruit of his lips, giving thanks to his name ?"—It is eminently fitted to warm the heart with love. We must love him who has so loved us as to give himself a ransom for our sins. Cold must be that heart, obtuse must be those affections, which are not kindled into an irrepressible glow by the atonement of Christ. The love of Christ must constrain all who rightly understand this subject, to love him in return. " Whom having not seen we love," expresses the spontaneous feeling of every saint. No believer but will be willing to say, " Lord, thou knowest all things, thou knowest that I love thee." This is indeed the test of personal Christianity. "If any man love not the Lord Jesus Christ, let him be anathema, maranatha." " Love the Lord, all ye his saints." How is it possible to come under the ardent rays of this burning love, and not feel induced to reflect its beams in kindred and reciprocal emotion! How is it possible for a gracious soul to treat love so dignified with neglect, love so free with ingratitude, love so productive with contempt, love so ardent with indifference, love so constant with even wavering affection!

Nor can anything be conceived better calculated to produce true humility, than the doctrine that man is utterly incapable of saving himself, and that such were his guilt, and corruption, and misery, that less could not suffice for his escape than the awful sufferings of the Son of God. Oh, who that duly considers this but must be deeply humbled and self-abased! What better fitted to stain the pride of human glory, and to fill with all lowliness of mind! The man who firmly believes and cordially embraces this truth, must see him self to be nothing, yea, and less than nothing. Self-righteousness, self-sufficiency, self-complacency, self-dependence can never be made to comport with Christ's having given himself a ransom for us, that he might redeem us from all iniquity.

It is no way at variance with this, that the doctrine should be viewed as calculated to fill the soul with hope, and joy, and exulting triumph. No limits can be set to the rapturous gladness which it is its native tendency to inspire. In the lowest depth of his humiliation, the believing soul, looking forward to the blessings, and anticipating the triumphs the cross of Christ is destined to secure, rejoices in hope of the glory of Cod. Seeing in it every reason for the highest moral delight and complacency, and feeling that all besides is nothing in comparison, he takes up the passionate yet dignified avowal, " God forbid that I should glory, save in the cross of our Lord Jesus Christ."

VI. *The atonement more or less affects all the divine dispensations toward our world.*

Even the creation of the world, there is every reason to believe, was with the view of its being a theatre on which to exhibit the work of man's redemption by the eternal Son. It is the workmanship of his hand. This is the purpose which it serves; and that it was framed with a view to its serving its purpose is surely no disputable assertion. Difficulties connected with that profound mystery, the origin of moral evil, may encumber this statement. But we are not bound to remove every difficulty from such a subject before being entitled to demand for it the assent of the mind. The apostle, in express terms, not only claims for Christ the honor of the world's creation, but asserts the purpose of its creation to terminate in Him:—" All things were created BY him, and FOR him." He is the *final* as well as the *efficient* cause of this world's creation. Our earth was selected as the chosen spot on which the mystery of redemption was to be displayed; and all the scenes of the mediatorial economy were here exhibited. The advent of the promised Messiah took place here; here was led his instructive life;

here were wrought his wondrous miracles; here were spoken his still more wondrous addresses; here were borne his mysterious sufferings; here was accomplished his awful decease; and here were achieved his glorious victories over men and devils, over sin and death.

This is indeed the glory of our world. That it was the abode of Christ and the scene of redemption, throws over it a surpassing lustre, imparts to it a matchless honor. "It is the glory of the world that he who formed it dwelt in it; of the air, that he breathed it; of the sun, that it shone on him; of the ground, that it bore him; of the sea, that he walked on it; of the elements, that they nourished him; of the waters, that they refreshed him; of us men, that he lived and died among us, yea, that he lived and died for us."* Yes; and we may add, had it only been that it was stained with his blood, it was honored by him beyond all human conception.—It is through the atonement also, that the things of this world come to be properly enjoyed, as it lays a foundation for that covenant-right to their possession which is essential to all true enjoyment. The righteous enjoy the good things of the present life, because they know they are secured for them by the blood of Emmanuel, and are taught to use them as the provision of a temporary state, looking forward to a better and an enduring portion in the skies. And thus it is, that to them the rose of the garden appears to wear a deeper blush, and the lily of the field to reflect a purer tint, and the sun to shine with a richer splendor, and the morning star to sparkle with a brighter beam, because they are the handiworks, as they are the consecrated emblems, of him who died on Calvary.

———————— "One spirit—His,
Who wore the platted thorns with bleeding brows,
Rules universal nature. Not a flower
But shows some touch, in freckle, streak, or stain,
Of his unrivalled pencil.————————
His presence who made all so fair, perceived,
Makes all still fairer."   COWPER.

The dispensation of providence regards the atonement as its centre. Redemption is the grand central

* M'Laurin.

point of providence, and atonement is the central point of redemption. The whole apparatus of redemption owes its being and its efficacy to the death of Christ; and every movement of the complicated wheels of providence derives its impulse from redemption. Preceding events look forward, succeeding events point backward, and meet as in a common centre in the cross. The course of providence, for four thousand years before the advent of the Son of God, prepared the way for this stupendous event; and the train of occurrences since only serves to follow up the great design of his coming. "The Lord reigneth—the government is upon his shoulders." "The world is, therefore, not a wandering star, abandoned in wrath, discarded from use, rushing to destruction, but is still held for a design, and turned to an account the most glorious. Its Maker has not denounced nor disowned his property. It may be a rebel, but he is still its sovereign: it may be a recusant, but he is still its Lord."*

The dispensation of mercy, in all its several stages, stands, of course, in intimate connection with the cross of Christ. Revelation, the record of these progressive dispensations, is everywhere sprinkled with the blood of atonement. History, type, prophecy, song, epistle, all breathe the sweet-smelling savor of this one theme; and their varied contents derive a character of unity from this pervading circumstance.

From Adam to Moses, the practice of sacrificing, we have seen, existed. Adam, Abel, Noah, Lot, Abraham, all presented their burnt-offerings, which, from the substance of which they consisted, and the language in which they were spoken of, appear to have been both designed and understood to prefigure the great Christian Expiation. Without this they have no meaning, no worth; but are a cruel mockery of man's misery, and a deception of human hopes.

The Mosiac economy had innumerable rites and institutions, calculated to convey distinct ideas of propitiation and vicarious suffering. But, without the atonement of Christ, they were meaningless, useless,

* Hamilton's Sermons.

artful all. The whole system was nothing better than a pompous parade of gaudy ceremonies: a criminal waste of valuable property; a wanton infliction of unnecessary pain on sentient unoffending creatures. The atonement of Christ is what gives it all its significancy, utility, and consistency.

The peculiarity of the New Testament dispensation consists in a free, full, unhampered proclamation of mercy and salvation in the Lord Jesus Christ, to all men. It is an offer of eternal life and every spiritual blessing to them that believe. "Holding forth the words of eternal life." "Come unto me, and be ye saved, all ye ends of the earth, for I am God, and besides me there is no Saviour." But on what ground do these universal proffers proceed? Whence derive they their consistency, and their power, but from the perfect all-sufficient atonement of the Son of God? "We preach Christ *crucified.*" "I determined not to know anything among you save Jesus Christ and him *crucified.*" "God forbid that I should glory save in the *cross* of our Lord Jesus Christ." This is the language held by its ministers; and, indeed, every individual benefit it bestows, they are accustomed to speak of in language which marks the same connection. Is it redemption? We have *redemption* through his blood, even the forgiveness of sins." Is it reconciliation? "God hath *reconciled* us to himself by Jesus Christ." Is it peace? "We have *peace* with God through our Lord Jesus Christ." Is it justification? "Being *justified* freely by his grace through the redemption that is in Christ Jesus." The Gospel minister's commission is sealed with the blood and stamped with the cross of Emmanuel; nor can he ever execute t, in consistency with the character and glory of God, unless he exhibit the sacrifice of Christ as the chief article of his message, the burden of his doctrine, the central orb of the Christian system which gives to every part its living energy, and binds the whole together in sweet and indissoluble union.

The divine forbearance towards our guilty race is greatly more extensive than either the efficacy of revelation of the dispensation of mercy. The history of the world is one continued illustration of this fact. The loud warnings which are uttered in the ears of mortal offenders, the apparent reluctance with which the sovereign Judge proceeds to execute his threatenings, and the manifest reservation even with which they are inflicted, bespeak the long-suffering and forbearance of God. "Judgment is his work—his strange work." "Yet forty days, and Nineveh shall be destroyed." "How shall I give thee up, Ephraim? how shall I deliver thee, Israel? how shall I make thee as Admah? how shall I set thee as Zeboim?" "Yea, many a time turned he his anger away, and did not stir up all his wrath." Now, how are we to account for this, in consistency with the character of God? On the principle of the atonement alone. Natural benevolence does not explain it, as this would have dictated the same course towards the angels who sinned, whereas the dispensation of forbearance is limited entirely to our race. Nor is it that He is waiting to see whether man will not clear himself of guilt, and return of his own accord to the path of duty. No. He knows that forbearance, in itself, can never secure salvation. Man may as soon annihilate himself or create a world, as emerge from guilt to innocence by his own merit, from corruption to holiness by his own power. It is with no such view, then, that the Almighty forbears to execute his just judgments on the workers of iniquity. The atonement of Christ explains the phenomenon, and gives consistency to this part of the divine procedure towards fallen man. The atoning death of Christ renders the salvation of men possible; and the execution of justice is suspended, that men may have time and opportunity to repent and be saved, for God is not willing that any should perish, but rather that they should turn unto him and live. But for the atonement, mankind had known as little of the divine forbearance as the fallen angels; the guilty pair had perished as soon as they had sinned; the instant of their disobedience and that of their death had been the same: at the eating of the forbid den fruit, not merely had "sky lowered, and muttered thunder," but the bolt had leapt from the heavens, and bursting on their heads, crushed them in their impotent rebellion.

Even the final judgment will exhibit a connection with the work of Christ. Not only is all judgment committed to the Son, as part of his mediatorial reward; but the equitable condemnation of the unbelieving and impenitent will derive its character and force from this source, while the sovereign acquittal of the righteous will rest upon the atonement as its proper foundation.

The eternal state, whether of bliss or of misery, will derive a character from this circumstance. In heaven, the relations of the redeemed to God and to the Lamb, shall take their rise from the atonement; all the communications of knowledge, and holiness, and felicity, shall flow through eternity in this channel; while every service they perform, shall find acceptance with God only on this ground. And in hell, it is not to be questioned, that the miseries of the damned shall be inconceivably aggravated by the contemptuous disregard they have shown to the way of escape provided for them by God in the death of his Son. The rejection of Christ gives a highly aggravated character to their sin; and the remembrance of this rejection will give weight and pungency to their misery. The blood of Christ, which extinguishes the fire of Tophet as regards such as believe, will have only the effect of making its flames burn more intensely as regards the finally impenitent. The thought of having despised Christ, and counted the blood of atonement a common thing, will haunt the wretched memories of the wicked forever and ever, inflicting on them, without cessation or diminished intensity, the horrific effects of its torturing power. "If I had not come and spoken unto them, they had not had sin, but now they have no cloak for their sin." "He that despised Moses' law died without mercy: of how much sorer punishment, suppose ye, shall he be thought worthy who hath trodden under foot the Son of God, and hath counted the blood of the covenant, wherewith he was sanctified, an unholy thing, and hath done despite unto the Spirit of grace?"

VII. In fine. *The atonement of Jesus Christ will form a theme of interesting and improving contemplation to the whole universe of moral creatures throughout eternity.*

The *saving* effects of this blessed fact are limited, it is true, to our race: not so its *moral* effects. These are wide as the universe. It is not the redeemed from among *men* only that sing praise to the Lamb; angels, beings of a higher order, more ethereal in their nature, and of more elevated endowments, strike their harps to the song, " Worthy is the Lamb that was slain." Angels desire to look into this mystery, and claim right to celebrate the praises of the Redeemer of men. And well they may. By the atonement of the Son of God, new and enlarged discoveries are made to them of the character of God. " Unto the principalities and powers in heavenly places are made known by the church the manifold wisdom of God." Without this, they could never have known even what they do of the natural and moral perfections of the Deity: and of his gracious character they could not have had so much as an idea. But here they have a display of infinite sovereignty, in saving men at all, and not leaving them, like the rebels of their own class, to perish in their sins; and of infinite love and mercy, in choosing for salvation, of the two races of sinful creatures, that which occupied the lowest place. These are views for which they are entirely indebted to the scheme of atonement; for had none been saved, they could have had no knowledge of mercy; had both orders of fallen creatures been saved, they could not have had the same display of sovereignty; and had angels been preferred to men, they could not have known that the mercy of God was the greatest possible. Marvellous wisdom! which thus, by overlooking the order of angels, gave them a brighter manifestation than could otherwise have been given of the character of God! What a scheme this for intelligent creatures of the highest rank to revolve through eternity! As moral creatures, too, angels cannot but feel interested in the atonement, which establishes the inviolable rectitude of the divine government. As benevolent in their dispositions, they must also take delight in what confers such an amount of dignity, and holiness, and happiness, on so large a number of human beings. And we have only to reflect, that the redeemed from among men are, in virtue of their redemption, introduced to the companionship of angels, to see that these celestial beings have another most powerful reason for contemplating, with the deepest interest, the atonement of Jesus. The things in heaven and things in earth are thus brought together into one. Men and angels are, in consequence, to engage in the same exercises, partake of the same privileges, share in and reflect the same glory. And it admits not of doubt, that this companionship will prove a source of knowledge and of happiness to even the " elder sons of light."

Thus extensive does the subject we have had under review appear to be in its influence. Men, some men only, are the subjects of Christ's atonement; but its moral bearing embraces not merely the human race, but the whole moral family of God. As a source of instruction, social happiness, and moral delight, it reaches far beyond the bounds of our earth. It not only scatters blessings over the plains of this lower world, but calls forth the benedictions of angels, awakens the sympathies of the heavenly hosts, and animates celestial beings to jubilant songs of thanksgiving and praise. Who, then, dare represent it as unimportant? Who can estimate the consequences of treating it with neglect? Rather let us count it all our salvation and all our desire. " To them that believe he is precious." " How shall we escape if we neglect SO GREAT SALVATION?"

PART II.

INTERCESSION.

SECTION I.

REALITY OF CHRIST'S INTERCESSION.

Intercession is the correlate of atonement. It is not, therefore, to be wondered at, that those who deny the doctrine of Christ's atonement, should have maintained the position that his intercession is only figurative. This is the view taken of the subject by Socinians, who resolve the intercession of Christ into his kingly office, understanding by it nothing more than the exercise of his regal power in communicating to men the blessings of his mediation. That the Saviour possesses and exerts such a power, is not by any means denied, but that it is the same thing as his intercession, and is all that is meant by this part of his work, may fairly be disputed on the most satisfactory grounds.

The relation which intercession bears to atonement has just been remarked. They are correlate ideas. They stand to each other in much the same character as do the ideas of creation and providence. The providence of God consists in upholding all things, or maintaining in being the creatures he has made; it is best conceived of as a continued putting forth of the creative energy. So the intercession of Christ is the continued efficacy of his expiatory merit; on which account it has been spoken of by some of the ancient writers as a perpetual oblation. If the providence of God were suspended all created being must be annihilated; and if Jesus were not to make intercession, the merit of his atonement would prove utterly unavailing. The arguments by which the reality of atonement has been established, thus support the reality of intercession. Admit the necessity and truth of Christ's atoning sacrifice, and the certainty and prevalence of his intercession within the vail naturally and irrefragably follow.

Christ's intercession is, indeed, essential to the fulfilment of the covenant of grace. As "mediator of the covenant" everything which he performs as a priest has a relation to this divine economy. The sacerdotal functions of oblation and intercession have regard respectively to the condition and the administration of the covenant. The stipulated condition of the covenant is, that satisfaction shall be made to the law and justice of God for the sins of those who are redeemed; and this is done by the sacrifice of Christ. The administration of the covenant comprehends whatever is con cerned with putting and maintaining the covenant children in possession of the blessings of redemption: and this takes its rise directly and immediately from the intercession of Christ. True it is, the agency of the Spirit and the instrumentality of means are concerned in this object; but, in the economy of man's salvation, the intercession of the Mediator is necessary alike to the operation of the one, and to the efficacy of the other. It is so arranged by infinite wisdom that all the good done to the souls of men, in connection with the covenant of grace, shall be begun, carried forward, completed, and maintained through eternity, in relation to Christ's intercession.

The perfection of his priesthood also demonstrates the reality of his intercession. That Christ's intercession belongs to his priestly, and not to his regal, office, is a necessary proof of its reality. And that it constitutes one of his sacerdotal functions, appears from the connection in which it is spoken of:—"He bare the sin of many, and made intercession for the transgressors."* To bear sin, means, we have seen, to make

* Isaiah liii. 12.

a onement; and it is here connected with making intercession. "Who is he that condemneth? It is Christ who died, yea rather that is risen again, who is even at the right hand of God, who also maketh intercession for us."* Christ died as a priest, and here his intercession stands connected with his death. But the connection is expressed in so many terms, in the following words:—"This man, because he continueth ever, hath an unchangeable *priesthood*: WHEREFORE he is able also to save them to the uttermost that come unto God by him, seeing he ever liveth to make *intercession* for them."† Moreover, he is spoken of as being a priest in heaven. Not on the cross only does he act in his sacerdotal character:—"He shall be a PRIEST UPON HIS THRONE."‡ His priestly office claims the stamp of perpetuity:—"Thou art a PRIEST FOREVER, after the order of Melchizedek."§ Heaven is the scene of his priestly acts:—"We have such an HIGH PRIEST who is set on the right hand of the throne of the Majesty in the HEAVENS."‖ If then, Christ is a priest on the throne of the heavens forever, there must be some sacerdotal act which he performs in this situation. And what is this act? Oblation it cannot be; he offered himself a sacrifice for sin *once* for all; by *one* offering he perfected forever them that are sanctified: and this one oblation was made upon earth. It can only, then, be intercession; and if it is denied that Christ is thus occupied in heaven, the name Priest is an empty sound, and you fix on him the degrading stigma of holding an office without a function, of accepting a title without a corresponding work. If farther proof be necessary, it is derived from the fact, that the intercession of Christ is ever represented as proceeding on the ground of his atonement. One passage may suffice in proof of this assertion; that, namely, in which his propitiation is exhibited as supporting his all-powerful, comforting advocacy:—"If any man sin, we have an ADVOCATE with the Father, Jesus Christ the righteous; and he is the PROPITIATION

* Rom. viii. 34.   † Heb. vii. 24, 25.   ‡ Zech. vi. 13.
§ Psalm cx. 4.   ‖ Heb. viii. 1.

for our sins."* But the best evidence of all, is that which is furnished by the act of the high priest under the law. It was not enough that he offered sacrifice on the brazen altar in the outer part of the tabernacle, on the day of expiation ; he must afterwards enter into the holy place, and burn sweet incense on the golden altar, after having sprinkled it seven times with the blood of atonement. " And Aaron shall take a censer full of burning coals of fire from off the altar before the Lord, and his hands full of sweet incense beaten small, and bring it within the vail. And he shall put the incense upon the fire before the Lord, that the cloud of the incense may cover the mercy-seat that is upon the testimony, that he die not."† The import of this significant ceremony we are not left to conjecture. " Christ is not entered into the holy places made with hands, which are the figures of the true; but into heaven itself, now to *appear in the presence of God for us.*"‡ " And another angel came and stood at the altar, having a golden *censer*, and there was given unto him much *incense*, that he should offer it with the prayers of all saints upon the *golden altar* which was before the throne. And the smoke of the *incense* which came *with the prayers of the saints*, ascended up before God out of the angel's hand."§ The intercession of Christ was significantly prefigured by this solemn act of the ancient high priest; and as the latter was, without doubt, a sacerdotal act, so also must be the former. In this way does it appear, that, for the reality of Christ's intercession, we have the same evidence as for the reality of his priesthood. If the one is figurative, the other is also figurative : if the one is real, the other is also real. And, unless it is meant to reduce the whole sacerdotal character of the Redeemer to a thin shadow, a mere figment, his intercession must be held to be a true and proper intercession.

We might even contend that the circumstances of the people of God render the intercession of Christ necessary. Numerous and daily are their wants: they

* 1 John ii. 1, 2. † Lev. xvi. 12, 13.
‡ Heb. ix. 24. § Rev. viii. 3, 4.

are made up of wants: their necessities are innumerable and constant. Blessings to supply these necessities, it is true, are procured by the atoning sacrifice of the Redeemer. But who shall apply to God for the bestowment of these purchased benefits? They cannot themselves; they have neither merit, nor skill, nor even at first inclination to apply for any such thing: they cannot plead their own cause; they are altogether unfit to appear in the presence of God for themselves; another must appear *for* them. Without the intercession, the purchase of Christ had thus been in vain, and the elect of God must have remained strangers forever to a single saving blessing.

The passages, then, which speak of the work of intercession, we regard as descriptive of a high and glorious function which is actually performed by the Saviour of sinners. A function, without a believing knowledge of which we can neither behold the Saviour's glory, nor understand the nature of man's salvation, nor experience the comforts of the redeemed.

It is no valid objection to the view we have given of this subject, that God loves his people, and has determined to confer on them the blessings purchased by his Son. If so, it has been asked, where is there need or room for Christ's intercession? The objection proceeds altogether on a mistaken conception regarding the use and object of the Saviour's intercession. It is not to awaken the love of the Father; it is not to obtain a decree in favor of those who are its subjects, that constitutes the object of this mediatorial function. Far be the impious thought! Its very existence is a fruit of God's love—an evidence of his gracious purpose. It is, that his Almighty love may be displayed, his sovereign decree fulfilled, in a way most consistent with the divine glory, most compatible with the honor of the divine government, most productive of the good of man, and most consonant with the interests of the moral universe at large. It is the method by which God has wisely determined to express his affection, and fulfil his purposes of mercy toward fallen men. And no objection on this ground can be urged against the intercession of Christ, which will not apply with equal force against our presenting a prayer on our own behalf, or on that of our fellow men.

Neither is there any validity in the objection, that intercession supposes something derogatory to the honor of the Redeemer. It is true, that the act of petitioning, in one point of view, implies inferiority in the petitioner with reference to the person petitioned. But, in the case before us, there is no inferiority supposed inconsistent either with the personal dignity or with the mediatorial glory of the Son of God. His person is divine, and on this the value of both his sacrifice and intercession greatly depends; but as they are official functions, whatever inferiority they may possess is wholly *official*, and affects not in the least his dignity as God. If it is not incompatible with his divine Majesty to offer himself as an oblation, no more can it be so to plead the cause of his people. If it was not derogatory to the honor of the Redeemer to assume the office, it cannot be derogatory to discharge its functions. The discharge of official duties can never disgrace an official functionary, unless the office itself be discreditable. This part of service is expressly represented as required of the only begotten of the Father: "Ask of me, and I shall give thee the heathen for thine inheritance, and the uttermost parts of the earth for thy possession;"* and so far from being dishonored by such a requirement, it is the very purpose for which he lives in official glory. "He ever LIVETH to make INTERCESSION for them."† It is to be remembered, too, that, in making intercession, he pleads not for himself, but for others. The humiliation attaching to personal supplication has no place here. To petition on behalf of another is compatible, not only with equality, but even with superiority in the petitioner over him with whom he intercedes. And, then, it is to be borne in mind, that an essential distinction exists, in respect of their nature, between the prayers presented by Christ in his state of humiliation, and those in his state of exaltation and glory. On earth,

* Psalm ii. 8. † Heb. vii. 25.

"he offered up prayers and supplications with strong crying and tears, unto him that was able to save him from death;" but no infirmities of this kind attach to his intercessory prayers on high; there all tears are wiped away from his, as from his people's eyes; there is nothing of servility or servitude supposed in these; they partake more of demand than of petition, of claim than of request; and evince rather the dignity of a claimant urging a right, than the poverty of a suppliant begging an unmerited favor. "Father, I will that they whom thou hast given me be with me where I am." Say not, then, that there is anything degrading in the supposition that Christ should make intercession. No. While his church has a want, while his people's necessities continue, he will count it his delight, his pleasure, his honor, his glory, to present their case to his Father, and to secure for them the bestowment of every needed boon.

SECTION II.

NATURE OF CHRIST'S INTERCESSION.

To intercede, means literally "to pass between." The term is used figuratively, to denote mediating between two parties with a view of reconciling differences, particularly in the way of supplicating in favor of one with another. In this sense, "intercession" is frequently affirmed of Christ in the scriptures :—"Who also maketh intercession for us."* "He ever liveth to make intercession for them."† The verb employed in these passages, (ἐντυγχάνειν,) when connected with the preposition that follows, (ὑπὲρ,) includes every form of acting in behalf of another; it is improper to limit it to prayer, as it denotes mediating in every possible way in which the interests of another can be promoted.

* Rom. v. 34. † Heb. vii. 25.

But other terms are employed in speaking of the same thing. It is expressed by *asking*:—"Ask of me, and I shall give thee the heathen for thine inheritance."* It is expressed by *praying*:—"I pray (ἐρωτῶ) for them; I pray not for the world;† which shows that supplication is included, though not to the exclusion of other ideas. It is also described by *advocacy*:—" If any man sin, we have an *advocate* (παράκλητον):—with the Father, Jesus Christ the righteous." This is a law term, which was in common use among the Greeks and Romans, to denote one who appeared in a court of justice to maintain the cause of a person accused,—an attorney, a pleader, a spokesman, a patron, who, placing himself in the room of his client, advocated his interests with all zeal and ability. The term is expressly applied to Christ in the passage quoted; and, in his own words, it is distinctly supposed to belong to him, when, consoling his disciples in prospect of his own removal from them, he says, "I will pray the Father, and he shall give you ANOTHER *comforter* (ἄλλον παράκλητον.) But, with reference to him, there must be understood this difference, that *his* plea is not the innocence of his clients but his own merits; *his* appeal is not to absolute justice but to sovereign mercy; what *he* sues for is not a legal right to which they are entitled, but a free favor to which in themselves they have no claim.

How the intercession of Christ, thus explained, is conducted—in what form this asking, praying, advocacy, is carried on, it does not become us either anxiously to inquire, or dogmatically to affirm. It becomes us rather to content ourselves with the account given of it in scripture. Beyond this, it is useless, and worse than useless, to conjecture.

It may be remarked, that, for one thing, Christ is said to *appear in the presence of God* for his people. "Christ is not entered into the holy places made with hands, which are the figures of the true; but into heaven itself, now *to appear in the presence of God for us*."‡ To this there seems to be an obvious reference in the preternatural vision of Stephen: "Behold

* Psalm ii. 8. † John xvii. 9. ‡ Heb. ix. 24.

I see the heavens opened, and *the Son of man standing on the right hand of God.*"* The same also is the reference in the apocalyptic vision, "And another angel came and *stood* at the altar, having a golden censer, &c."† His presenting himself before God is denoted by his *appearing* and *standing,* language which plainly enough marks some sort of official activity. This is the first thing implied in his intercession; when our case is called, so to speak, at the bar of heaven, he *appears* in our room; when we are summoned to appear, he *stands* up in our name.

But appearance is not all. He is farther said to *exhibit his atoning sacrifice,* as the ground on which the blessings for which he pleads are to be conferred on his people. The Hebrew high priest's entering into the sanctuary, on the day of expiation, prefigured the intercession of Christ. But it was not a simple appearance within the holy place that was made by this typical functionary; he carried with him the blood of the victim which had just been offered in the outer apartment, and sprinkled it seven times on the mercy-seat and the ark of the covenant. Without this his appearance could be of no avail, his entrance could have no efficacy; corresponding to which is Christ's *presenting the memorials of his atonement* before God in heaven. "Christ being come an high priest of good things to come, by a greater and more perfect tabernacle, not made with hands, that is to say, not of this building; neither by the blood of goats and calves, but BY HIS OWN BLOOD, he entered in once into the holy place, having obtained eternal redemption for us."‡ To the same circumstance does the apostle refer when he says, "It was therefore necessary that the patterns of things in the heavens should be purified with these; but THE HEAVENLY THINGS THEMSELVES WITH BETTER SACRIFICES than these."§ By his blood and sacrifice, represented in these passages as carried by him into heaven, it is almost unnecessary to remark, we are not to understand the material blood which flowed in the garden and on the cross, but the merit of his sufferings

---

* Acts vii. 56. † Rev. viii. 2. ‡ Heb. ix. 11, 12. § Heb. ix. 23

and death, the virtue of his atonement, the substance of his sacrifice, the whole essence of his passion. The intercession is founded on the oblation. The former is nothing without the latter. It may, without impropriety, be said that it is the sacrifice which intercedes: it is the blood of Jesus Christ in heaven which cries to God on our behalf: "The blood of sprinkling SPEAKETH better things than that of Abel."* Even in the midst of the throne, he stands " a Lamb as it had been slain."† The vestments of mediatorial exaltation conceal not the marks of mediatorial suffering; the diadem of glory hides not the impression left by the crown of thorns; he is still red in his apparel, and his garments dyed with blood; the scars of conflict are visible in the body of the Conqueror. His wounds are still open, and every mouth pleads our cause with God. His death pleads for our life; his blood cries for our safety; his tears procure our comfort; and everlasting joy is borne to us on the breeze of his deep-drawn sighs.

It is not difficult for us to understand, how intercession is made for us in heaven by the memorials of the Saviour's sacrifice. The language of signs is no strange thing among men. God has condescended to allow himself to be addressed in the same way:— " The bow shall be in the cloud, and I WILL LOOK UPON IT that I may remember the everlasting covenant between God and every living creature of all flesh that is upon the earth."‡ Or, to adduce an example more directly bearing on the present subject:—" And the blood shall be to you for a token upon the houses where you are: and WHEN I SEE THE BLOOD, I will pass over you."§ In like manner, there is a *rainbow*, round about the throne like unto an emerald, which pleads with God our exemption from the deluge of wrath, and which derives its vivid tints from the rays of the Saviour's love, refracted by the shower of divine anger, and reflected from the dark cloud of his suffering. It is when he *sees the blood of the everlasting covenant*, that Jehovah passes by those who were de-

* Heb. xii. 21. † Rev. v. 6. ‡ Gen. ix. 16. § Exod. xii. 13.

serving of destruction. Even profane history has been happily adduced in illustration of this subject. Amintas had performed meritorious services in behalf of the commonwealth, in course of which he had lost a hand. When his brother Æchylus is about to be condemned to death for some offence of which he has been guilty, Amintas rushes into the court; without uttering a syllable he holds up the mutilated limb; the judges are moved; and Æchylus is set free. Thus the sacrifice of our Redeemer,—the wounds in his hands and his feet, and his transfixed side, plead the cause of his people with perfect clearness, and infallible power. The advocate and the propitiation are the same: "We have an *advocate* with the Father—He is the *propitiation* for our sins."

In the intercession of Christ there is also included an *intimation of his will* that the purchased blessings of redemption be conferred. In whatever form conducted, it supposes substantial prayer or petition. There is the expressing of a wish, the intimating of a request. "Father, I WILL that they also whom thou hast given me be with me where I am."* "Simon, Simon, Satan hath desired to have you that he might sift you as wheat: but I have PRAYED for thee that thy faith fail not."† This seems to correspond to that part of the function of the Levitical high priest, which consisted in burning incense on the golden altar, within the sanctuary, on the day of expiation. It was appointed that he should "take a censer full of burning coals of fire from off the altar before the Lord, and his hands full of SWEET INCENSE beaten small, and bring it within the vail, and put the incense upon the fire before the Lord, that the cloud of the incense may cover the mercy-seat that is upon the testimony." The intercessory prayers or requests of the Saviour himself, not the prayers of his people which he presents, constitute the antitype of this expressive symbol Incense and the prayers of saints do not yield corresponding ideas. It is the prayers of Christ which breathe the sweetness, and produce the effects, of in-

* John xvii. 24. † Luke xxii. 31, 32.

cense. Accordingly, in the vision of the angel seen by John, " the smoke of the incense came up WITH the prayers of the saints out of the angel's hand :" thus demonstrating that the incense and the prayers of the saints do not mean the same thing. And what can we understand by this cloud of incense, but those innumerable intimations of the Saviour's will, which, in performing his work of intercession, ascend to God with so sweet a savor, and such glorious results ?

We take not upon us to determine the question, whether these requests of Christ are conveyed vocally or symbolically, by words or by signs. Indeed, we are inclined to think the question is unworthy of being entertained at all. It seems foolish and useless, if not hurtful and presumptuous, to speculate on this point. The majority of sober writers incline to the opinion, that the intercession is conducted silently, without the use of spoken language altogether. Without calling in question the soundness of this conclusion, we must be allowed to say that we are little satisfied with some of the arguments by which it is supported. To say that words are *unnecessary* to convey to God the Saviour's will, is saying only what might with equal truth be affirmed of the exhibition of his sacrifice. It is not because it is *necessary* to express his will, that Christ appears before God a Lamb as if he had been slain. It is not to remind God of what he would otherwise forget, or to make known to him what he would not otherwise know, or to incline him to that to which he would be otherwise indisposed, that Christ's intercession is introduced at all. No. It is to illustrate the divine majesty and holiness; to display the wisdom, grace, and merit of the Son ; and the more to impress the redeemed themselves with their obligations to deep and lasting gratitude ;—these are the purposes which this part of the mediatorial economy is designed to subserve. And if for ends like these vocal utterance could be shown to be better adapted than silent symbols, we can see no reason why it should not be supposed to be used. Besides, what are words but signs? They are nothing more than symbols;

symbols, it is true, of a particular kind, but, after all only symbols of thoughts and ideas. We are not to be understood, in these remarks, as maintaining the position that vocal language *is* employed by Christ in making intercession; we only object to some parts of the reasoning to which those who oppose this view of the subject have recourse. We express no opinion of our own. We regard the whole question as vain and trifling. Without indulging in foolish conjectures, it should be enough for us to know, that the intercession of our Divine Advocate is conducted in the best possible way, for promoting the glory of God, his own honor, and the good of his people. And one thing is certain, that such is the efficacy of the Saviour's blood, such the value of his death, such the merit of his sacrifice, that the memorials of his atonement, exhibited before God in heaven, advocate our cause more powerfully than could ever be done by the language of men. No tongue of orator, or eloquence of angel, can ever plead so effectually in favor of guilty sinners, as " the blood of sprinkling which speaketh better things than that of Abel."

SECTION III.

MATTER OF CHRIST'S INTERCESSION.

The *persons* for whom, and the *things* for which, Christ intercedes, are different points, which are, nevertheless, intimately connected with one another. The latter is determined by the former, and on this it may be proper to offer a few remarks before proceeding to what may be regarded as the principal subject of this section.

In general, however, it may be remarked, both with regard to persons and things, that the extent of intercession must be regulated by that of atonement. As it is unreasonable to suppose Christ to make atonement for any for whom he does not intercede, so it were preposterous to allege that he intercedes for any but those for whose sins he has atoned, or that the matter of his intercession includes anything not purchased with his blood. Intercession and atonement are correlates, not merely in nature, but in extent. For whomsoever and for whatsoever he has procured by his blood, does he plead before the throne of God. This is a leading principle which may serve to guide us in the observations we have to offer on this department of our subject.

With respect to persons, we observe, that Christ makes intercession for *the elect only, and for all and each of the elect.* That he intercedes for the elect only is abundantly plain from the speciality of God's sovereign purpose of mercy, from the definite extent of the atonement, and from the explicit testimony of the Scriptures. It has already been adverted to in the former part of our work.* Indeed, wherever the intercession is spoken of, this limitation of the objects is expressed or clearly implied. Paul says, " who also maketh intercession FOR US." Not for all, observe, but for the *elect* spoken of in the preceding verse. Again, " He ever liveth to make intercession for THEM." For whom? For them only who, as he says in the clause immediately going before, *come unto God by Christ.* To the same purpose is the testimony of John:—" If any man sin, WE have an advocate with the Father;" speaking in his own name and that of the Christian brethren to whom his epistle is addressed. With this agrees the language of Christ's intercessory prayer on earth:—" I pray for THEM: I pray not for the world." Who they are that are here referred to by the pronoun *them,* may be judged from the expression that occurs so frequently throughout the prayer—" the men which thou gavest me out of the world.' It is utterly absurd and pernicious, as well as unscriptural, to suppose that he makes intercession for those who live and die

* See p. 203.

in unbelief, who continue to disown his mediatory office, and to place reliance on other grounds of salvation than his infinite merits. With regard to all such, he must be understood as saying, "Their drink-offerings of blood WILL I NOT OFFER, NOR TAKE UP THEIR NAMES INTO MY LIPS."*

There are some passages of scripture urged in opposition to the sentiment thus expressed and supported. In the same intercessory prayer to which we have appealed, it is said, " Neither pray I for these alone, but for them also who shall believe on me through their word."† But only let our affirmation be marked, and no contrariety will be found to it in this verse. We said, not that Christ intercedes for *believers* only, but for the *elect* only. All the elect are at one time unbelievers, many continue long in this condition, and it is only in consequence of Christ's intercession, as we shall afterwards see more particularly, that they are ever brought out of this state. Those who *have* believed, and those who *shall* believe, are both included in " them which are given" to the Son. After this, the expression in the fifty-third chapter of Isaiah's prophecy—" he made intercession for the *transgressors*" —can give no difficulty; whether "the transgressors" are those whose sins he bore, or those who were active in effecting his crucifixion, the passage admits of easy explanation. It is not said that he made intercession for *all* transgressors, and we know that the character which the term delineates belongs by nature to the whole number of the elect. If the instruments of his crucifixion are meant, then is the expression explained at once by the prayer on the cross, " Father, forgive them, for they know not what they do."‡ We are aware that some excellent divines regard this prayer as not intercessory, but merely as a part of that moral duty required of Christ in fulfilment of the law which enjoins the forgiveness of offences.§ But, without

---

* Psalm xvi. 4.   † John xvii. 20.   ‡ Luke xxii. 34.

§ " We may, we must," says Dr. Owen, " grant a twofold praying in our Saviour; one by virtue of his office, as he was mediator; the other in answer of his duty, as he was subject to the law; but yet those things which he did in obedience to the law as a private person, were

taking upon us to determine this point, it may be observed, that even on the contrary supposition the passage is easily explained. We see no reason why it should not be admitted, that Christ made official intercession for his murderers. Were not the five thousand, who were converted by the preaching of Peter, openly charged by that apostle, as persons who " denied the Holy One and the Just, and desired a murderer to be granted unto them," and who " *killed* the Prince of Life ?" And as to the chief priests, who acted so prominent a part in that scene of crime, are we not afterwards informed, that " the word of God increased, and the number of the disciples multiplied in Jerusalem greatly ; and a *great company of the* PRIESTS *were* obedient to the faith ?" But this only proves the sovereign grace of God and the infinite merit of Christ's blood, in including in the number of the elect and the saved the basest and most guilty among men, not that the intercession of Christ is general.

Christ makes intercession for *all* the elect. Whatever their state, believers or unbelievers, they are remembered according as they require. " Neither pray I for *these* alone, but for them also which *shall believe* on me through their word." Whatever the age of the world in which they live, from the entrance of sin to the end of time, they are included in his prayers. We are apt to conceive of the work of intercession as conducted only since the Saviour's ascension, or at most since his appearance on earth. But he was always

---

not acts of mediation, nor works of him as mediator, though of him who was mediator. Now, as he was subject to the law, our Saviour was bound to forgive offences and wrongs done unto him, and to pray for his enemies ; as also he had taught us to do, whereof in this he gave us an example ; Matt. v. 44 :—' I say unto you, love your enemies, bless them that curse you, do good to them that hate you, and pray for them who despitefully use you, and persecute you ;' which, doubtless, he inferreth from that law, Lev. xix. 18, ' Thou shalt not avenge nor bear any grudge against the children of thy people, but shalt love thy neighbor as thyself ;' quite contrary to the wicked gloss put upon it by the Pharisees : and in this sense, our Saviour here, as a private person, to whom revenge was forbidden, pardon enjoined, prayer commanded, prays for his very enemies and crucifiers ; which doth not at all concern his interceding for us as mediator, wherein he was always heard, and so is nothing to the purpose in hand."—*Owen's Works*, vol. v. p. 275.

the Angel of God's presence who saved his people "He bare them, and carried them" on his heart "*al. the days of old.*" And before his incarnation, we have one distinct act of intercession on record:—" Then the angel of the Lord answered and said, O Lord of hosts, how long wilt thou not have mercy on Jerusalem, and on the cities of Judah, against which thou hast had indignation these threescore and ten years? And the Lord answered the angel that talked with me, with good words and comfortable words."* Among the innumerable multitude of the chosen of God, not one shall ever be omitted, in this part of his sacerdotal function. Out of the hand of the Angel of the covenant ascend continually, amid the cloud of incense, " the prayers of ALL saints." As on the Aaronic pectoral, worn by the high priest of old when he entered into the most holy place, were engraven all the names of the children of Israel, so on the heart of our Intercessor within the vail, are borne all the chosen of God.

Nor is it for all in the mass, that the Saviour makes intercession. He prays for *each* by himself. Even as respects believers, his intercession is not general, but particular. With a speciality such as might be supposed if there were only one, does he attend to the interests of each individual in the vast number of those given him by the Father. A general remembrance of them would not suffice. Their cases are various; not two of them are exactly alike. But, with infinite compassion and skill, is every special case of each individual presented by this divine Advocate to his Father. "Simon, Simon, Satan hath desired to have you, that he may sift you as wheat; but I have prayed for THEE that thy faith fail not." "He that overcometh, I will not blot out his name out of the book of life, but I will confess HIS NAME before my Father, and before his angels."†

Now, by these remarks on the persons for whom Christ intercedes, we are prepared to enter on the SUBJECT-MATTER of his intercession.

Christ intercedes that the chosen of God may be

* Zech. i. 12, 13.   † Luke xxii. 31, 32. Rev. iii. 5.

brought into a gracious state. They mingle originally with the world lying in wickedness, are enemies to God in their mind by wicked works, rebels against the divine authority, and sinners before the Lord exceedingly. There is no visible distinction between them and the world; they are in the same state of condemnation, they possess the same character of ungodliness, and they merit the same punishment. But there *is* a distinction, and *that* one of immense importance; they are chosen of God; they are given to Christ to be redeemed; the eye of the omniscient Saviour is upon them; and, when the period fixed in the arrangements of infinite mercy for their salvation arrives, he pleads his merits for the bestowment of the primary blessings of the new life. The blessings of grace may be viewed, as they affect respectively the commencement, the progress, or the consummation of the new life. It is not for the two latter merely that Jesus makes intercession, but also for the first; for justification, regeneration, and adoption, as well as for sanctification, and eternal glory. " Ask of me, and I shall give thee the heathen for thine inheritance." The heathen, and consequently those, who, in respect of condemnation, are not better than heathen, must be prayed for, in order to their being brought into a fit state to be characterized as the inheritance of Christ Justification is an act of acquittal from condemnation, the ground of which is the sacrifice of the Redeemer; but as Satan, the law, and the justice of God accuse the sinner of guilt, the Advocate with the Father must plead the merits of his sacrifice in answer to these accusations, before the act of acquittal can be pronounced. The procuring cause of justification is the Saviour's merits, but the immediate cause of actual justification is the Saviour's intercession. Hence, says the apostle, " Who shall lay anything to the charge of God's elect? who is he that condemneth? It is Christ that died, yea rather that is risen again, who is even at the right hand of God, who also maketh intercession for us."* Regeneration is a result of the

* Rom. viii. 33, 34.

Spirit's efficient power on the soul; but the intercession of Christ is connected, in the economy of redemption, with the gift of the Spirit for this end. "I will pray the Father, and he shall give you another Comforter, even the Spirit of truth; whom the world cannot receive, because it seeth him not, neither knoweth him: but ye know him, for he dwelleth with you, and shall be in you."* In like manner, in order to adoption or admission to the family of God, the Saviour must plead the ground of admission as that on which the act in question proceeds.

Thus does it appear that, but for the intercession of Christ, men would never be brought into a state of grace, but remain forever in condemnation and sin. The intercessor within the vail, however, looks down with omniscient inspection on the whole family of mankind: he sets an eye of special recognition on those who were given to him by the Father; these are all well known to him, for "the Lord knoweth them that are his;" their names are all written in the Lamb's book of life, they are engraven on the palms of his hands, on the tablets of his heart; when, in the lapse of time, the period fixed for the salvation of each occurs, he carries their case to the throne of God; the Father hears; the Spirit is sent; and the sinner is turned from darkness to light, from the power of Satan unto God. Means may have been at work for long to accomplish this end. This Scriptures may have been read; the Gospel may have been heard; there may have been the entreaty, and expostulation, and prayers of deeply interested friends; the providence of God may have prepared the way; the law may have uttered its thunders, the Gospel may have whispered its comforts, and deep serious thoughtfulness may have been produced. But not one, or all of these together, could make the man a new creature, and convert the sinner into a saint. Yet a change *is* effected, a visible alteration to the better is produced: and the true explanation of this change is to be found in the efficacy of Christ's intercession. It is this that has put all the

* John xiv. 16

wheels in motion; it is this that has given power and efficacy to the means: the proper and simple account of the whole matter is, that an unknown Friend in Heaven has spoken for the elect sinner to the King.

The need for Christ's intercession does not end on being brought into a gracious state. Saints, as well as sinners, require an interest in this function of the great High Priest. It is thus that *the pardon of the daily sins of the people of God* is procured. Believers sin, as well as others. "In many things we offend all." "If we say we have no sin we deceive ourselves, and the truth is not in us." True, it is written, " whosoever is born of God doth not commit sin; for his seed remaineth in him; and he cannot sin because he is born of God." But, in consistency with the other assertion just quoted of the same writer, this can mean nothing more than that a true child of God cannot sin with complacency, or so as to be brought under final condemnation. The reason of this is, not that the sins of such are less criminal than those of others, for, besides involving rebellion against the same authority, and a violation of the same holy, just, and good law, they are peculiarly aggravated by the obligations arising from the benefits that have been received. But the reason is, the interest which such have in the justifying righteousness of Christ, to which constant efficacy is given by his intercession. This is the believer's security from the daily condemnation to which his daily transgressions expose him. The act of justification is pronounced at once; the state of justification continues forever. The security of this permanent state is the same with that which constitutes the ground of the primary act—the righteousness of Emmanuel: and the intercession is what secures the constant efficacy of this perfect righteousness. The Apostle John asserts thus much:—"If any man sin, we have an Advocate with the Father, Jesus Christ the righteous, and he is the propitiation for our sins."*
But for his advocacy, the sins which the people of God daily commit would procure for them condemnation,

* 1 John ii. 2, 3.

justifying grace would be withdrawn, and the rich promises of saving mercy would be virtually cancelled. Believers, therefore, need, not only to be warned against temptations to sin, but to be furnished with encouragement in case of its being committed: despondency in the latter case may prove as hurtful as security in the former. And their consolation springs from Christ's intercession; but for which, amid the daily shortcomings arising from the corruptions of nature, the snares of the world, and the wiles of Satan, they must be utterly miserable. But let it not be supposed from this, that the intercession of Christ gives any encouragement to men to sin. To hold out the comforting prospect of pardon when sin has been committed, is a very different thing from holding out an inducement to commit sin. It is for the former, not the latter, purpose, that the doctrine of Christ's intercession is introduced in the Scriptures. "*If* any man sin, we have an Advocate:" not "*that* any man may sin," &c. The latter is a fearful abuse against which we must be ever on our guard.

By his intercession, Christ, farther, *protects his people against the accusations and temptations of Satan.* He came to destroy the works of the devil. He was predicted of old as he who should bruise the serpent's head: and for this purpose was he manifested in due time. He cast out the unclean spirits with a word; he vanquished Satan in single combat in the wilderness; and by his death, did he destroy him that had the power of death, that is the devil. The same work he still carries on in glory in the character of Intercessor, answering the accusations brought against his people, and protecting them from the assaults of the adversary. Satan is the accuser of the brethren; he prefers heavy charges against the disciples of Christ at the bar of conscience, and, through his human agents, at the bar of public opinion. These, as being well known to Him, may be understood to be preferred at the bar of God. Some of them are true, others false; but Christ, as the advocate with the Father, answers them all. He refutes such as are false by showing their groundlessness; and for the forgiveness of such as are true he pleads the merit of his blood. In proof of the latter, we may refer to the oft-quoted passage in the epistle of John:—" If any man sin, we have an Advocate with the Father, Jesus Christ the righteous: and he is the propitiation for our sins." In support of the former, we may refer to the case of Joshua:—" And he showed me Joshua the high priest standing before the angel of the Lord, and Satan standing at his right hand to resist him. And the Lord said unto Satan, the Lord rebuke thee, O Satan; even the Lord that hath chosen Jerusalem rebuke thee: is not this a brand plucked out of the fire?"* Here are three characters introduced to notice:—the *panel* at the bar, " Joshua the high priest;" the public *prosecutor*, " Satan ;" and the *advocate*, " the Angel of Jehovah." Joshua had just escaped from Babylon, where, it is taken for granted, he had been guilty of many crimes, especially of neglecting the worship of the true God, conforming to the idolatrous customs of the heathen, and forming alliances with the enemies of Israel. These, and similar accusations, are brought against him by Satan. But the Angel of the Lord stands up in his behalf against the accuser; answers satisfactorily every charge; and brings off his client in triumph. In this we have a specimen of the manner in which he acts towards his people in similar circumstances. He who, having died and risen again, also maketh intercession for us, is entitled, by way of eminence, to say, " Who shall lay anything to the charge of God's elect?"

Nor is the intercession of Christ of less avail in procuring strength to resist the temptations of Satan. Many are the assaults made by the adversary on the children of God. They are not ignorant of his devices. These assaults are at once formidable from their number, appalling from their strength, and dangerous from their skill. They are managed with great dexterity, every art of fear and hope, smile and frown, allurement and terror, being employed to secure success · and the

* Zech. iii. 1, 2.

nature or form of the suggestion being cunningly adapted to every peculiarity of individual character or situation, so as to lead men to think evil of God, to distrust the Saviour, or to grieve the Holy Spirit; to neglect duty, or to practise iniquity; to despair of salvation, or presumptuously to rest on a false hope. Thus exposed, unless the people of God had on their side one more skilful and more powerful still, one willing as well as able to counteract the working of this mighty adversary, they must necessarily fall a prey to his subtlety, and sink beneath the weight of his infernal artillery. The advocacy of Christ is their safety. "Simon, Simon, behold Satan hath desired to have you, that he might sift you as wheat; but I have prayed for thee, that thy faith fail not." By the intercessory prayer of their divine Advocate, their faith is rendered firm and immovable; they are strengthened to fight and to overcome; they resist the devil, and he flees from them: instead of shrinking from his attack, they confront him boldly; they say, with undaunted countenance, "Get thee behind us, Satan;" and the stripling combatant comes off more than conqueror, leaving his vaunting adversary stretched on the field. The faith of a believer, invigorated by the intercession of his Saviour, must ever prove more than a match for the heaviest assault of the Prince of darkness. This is a shield which no arrow can pierce; and any impression that even the most formidable temptation can make upon it is like that of a leaden bullet discharged against a brazen wall.

The *progressive sanctification of the saints, and their general perseverance* stand connected with the intercession of Christ. The whole scheme of salvation has for its end the holiness of its subjects. This end, everything about it is adapted as well as designed to promote. The sacrifice of Christ is fitted to advance moral purity in the soul; the blood of God's Son cleanses from all sin; it is a fountain opened for sin and for uncleanness. His intercession has the same effect. If he was manifested on earth to take away sin in its guilt, he interposes in heaven to take away sin in its defilement. "I pray not that thou shouldest take them out of the world, *but that thou shouldest keep them from the evil.—Sanctify them* through thy truth, thy word is truth."* From this it would seem, that believers are indebted to the intercession of the Redeemer, for all that repugnance to sin which leads them to crucify the flesh, to mortify the deeds of the body, to deny ungodliness and worldly lusts, and to abstain from all appearance of evil; and for all that love of holiness which prompts them to indulge pure thoughts, to cherish sacred desires, to form spiritual resolutions, and to practise sanctified obedience. The expulsion of sin, the implantation of the principle of righteousness, and the maintenance of habitual holiness, all proceed directly from this source. Sanctification in life, as well as in nature, is one of the gifts which the ascended Mediator has received for the rebellious, and with the bestowment of which his advocacy on high is inseparably connected. Without this, indeed, never could the believer subdue a single corruption, or think a single hallowed thought, or feel a single pure emotion, or speak a single holy word, or perform a single unpolluted act.

And thus is the perseverance of the saints in general secured. Accusations, after being answered, may be renewed; temptations, once resisted, may be repeated; holiness, once imparted, may have its strength weakened, or its lustre obscured. It is necessary that perseverance to the end, in acquittal, resistance, and sanctification, be secured. And this is effected in the same way as the incipient benefit. "I have prayed for thee, that thy faith fail not." If the faith fail not, there can be no accusation without its answer, no temptation but is sure to be repelled, nor any kind or degree of holiness finally unattained. But the stability of the believer arises not from his faith, nor from anything about himself, not even from the work of grace in his soul; but from that to which he is indebted for the stability of his faith itself, namely, the intercession of Christ *"I have prayed for thee,* that thy faith fai'

* John xvii. 15, 17.

not." Here lies the secret of the saints' perseverance If Christ only persevere to pray for them, they cannot fail to persevere in the enjoyment of what he has procured, and the practice of what he has commanded. And does he not thus persevere? "HE EVER LIVETH TO MAKE INTERCESSION FOR THEM."

By the intercession of Christ *peace is maintained, and intercourse kept up between God and men.* He *made* peace by the blood of his cross; by presenting this blood in heaven is this peace *maintained.* He hath reconciled us to God by his death; but we need to be upheld in reconciliation by his life of intercession. There are many things at work which have a tendency to disturb this peace, to break in on this state of reconciliation. Sin separates between believers and their God; and the accusations of Satan and of a guilty conscience, tend to deprive them of all inward tranquillity. But, by means of the Saviour's intercession, the propitiation for sin shall be so applied, and the blood of sprinkling be so brought home to the conscience, that any interruption of intercourse or of peace, shall be but partial and temporary. "For a small moment have I forsaken thee, but with great mercies will I gather thee. In a little wrath I hid my face from thee for a moment: but, with everlasting kindness will I have mercy on thee, saith the Lord thy Redeemer. For the mountains shall depart, and the hills be removed: but my kindness shall not depart from thee, neither shall the covenant of my peace be removed, saith the Lord that hath mercy on thee."* Hence the people of God have ever access to him for the supply of their daily wants. Not a day, not an hour, but they have business to transact in the court of heaven. They have requests to prefer: sins to be pardoned; wants to be supplied; iniquities to confess with shame; blessings to acknowledge with gratitude. And how shall they approach a throne of such awful majesty; how enter a court of such inexorable justice! The mediatorial Angel before the throne, the Advocate at the bar, is their encouragement. "Through him

* Isaiah liv. 7, 8, 10.

we have access by one Spirit unto the Father—In him we have boldness and access with confidence—Seeing that we have a great High Priest that is passed into the heavens, let us come boldly unto the throne of grace—Having an High Priest over the house of God, let us draw near with a true heart, in full assurance of faith."*

It is through the intercession of Christ that the *services of the people of God are rendered acceptable.* The services required of them are special, manifold, great, and arduous. The whole moral law is the measure of these services. And it is a matter of no small consequence for them to know, not only in what strength these services may be performed, but by what merit they can be accepted. If they are not to be received and acknowledged by God, the performance of them must be nullified. The law requires perfection, but the services of the people of God are at best imperfect; the law requires unblemished obedience, but their services are at best tainted with pollution. How then shall they be accepted? Through the intercession of Christ. This makes up for all their deficiencies; this removes all their blemishes. The prayers of the saints ascend up before God out of the Angel's hand, n which is held a golden censer with much incense. And what is true of the prayers of the saints is true also of all their other services—their songs of praise, their tears of penitence, their works of faith and labors of love, their deeds of mercy, and their acts of holy obedience. *Their burnt-offerings and their sacrifices shall be accepted upon mine altar.*"† It is in this way that God overlooks all their imperfections; he sees no iniquity in Jacob, nor perverseness in Israel; he smells a sweet savor in the performances of his children; their sacrifices of righteousness are well-pleasing and acceptable in his sight; and, although in themselves like " pillars of smoke," dark, confused, and ill-savored, they come up before him " perfumed with myrrh and frankincense, and all the powders of the merchant." Like Aaron of old, our great High Priest has on his

* Eph. ii. 18; iii. 12. Heb. iv. 14, 16; x. 21, 22. † Isa. lvi. 7.

forehead the inscription, HOLINESS TO THE LORD, that he " may bear the iniquity of the holy things which the children of Israel shall hallow in all their holy gifts."* So far from the perfomances of men being the ground of their acceptance with God, it thus appears, that for the acceptance of our performances themselves we are indebted to the merits of another. Our services, as well as our persons, are accepted in the Beloved. By expecting to be accepted for anything that we do, we set aside the Saviour's atonement; by expecting that anything we do shall be accepted on account of its intrinsic excellence, we set aside the Saviour's intercession. And it is thus we are enabled to understand how it comes about, that " a cup of cold water given to a disciple in the name of a disciple shall not lose its reward," while " the ploughing of the wicked is sin."

In fine, the intercession of Christ secures *the complete salvation of the chosen of God, their entrance into heaven, and their everlasting continuance in a state of perfect blessedness.* God is a rock, and his work is perfect. What he begins, he completes; nor rests till he has secured for his redeemed perfect acquittal beyond the reach of accusation, deliverance from all temptation, immaculate holiness, and uninterrupted and permanent peace. It is by his intercession that he thus saves to the uttermost. " Wherefore he is *able also to save them to the uttermost* that come unto God by him, *seeing he ever liveth to make intercession for them.*"† The work of salvation being thus completed, the redeemed are admitted into heaven, for which they are prepared. Their reception into glory is the matter of distinct request on the part of the Saviour. " Father, I will that they also whom thou hast given me be with me where I am, that they may behold my glory which thou hast given me."‡ The title of admission, it is true, is the Saviour's death; but the immediate cause of their admission is his intercession. It is by this that the title, so to speak, is carried into heaven, and presented to God, and plead as the ground on which their admission is to take place.

* Exod. xxviii. 38.   † Heb. vii 25.   ‡ John xvii. 24.

He entered into heaven, not without blood, to appear in the presence of God for us. He goes to the portals of the upper sanctuary, holding in his hand the memorials of his sacrifice; at his approach the celestial gates fly open; he enters in the name and on behalf of his people; he opens and no one can shut, till all his redeemed and chosen have followed him thither; and, then, he shuts and no one can open, either to invade their peace or to pluck one of the countless multitude from their happy abode.

The permanent continuance of the redeemed in the state of glory stands connected, in the same manner, with the intercession of Jesus. "He is a priest *forever.*" Not only is everlasting glory the *effect* of his intercession; but it is the *subject of* everlasting intercession. "He *ever liveth* to make intercession." The perpetuity of heavenly blessings, and the acceptance of celestial services, must all be traced to this source. Not a ray of light, not a smile of favor, not a thrill of gladness, not a note of joy, for which the inhabitants of heaven are not indebted to the Angel standing with the golden censer full of incense, before the throne. Remove this illustrious personage from his situation; divest him of his official character; put out of view his sacerdotal function; and all security for the continuance of celestial benefits is gone,—the crowns fall from the heads of the redeemed, the palms of victory drop from their hands, the harps of gold are unstrung, and the shouts of halleluiah cease forever; nay, heaven must discharge itself of its human inhabitants, and the whole be sent away into irremediable perdition! But no such appalling catastrophe need ever be feared: CHRIST EVER LIVETH TO MAKE INTERCESSION!

SECTION IV.

PROPERTIES OF CHRIST'S INTERCESSION.

From the character of the advocate, we may judge what will be the qualities of his advocacy. Possessed of infinite wisdom and knowledge, the intercession of Christ cannot but be eminently *skilful*. A skilful advocate must know well the case of his client, the character of the judge with whom he has to deal, and the law according to which he must plead. Christ's knowledge of all these is perfect. He knows perfectly all his people, and all their cases. "He needeth not that any should testify of man; for he knows what is in man." "He searcheth the reins and hearts." All the exercises and doings of his children are thoroughly understood by him. Their wants, necessities, sins, and infirmities, are better known to him than to themselves; even their inward breathings and secret groanings are as well understood as "the well set phrase of the orator." Nor this only in respect of his intuitive omniscience as God, but of his experimental knowledge as man. Experience must add powerfully to the skill of an intercessor; and this advantage is possessed by Christ in an eminent degree. "For in that he himself hath suffered, being tempted, he is able to succor them that are tempted." Had he no other knowledge of his people than what is derived from their own statements and prayers, he could not plead their cause with skill. They are often generally ignorant of themselves, form the most mistaken ideas, entertain the most inadequate views of their own wants, and are unable properly to express even what they may adequately feel. Their petitions for themselves are often, from these causes, defective, erring, and stammering. But never so those of their divine Intercessor on their behalf. By him, their thoughts, affections, and desires, are fully appreciated, and their case represented with consummate skill.

He knows, too, Him with whom he has to plead. Much of an advocate's skill must depend upon this, so as to be able to adapt his manner of pleading to the temper and disposition of the judge. Our Intercessor is thoroughly acquainted with the character of God. "No one knoweth the Father but the Son." He is thus qualified to adapt his appeals to features of the divine character corresponding to their nature. Are his people weak? He goes, on their behalf, to God as *the Lord of Hosts*. Have they fallen into sin, and are in need of pardon? He addresses God as a *God of holiness*. Does he plead the fulfilment of promises? He makes his appeal to the *righteousness* of Jehovah.

Nor is he less skilfully acquainted with the law according to which his intercessions are to be regulated. And it is not, as is too often the case among men, by evading, or concealing, or perverting, or explaining away the law, that this advocate exhibits his skill. No; he admits its authority, vindicates its claims, and maintains inviolably the rectitude of all its sanctions. Nor does he ever attempt to make it appear that those for whom he pleads have not violated its requirements, and rendered themselves obnoxious to its punishments. But his ability is shown in skilfully pleading the fulness of his own merits, by which satisfaction has been given to the law, and every blessing secured in consistency with the claims of infinite equity. Such, in short, is his skill, that he asks whatever his people need, only what they need, what has actually been procured for them, and what it every way comports with the character and law of God to confer; so that no cause can ever fail in his hands from want of knowledge or wisdom to conduct it.

Moral purity characterizes the intercession of Christ. The necessity of this was set forth under the law, in the altar of incense being of pure gold. Both the pleader and the plea must be holy. Christ intercedes not for *sin*, but for sinners. The tendency of all that he asks is to purify from all iniquity, and to perfect holiness in the fear of the Lord. No request of a contrary character could ever be presented to a holy and righteous God, or could ever possibly be granted. Nor could anything of this kind ever comport with the character of the Advocate himself. He is no corrupt venal pleader. He is the righteous Lord that loveth righteousness. To this is the efficacy of his intercession ascribed by the apostle :—" He is able to save them to the uttermost that come unto God by him, seeing he ever liveth to make intercession for them. For *such an high priest became us who is holy, harmless, undefiled, separate from sinners.*" Corruption in an advocate, if detected, is sufficient to blast his cause even at the bar of man. And the slightest taint of impurity in Christ would have disqualified him for conducting a successful advocacy on behalf of his people, at the bar of God. Corruption may be concealed from an earthly judge, but no degree of it could escape undetected by the omniscient Judge of all. The intercession of Christ is as pure and sinless as his sacrifice. Everything about it is holy,—the matter in which it consists, the plea on which it rests, the place in which it is conducted, the person by whom it is managed, and the judge before whom it is transacted. Truly may our Advocate with the Father be described as " Jesus Christ THE RIGHTEOUS."

Jesus Christ is a *compassionate* intercessor. The advocate who is to plead the cause of the wretched must not be hard-hearted and unfeeling ; he must be able to enter into their feelings, and to make their case his own. Without this he can never expect to succeed ; but, thus qualified, it is scarcely possible for him to fail. His language, looks, tones, and whole manner, indeed, will acquire a more melting influence, in proportion to the depth of the compassion with which he is touched. So of Christ it is said, that it behooved him to be a " merciful," as well as a " faithful," high priest ; and, had he not been merciful, he could not have been faithful. But " in him compassions flow ;" the compassions, not of divinity merely, but of humanity ; of a humanity, too, the sensibilities of which were exquisitely fine, from its being unaffected by the blunting influence of sin. And even the delicate sensibilities of his holy human nature were heightened by his personal experiences. He who pleads the cause of those in whose miseries himself once shared, must be admirably fitted to do it with effect. " We have not an high priest who cannot be touched with the feeling of our infirmities; but who was, in all respects, tempted like as we are, yet without sin." He tasted of all the sorrows of human life. Of the severest afflictions, the bitterest temptations, the most pungent sorrows, the most awful privations, he had full and frequent trial. He was not only cast into the same mould as his people with respect to nature, but into the same furnace with respect to affliction. And, although he had no knowledge of the evil of sin from personal feeling well he knew its weight and its bitterness from having had its guilt imputed and its punishment exacted of him. Nor let any one object, that, although this might be the case while Christ was on earth, it cannot be expected to continue now that he is in heaven. His exaltation to glory has wrought no change on his nature or his affections. He is the same in heaven that he was upon earth. He is still possessed of human nature —God-man—Emmanuel, God with us. And it is not more certain that, in his exalted state, human blood flows in his veins, than that human sympathies glow in his breast. He feels more for the objects of his intercession than man or angel can do, nay, than they can even do for themselves. The pity of Christians for themselves can never equal the pity with which they are regarded by their Saviour: for theirs is the pity of a corrupted nature, his of uncontaminated humanity; theirs the pity of mere human nature, his of human nature indissolubly linked with all the tender mercies of Deity.

Much importance attaches to the *promptitude* of an intercessor. The value of a bestowment often depends on the time of its being conferred. Allow the crisis to pass, and the gift loses its value. A successful advocate must seize the earliest opportunity for taking up and introducing the cause of his client. This is a property of our Lord's intercession. He is ready to receive the applications, and to present the cases of his people. He is never absent from his place; they know always where he is to be found: he is ever at the right hand of God, waiting to undertake what they may commit to his charge. Nor, after it is committed, does it run any risk of being lost through neglect. No; as he is of "quick understanding" to perceive, so is he of prompt activity to prosecute, whatever he undertakes. The attitude in which he was beheld by the proto-martyr, in his remarkable vision, indicates at once readiness to undertake and activity to prosecute whatever is committed to him. He was seen *standing:* "He looked up steadfastly into heaven, and saw the glory of God, and Jesus STANDING on the right hand of God."* With what promptitude, for example, does he interpose in behalf of the church, when, in the dispensations of providence, a fit time for the restoration of Jerusalem presents itself:—" O Lord of hosts, how long wilt thou not have mercy on Jerusalem, and on the cities of Judah, against which thou hast had indignation these threescore and ten years?" This gives the people of God encouragement to go with boldness to the throne of grace, that they may obtain mercy, and find grace to help *in the time of need.* Their times of need are well known to the Advocate with the Father, and not one of them will he suffer to pass unnoticed, or unimproved. Christians may themselves overlook the fit time for making application to God, but not so their glorious Intercessor. They may rely on him with perfect confidence, that when they sin, he will plead for pardon; when they are accused, he will vindicate their character; when they are afflicted, he will procure them succor; when they are tempted, he will pray for them that their faith fail not; and when they perform with diligence their duties, he will give them acceptance with the Father. We would not have them to expect that he will procure them comforts unless they make

* Acts vii. 55.

application for them, for, in that case, they could neither be relished nor felt; but when they do make earnest and believing application, they will find that the blessings are already procured, and ready to be put into their hands. If they but open their mouths wide, he will see to it that they are filled abundantly. He can solicit blessings from the Father, and bestow them on his disciples, at the same time. While he presents the golden censer at the altar of burnt-incense on high, he can extend the sceptre of mercy to the humble suppliant below. The work of intercession can occasion no delay in the communication of needed benefits for to plead their bestowment, and actually to bestow them, are the work of the same moment.

The preceding remarks prepare us to hear of the *earnestness* of Christ's intercession. His skill, compassion, and promptitude, all suppose this. This is an essential property in successful pleading, whether for ourselves or for others. It is more apt, certainly, to occur in the former case than in the latter; many, who exhibit all the warmth of animation in petitioning for themselves, being cold enough in presenting requests for others. But it is not so in the present instance. Nothing can exceed the fervor of our Saviour's intercession. The earnestness he displayed in laying the foundation of our salvation in his sufferings on earth, when he was straitened till his bloody baptism should be accomplished, and used strong crying and tears, may be taken as a pledge that he will not be less earnest in carrying out his benevolent undertaking to its completion in heaven. The specimen of intercession which he gave before he left our world, so full of holy ardor and vehemence, may serve to give us some idea of the warmth with which the same work is conducted in the sanctuary above. The affection, too, which he bears to his people, cannot but give a peculiar eagerness to his supplications on their behalf. He bears them upon his heart, as the names of the children of Israel were engraven on the breastplate worn by the high priest of old when he went into the holy of holies, and the burning coals of fire with which the incense-censer was filled, were an apt, though faint representation, of the holy ardor with which the love of the Redeemer glows when he ministers as our intercessor before the throne of God. He is no cold, selfish pleader; his soul is in the work; his prayers are the prayers of the heart; love prompts all his requests, selects the best arguments, and urges the strongest pleas. "Who is this that *engaged his heart* to approach unto me? saith the Lord." Yes, Christians, your prayers for yourselves are nothing like so fervent as those of the Redeemer for you. Oh, how shamefully cold, and languid, and lifeless, and formal, in many cases, are your petitions! How often do you use words without feeling, and put forth a frothy vehemence of language when there is no corresponding ardency within! Every saint must have something of this kind with which to accuse himself; but no such charge can be brought against Christ. His intercessions ever exceed in ardency, our warmest addresses, our most vehement appeals. We can never be said to plead with *all* our heart; he never pleads in any other way.

The *authoritative* character of our Lord's intercession should not be overlooked. It is not enough that an advocate be a person of skill, integrity, compassion, and zeal; he must also be authorized; he must bear a commission; he must be regularly licensed to practise at the bar. There must be a legal, as well as an intellectual and moral, qualification. This, in the case of Christ, is undoubted. He does not assume of himself the office of intercessor, nor does he derive his commission from his people, but from God. "*I will cause him* to draw near, and he shall approach unto me: saith the Lord." His intercession is a part of his sacerdotal functions; and we know "*Christ glorified not himself* to be made an high priest, but He that said unto him, Thou art my Son, to-day have I begotten thee." His general suretyship implies such a special commission; for it supposes a right to see all the stipulations of the covenant fulfilled, all the debts of the covenant children discharged, and payment made of every purchased benefit. The very manner in which he conducts his intercession carries in it thus much. He sues for the new covenant blessings, more as a matter of right than of favor; he demands rather than petitions; he claims rather than begs. There is a tone about his request—" Father, I *will*"—that bespeaks the authority under which he acts. They savor of the *throne* not less than of the *altar*. He is a Priest upon his Throne.

Betwixt the intercession of Christ and advocacy among men, there are, as we have seen, many points of resemblance, but in other respects, it is altogether *peculiar*. It possesses a character of utter exclusiveness; neither man nor angel must invade it; so absolute is it, indeed, as to exclude even the other persons of the Godhead. This peculiarity was set forth in the type. No man, not even the king himself, might intrude into the functions of the priesthood in general; nor was any one but the high priest permitted to carry incense, on the day of expiation, into the holy of holies. There is none else in heaven or in earth, either qualified, or authorized, or required, to make intercession. "No ONE cometh unto the Father BUT BY HIM." "Through HIM we have access by one Spirit unto the Father." "There is ONE mediator between God and men, the man Christ Jesus." The saints may, indeed, lawfully intercede for one another, but in a way very different from Christ. They intercede on earth, he in heaven; he on the footing of his own merit, they altogether denied to everything like personal worth as the ground on which they trust for being heard. Angels may not intrude on this high and peculiar function of the Lord of angels. They are often said to praise, but never, that we are aware of, to pray. Nor can they have any personal disposable merit to form the foundation of vicarious intercessions. To represent either angels or men as joint intercessors with Christ, as is done by the church of Rome, is to be guilty of a daring invasion of a high and exclusive prerogative of the one Mediator. To the entrance into the holy place not made with hands, in the sense in which we are now speaking of it, the language of the prophet may be fitly accommodated :—" This gate shall be shut, it shall not be opened, and no man shall enter in by it ; because the Lord, the God of Israel, hath entered in by it, therefore it shall be shut. It is for the Prince."* Yes, Messiah the Prince, the Prince of peace, claims the work of intercession as his peculiar prerogative. It is a prerogative, indeed, which he claims as his to the exclusion, as we have said, even of the other persons of the Godhead. The Father, as the representative of Deity, sustaining the character of the judicial sovereign with whom the intercession must be transacted, cannot be supposed to act in the capacity of intercessor. We read, indeed, of the Spirit's intercession—" The Spirit maketh intercession for the saints according to the will of God."—but it is essentially different from that of Christ. We cannot, at present, enter minutely into all the distinctions between them. That of Christ is personal ; that of the Spirit moral. The Spirit does not stand up, as does Christ, before God in the court of heaven, and literally plead the cause of men. Such a supposition, besides implying a reflection on the perfection of Christ's work, is at variance with the exclusive divinity of the Spirit, he having no human nature as Christ has in which he can appropriately appear in the capacity of a pleader. The Spirit's intercession consists in the moral influence he exerts on the souls of the people of God, in leading them out to pray for themselves, by discovering to them the matter of prayer ; by imparting a disposition or inclination to pray ; by fixing the mind on the subject of prayer ; by giving enlargement, freedom, and confidence in the exercise ; and by directing them in the use of proper arguments. From this it will plainly enough appear, in what the intercession of Christ and that of the Holy Spirit differ from one another. They differ in their *nature*, the one being meritorious and the other moral ; in their *objects*, that of the one being to remove the obstacles to man's salvation that exist on the part of God, that of the other to remove those which exist on

* Ezek. xliv. 2, 3.

the part of man; in their *locality*, the one being in heaven, the other on earth; in the *relation* which they bear to their subjects, the one being without men, the other within; and in their *effects*, the one enabling to pray, the other rendering prayer acceptable to God. It thus appears that the intercession of the Spirit interferes in no point whatever with that of Christ, but leaves it in all its naked peculiarity or exclusiveness.

The *prevalence* or efficacy of Christ's intercession is a feature on which we might descant at great length. It is an inviting theme, so full is it of comfort and encouragement. It often happens, among men, that the most urgent petitions, the most touching appeals on behalf of the oppressed, the wretched, and the needy, are permitted to remain disregarded and unheard. But not one request of our divine Advocate can possibly share this fate. Him the Father heareth always. This view admits of ample confirmation and illustration. It was typified, indeed, under the law, by the success which attended the entrance of the high priest into the holy of holies on the day of expiation; for, had he not been accepted, the fire would have been extinguished on the golden altar, the censer of incense would have dropped from his hand, and he would never have been permitted to return to bless the people. In the twenty-first Psalm, which, from the lofty terms in which it is conceived, must have a higher reference than to the literal David, we read, " Thou hast given him his heart's desire, and hast not withholden the request of his lips."* Nor did Christ ever, while on earth, intercede in vain. " Father, I thank thee that thou hast heard me," is his own testimony on one particular occasion, to which he subjoins the general affirmation, " And I knew that thou hearest me always."† The apostle assures us, that " when in the days of his flesh he had offered up prayers and supplications with strong crying and tears, he was heard in that he feared."‡ One request only was he ever denied, " Father, if it be possible let this cup pass from me." But this was no part of his intercession:

* Psalm xxi. 2.   † John xi. 81, 42.   ‡ Heb. v. 7.

it was the natural shrinking of his holy human nature from the awful scene that was before him; and, instead of militating against our position, it gives it support, inasmuch as his drinking the bitter cup of mingled woe, which could not possibly pass from him, laid a meritorious foundation for the success of his advocacy. If that one prayer had been heard on his own behalf, not another could have been heard on ours. When the character of the intercessor is considered, there can be no reason to dread his ever being unheard. The dignity of his person must give weight and influence to his petitions; the relation in which he stands to God as a Son, cannot but have its effect; nor are his personal and official qualifications here to be forgotten. That one who is infinitely wise, and holy, and compassionate; whose diligence, and zeal, and affection are boundless; who acts moreover under the high authority of a divine commission, should fail in his suit is utterly impossible. Were he man only, or even angel, failure were not impossible; but being the Son of God, Jehovah's fellow, it must be that as a Prince he has power with God and shall prevail. The foundation on which his intercession rests affords farther security. It proceeds on the footing of his atonement. He asks nothing for which he has not paid the full price of his precious blood. What he seeks is what he has merited; and he who has "accepted his sacrifice" cannot but "grant him his heart's desire," cannot "withhold from him the request of his lips." Nor is there in the matter of his intercession, as before delineated, anything but what is good in itself, agreeable to the will of God, and fitted to advance the glories of the Godhead. The objects, too, for whom he pleads, are all the chosen of God, the children, the friends of Him with whom he pleads, dear to *his* heart as to his own, alike the objects of his complacent affection and esteem. "The Father himself loveth them." Add to all these considerations, the security arising from the results of Christ's intercession that have been already realized. How many souls have been converted, how many sins pardoned, how many temptations repelled, how many acts of holy obedience performed and accepted, how many sons brought to full and eternal glory, in all of which the efficacy of Christ's intercession has been proved by the best of all evidence—its actual effects! So abundant, thus, is the evidence of its prevalence, that the timid can have no reason for distrust, the unbeliever no excuse for neglect.

It only remains to observe the *constancy* of Christ's intercession. He is continually employed in this work His oblation was the work of comparatively a short period, but his intercession never ceases. Human benevolence may become languid, may intermit for a time, or may finally die away altogether. But not so the benevolence which prompts the petitions of our Advocate. He can never become languid from ignorance of his people's wants, for he is omniscient; nor from want of affection, for his love is abiding; nor from want of merit, for his sacrifice is of unfailing virtue; nor from fatigue, for he is the almighty and immutable God. Nothing can ever occasion a suspension. A moment's intermission would prove fatal to the eternal interests of all the elect. But, while attending to the case of one, he has no need to suspend attention to that of another. Innumerable as are his applicants, he attends to the wants of each as if there were not another that needed his care. Multiplicity cannot bewilder, variety cannot divide, importance cannot oppress his thoughts. To him the care of millions is no burden. Ten thousand claims meet with the same attention as if there were but one. His understanding, his love, his merit, his power, are all infinite; and we must beware of measuring him by the low standard of our own limited capacities. Nor can his intercession ever come to an end. There will be need for it forever. So long as his people sin, he will plead for pardon; so long as they are tempted, he will procure them strength to resist; so long as they continue to perform services, he will continue to give them acceptance; so long as they are in the wilderness, he will procure them guidance and safety;

nay so long as the blessings of Heaven are enjoyed, will he plead his merits as the ground on which they are bestowed. Through eternity will he continue to plead on behalf of his people. Never shall they cease to be the objects of his care; never shall their names be erased from his breast; never shall their cause be taken from his lips; never shall the odor-breathing censer drop from his hand; nor shall his blessed merits ever cease to rise up in a cloud of fragrant incense before the Lord. HE EVER LIVETH TO MAKE INTERCESSION FOR THEM.

SECTION V.

RESULTS OF CHRIST'S INTERCESSION.

THE intercession of Christ affords a bright display of the *love of God*. In appointing for men an advocate at all, and especially such an advocate, this feature of the divine character, so conspicuous in every other part of redemption, is strikingly developed. Without this appointment, the purchased salvation could never have been enjoyed; man could never have successfully plead his own cause; and the evils to which he is constantly exposed, must inevitably have wrought his ruin. His services could never have been accepted; temptations must have placed him in daily jeopardy; and his sins should have brought him, without fail, under condemnation. Without it, even the people of God could never reach final salvation; not a prayer which they might offer could be heard; not a service they might perform could be accepted; not an assault of Satan could they repel; and the very first sin, however small, that they should commit, would sink them to perdition. How, then, is the love of God displayed in providing for men an advocate to plead their cause, and to secure them against such fatal consequences! And, then, such an advocate; not a man like ourselves, not an angel of light, not a seraph of glory, but his Son, his own Son, his only begotten, well-beloved Son, equal to himself in every divine perfection, the noblest personage in the universe. Herein is love! Let us contemplate it with grateful adoration, and dwell upon the delightful theme till our enraptured hearts reciprocate the emotion, till we can say, " We love him because he so loved us."

How does the subject illustrate, also, *the love of the Son!* This is equally apparent, in his being pleased to identify himself, by becoming their advocate, with guilty, polluted, rebellious, worthless, wretched creatures of our fallen race. This he was under no obligation to do; it was his own spontaneous act, flowing from the good pleasure of his will. And, when his personal dignity is considered, his love is enhanced by the condescension supposed; for, although exalted far above all principalities and powers, and having a name above every name,—though having all things under his feet, and receiving the homage of angels, and regulating the affairs of the universe, he disdains not to espouse the cause of us mortal worms, and to become our suppliant with the Father. As love induced him to undertake the work, so is it evinced in the promptitude, and earnestness, and diligence, and zeal, and ceaseless constancy, with which it is prosecuted, laying us under obligations to regard with admiration, and to acknowledge with gratitude, such disinterested affection.

The intercession supplies an argument of no mean force for the *divinity* of Christ. This doctrine, indeed, runs like a golden thread through the whole system of man's salvation, connect ng itself with every part, and giving strength and consistency to the whole. It is no less necessary to the efficacy of his intercession than to the worth of his sacrifice. To know minutely all the cases of so many millions of people; to listen to, and understand, such a multitude of simultaneous applications; to represent them all with perfect skill, and in due order; to give effect to all the pleas demanded by their endless variety, must require qualifications nothing short of divine. No finite being could ever be fit for such an undertaking. What finite mind could understand the matter! What finite power could sustain the load! What finite worth could secure success! An undertaking this, sufficient to confound and crush to the dust the mightiest of creatures, nay, all created being combined. None but a divine person is qualified to be the intercessor of elect sinners. Such is our Advocate with the Father. "This is the true God, and eternal life."

The intercession of Christ confirms *the efficacy of his death*. It all proceeds on the ground of his atonement. But for this a single petition could not have been presented on our behalf. The high priest's entering into the sanctuary with the censer of incense, supposed the expiatory sacrifice to have been previously offered, for he had to carry with him its blood. In like manner, our Lord's intercession supposes his sacrifice to have been previously offered and accepted, and every act of intercessory interposition establishes the efficacy of his meritorious death. If at any time our faith in the latter truth happen to be staggered, if we want confirmation of this fundamental verity, we have only to look on high, and contemplate the Angel standing at the altar, having a golden censer with much incense, and to behold the smoke of the incense, with the prayers of the saints, ascending up before God out of the Angel's hand.

It gives *perfect security* to the people of God. Their present state is imperfect. The matter of Christ's intercession supposes this; there would be no need for him to pray for pardon if there were not guilt, or for satisfaction if there were not corruption; so that the sinless perfection to which some presumptuously lay claim, is not more at variance with Christian humility than with the work in which the Saviour is engaged. But against the despondency which this imperfection might otherwise occasion, the people of God have the security of final perfection, arising from the work of intercession. Their security springs not from anything naturally indestructible in the principle of the new life of which they are possessed, nor from any want of criminality in the sins they commit, nor from anything less dangerous in the circumstances in which they are placed; but wholly from the intercession of Christ. The principle of the new life may, in itself, be liable to decay, but Christ by his intercession will uphold it; their sins may deserve condemnation, but he intercedes for pardon; they may be openly exposed to danger, but his intercession interposes a shield of infallible protection. Not a sin can they commit, for which his merits cannot secure forgiveness; not an accusation can be charged upon them which he has not skill to answer; not a temptation can assail them which he has not power to repel; not a service can they perform, however imperfect, to which he cannot give acceptance in the sight of God. Their final salvation is thus rendered absolutely secure, and in a spirit, not of haughty self-confidence, but of humble dependence on the Advocate with the Father, may they bid defiance to all opposition, and calmly trust that the gates of hell shall not prevail against them. The church is thus surrounded as with a wall of adamant, which no enemy can either penetrate or overthrow. Infidelity may open wide its mouth, and heresy may pour forth its polluted streams, and persecution may light its fires, and immorality may spread its thousand snares, and war and famine and pestilence may spread devastation all around, but not one, nor all of these together, can prove a match for that Angel-intercessor who cries with a loud voice, " Hurt not the earth, neither the sea, nor the trees, till we have sealed the servants of our God in their foreheads."

How ought the people of God to beware of *dishonoring Christ's intercession*. It has already been remarked what an abuse of this function takes place when encouragement is taken from it to indulge in sin. But it is also dishonored by being neglected or overlooked. This we fear is no uncommon occurrence. There is a disposition in many to regard what Christ *has done*, to the neglect of what he *is doing*. Not that we would have men to think less of the former, but more of the latter. Surely the preceding pages have been read to little purpose, if they have not left the impression on the mind that the *present* work of Christ in heaven is of no inferior moment. Much is said of it in the Scriptures, not a little is made of it by the inspired writers. The purpose for which the Saviour lives in mediatorial glory cannot be of small importance; "he ever liveth to make intercession;" "if when we were enemies we were reconciled to God by the *death* of his Son, MUCH MORE, being reconciled, we shall be saved by his *life*." Let us then think highly, and think much, of the intercession as well as the death of Christ. Let us see, too, that we restrain not prayer before God. This would be to do what we can to nullify the Saviour's character as an advocate, as, in this case, he could have no service to offer, no cause to undertake, no matter to perfume with the fragrance of his merits. Such as would put honor on Christ's intercession must "pray without ceasing." Nor let any indulge unreasonable despondency. The intercession of Christ ought to prove an antidote to every such feeling. Hear how the apostle reasons on the subject:—"He is able to save unto the uttermost all that come unto God by him, seeing he ever liveth to make intercession for them." To those who have right views of this truth, there can be no room for despair. Yet there are professing Christians who give themselves up to a morbid melancholy, brooding over their sins and short-comings, which could be warranted only on the supposition that there were no advocate with the Father, no intercessor within the vail, no days-man to plead their cause and secure their salvation. A view of the fact and properties of the Saviour's intercession should charm away all gloomy forebodings; and Christians, who feel as if cast out from God's sight, would we exhort to look again to that Holy Temple where pleads the Minister of the upper sanctuary, and to be no more sad.

Let all *seek an interest in, and daily improve*, this view of the Saviour's character and work. Those who are duly sensible of their situation will be disposed, like the Israelites, when they were bitten with the fiery serpents, to look around for some one to pray for them. To whom can they go with safety but to Christ? He alone can pray for the people. Let them believe in his name, trust in his merits, and obey his commands, and they may lay their account with sharing in the benefits of his intercession. Daily they need, and they may daily have recourse to him, in this character. Oh that men would consider the misery of being without an interest in this part of the Saviour's work! To be without the prayers of our friends is deemed a calamity. To be denied the intercession of such men as Noah, Daniel, and Job, is justly represented in Scripture as no light thing. "Pray not thou for this people, neither lift a cry or a prayer for them," is one of the heaviest judgments that can befall a backsliding nation. How dreadful beyond all conception, then, must it be to have no interest in the prayers of Christ! But this is not all, for not to have his prayers *for* us is to have them *against us.* He prays for the destruction of his enemies. That blood which speaks so powerfully for the salvation of those who believe, cries loudly for vengeance on such as despise and abuse it. Let the unbelieving and ungodly ponder this, and tremble. And who can tell the happiness which an interest in the intercession of Christ is fitted to yield! It is a doctrine full of comfort to saints, as of terror to sinners. It is calculated to fill the heart with joy, to know that, whatever may be their sinful weaknesses and infirmities, they shall not bring them into condemnation—that, whatever be their temptations, their faith shall not be permitted to fail,—that, whatever their backsliding, they shall not finally fall away,—that however weak, and cold, and confused, their devotions, they shall be rendered, nevertheless, a sweet-smelling savor to God. In sin and duty, in health and sickness, in prosperity and adversity, in life and death, the doctrine of Christ's intercession gives joy and comfort to the believer. Be it, then, the concern of all who read these pages, earnestly to seek such an interest in what the Saviour has done and is still doing, that they may be able to assume as their own, the triumphant appeal of the apostle:—"Who shall lay anything to the charge of God's elect? It is God that justifieth. Who is he that condemneth? It is Christ that died, yea, rather that is risen again, who is even at the right hand of God, WHO ALSO MAKETH INTERCESSION FOR US. Who shall separate us from the love of Christ?"

Thus have we brought to a conclusion our inquiries into these deeply interesting subjects. And we cannot part with our readers, without reminding them of the necessity of making a personal application of the glorious truths which have occupied their attention, before turning their thoughts to anything else. Let them not regard them as matters of curious speculation, or content themselves with a mere doctrinal belief. To their being rightly appreciated, and properly improved, they must become the subjects of a saving faith. No doctrines stand more closely connected with the eternal salvation of the soul. Let not the reader, then, rise from the perusal of these pages, without seriously and conscientiously asking himself these questions:—Am I interested in the atonement and intercession of Jesus Christ? Have I faith in the sacrifice of the great High Priest? Has my soul then been sprinkled with his precious blood? Does he plead in my behalf with the Father? Is my name engraven on his heart? Have I any good reason to conclude, that he is even now praying that my sins may be forgiven, that my faith may not fail in the hour of temptation, and that I may be kept from the evil which is in the world? Were I called, at this moment, to recline my head on the pillow of death, could I indulge the comforting assurance that the Advocate within the vail, whom the Father heareth always, would present on my behalf the request, "Father, I will that he whom thou hast given me be with me where I am," and that, in answer to this prayer, my disembodied spirit should be ushered, in perfect holiness, into the immediate and unclouded presence of my covenant God, and into all the glories of the heavenly kingdom? These are solemn questions. Let no one neglect to put them to himself, or hesitate to press them, till, if no favorable answer can be candidly returned, at least such convictions have been awakened, as no occupation can dissipate, no exercise allay but a believing appropriation of the blood and advocacy of the great High Priest of our profession. May the Spirit of all grace, whose prerogative it is to take the things and show them unto men, be pleased to grant, that the perusal of these sheets may thus prove the means of salvation to many; and to the only wise God, our Saviour, be all the glory. Amen!

INDEX.

Abel's sacrifice, 80.
Absurdity of supposing Christ's atonement to be indefinite, . 98.
Acceptance of sacrifices, a proof of their divine origin, 79.
"All men," passages in which the phrase occurs explained, 222.
Ancient sacrifices, 66. Vicarious nature, 71. Use and design, 88.
Antiquity of sacrificing, 67.
Apostolical writings, proof of atonement from, 136.
Application of atonement limited, 188.
Appointment of God, an element in the value of Christ's atonement, 180.
Atonement, doctrine defined, 12. Term explained, 13. Objections to, considered, 20. Necessity of, shown, 47. Proof of reality, 67. Matter, 149. Value, 160. Extent, 184. Results, 234.

Cain, expostulation of God with, 82.
Causation, law of, observed in man's salvation, 160.
Christ, legally though not personally guilty, 36. Suffered voluntarily, 37, 176. His divine dignity, 163. His innocence, 170. Originally under no law, 176.
Coats of skin used by our first parents, 69.
Creation, how connected with atonement, 331.
Curse, in what sense Christ made a, 140.

Death of Christ voluntary, 177.
Definite atonement explained, 185.
Divinity of Christ, essential to value of atonement, 163.

Efficacy of Christ's death, proved by his intercession, 277.
Elect, only for such Christ makes intercession, 269.
Example, not sufficient to account for the sufferings of Christ, 133.
Expiation, term explained, 17.
Extent of Christ's atonement explained, 184. Proved to be definite, 178.

"For," the preposition, in what sense used in connection with the work of Christ, 142.
Forbearance of God connected with the atonement, 239.

God not changed by atonement, 24. His perfections, 48. His character illustrated, 234.
Goodness of God, 52.
Good works not sufficient to obtain pardon, 61.
Guilt, in what sense it belonged to Christ, 36.

Heathen sacrifices vicarious, 72.
Hebrews, importance of epistle to, 115.

"Himself," import of Christ's sacrifice being said to be, 164.
Holiness of God, 50.
Holiness of Christ, 170. Holiness of his life, 171. Holiness of his nature, 172.
Honor of Christ, not impugned by his atonement being definite, 205. Intercession not incompatible with, 261.
Humanity of Christ, necessary to the worth of his atonement, 169. Its perfect purity, 170.

Inefficacy of every expedient but atonement to procure pardon of sin, 57. Of repentance, 58. Of good works, 61.
Infinite intrinsic worth of Christ's death, 185.
Innocent suffering for the guilty, no valid objection to Christ's atonement, 33.
Intercession of Christ, 256. Correlate of atonement, 256. Reality, 256. Term explained, 262. Wherein consists, 263. How performed, 267. For whom made, 269. For what, 272. Its properties, 284.

Judgment, final, affected by atonement, 253.
Justice of God, 50.
Justice and mercy consistent, 22.

Law of God, renders atonement necessary to pardon, 53. Cannot be relaxed, 54.
Levitical institutes ought to be studied, 115.
Levitical sacrifices, 93. Many of them propitiatory, 95. Not sufficient to take away sin, 98. Prefigurative of Christ, 101. Erroneous views taken of their design, 109.
Love of God, not caused by atonement, 21. Displayed in Christ's intercession, 265.

Matter, of Christ's atonement, 149. Of his intercession, 269.
Middle system described, 11.
Miraculous conception of Christ, a proof of the spotlessness of his human nature, 173.
Moral government of God, renders atonement necessary to pardon, 53. Vindicated and established by the atonement, 154.

Nature of Christ's intercession, 262.
Necessity, in what sense affirmed of atonement, 47.
Noah's sacrifice vicarious, 74.

Objections, to atonement considered, 20. To divine origin of sacrifice answered, 85.
Origin of primitive sacrifice, 75. Not human, ib. Divine, ib.

Pardon, strictly gracious notwithstanding the atonement, 23. Included in matter of Christ's intercession, 275.
Paschal lamb, a proper sacrifice, 107.
Passover, prefigurative of Christ, 107.
Patriarchal sacrifices, vicarious, 73.
Perfections of God prove necessity of atonement, 48. Illustrated by the atonement, 234.
Possibility of those perishing for whom Christ died, passages which seem to imply, explained, 227.
Propitiation, term explained, 15. Passages in which applied to work of Christ, 137.

Prophecy, proof of atonement from, 116.
Providence, affected by atonement, 248.
Punitive character of Christ's sufferings, 121.

Ransom, work of Christ so called, 138.
Reconciliation, term explained, 14. In what sense affirmed of God, 24. Work of Christ so called, 136.
Rectitude of the divine character, an argumen for atonement being definite, 190.
Redemption, term explained, 15. Work of Christ so called, 138.
Redundancy, supposed in the merits of Christ's death, an objection to atonement being definite, 207.
Repentance, insufficient to procure pardon of sin, 58.
Results, of Christ's atonement, 234.

Sacrifice, in what sense God said not to desire, 87. Work of Christ so called, 141.
Sacrifices, of great antiquity, 67. Universal prevalence, 70. Heathen, 72. Levitical, 93. Erroneous views respecting the design of the legal sacrifices, 109. Why the services of believers called sacrifices, 141. Cessation at death of Christ, 109.
Salvation, imperfect views taken of by enemies of atonement, 44. Complete, secured by Christ's atonement, 240.
Satan, his accusations and temptations included in the matter of Christ's intercession, 276.
Satisfaction, term explained, 16.
Scape-goat, ceremony of, 97, 122.
Security of the people of God springs from the intercession of Christ, 298.
Services of God's people rendered acceptable by the intercession of Christ, 280.
Silence of Scripture, improperly adduced against divine origin of sacrifice, 85.
Sin, inadequate views of, taken by the enemies of atonement, 44. In what sense Christ made sin, 140. Exceeding evil of sin shown by atonement, 239.
Socinian system described, 10.
Subjection to the law, different kinds of, 150.
Substitution, term explained, 17. Passages in which language of, applied to Christ's work, 141.
Sufferings of Christ, an argument for atonement, 127. Punitive character of, 121. Substitutionary, 124. Their continuance, 127. Their variety, 128. Not explained on the principle of retributive justice, 130; nor of discipline, ib.; nor of being confirmatory of his doctrine, 131; nor of example, 133. Sufferings of his soul, 155. Not the same as those of lost spirits, 158.

Terms explained, 13.
Truth of God, 49.

Universe of moral creatures interested in the atonement by Christ, 251.
Universality of sacrifices, 70.
Universal offer of the Gospel, 209.
Universal terms employed in speaking of the subjects of Christ's atonement, explained, 214.
Unique character of Christ's atonement, 41.

Use and design, of ancient sacrifices to prefigure Christ, 88. Of levitical sacrifices, 101.

Value of Christ's atonement, 160. From what it does not proceed, 162. From what it does, 163.
Vicarious, what the word means, 17.

"World," "whole world," &c., passages in which these terms occur explained, 219.
Worth of Christ's sacrifice, divine, 164.